Anonymous

Calliope

The musical miscellany

Anonymous

Calliope
The musical miscellany

ISBN/EAN: 9783337126452

Printed in Europe, USA, Canada, Australia, Japan

Cover: Foto ©Thomas Meinert / pixelio.de

More available books at **www.hansebooks.com**

CALLIOPE:

OR, THE

MUSICAL MISCELLANY.

A SELECT COLLECTION

OF THE MOST APPROVED

ENGLISH, SCOTS, AND IRISH SONGS,

SET TO MUSIC.

LONDON:
Printed for C. ELLIOT and T. KAY,
Opposite Somerset-Place, N° 332, Strand;
And C. ELLIOT, Edinburgh.

ADVERTISEMENT.

THE Publisher of the following compilation having come by accident into the possession of the first 192 pages, which were printed off under the inspection of the Editor of the Musical Miscellany, (a collection published at Perth in 1786, and very favourably received by the Public), he immediately resolved to finish the volume on a more enlarged plan than that of the Musical Miscellany; of which, however, this may properly be considered as a new edition, although under a different title. Accordingly, no pains have been spared to render it as complete as possible. Every popular and fashionable song, whether English, Scots, or Irish, has been inserted; at least the Publisher hopes that very few, if any, have been omitted. How far the present Editor has succeeded must be determined by a candid Public.

It is presumed that no Collection of Songs with the Music, hitherto published in *Great Britain or Ireland*, of the same size and extent, has been afforded at so low a price as the present.

EDINBURGH,
April 1788.

INDEX.

	Page.
A COBLER there was and he liv'd in a stall	248
Adieu ye groves	150
Ah, why must words my flame reveal	72
Ah, Chloris! cou'd I now but sit	438
Ah, ma chere! my pretty dear	398
A fig for all your whining stuff	344
A lass that was laden with care	270
A master I have, and I am his man	359
Alas, my heart! alas, my heart	396
All in the Downs the fleet was moor'd	408
All ye who wou'd wish to succeed with a lass	228
And gin ye meet a bonny lassie	404
Assist me, ye lads, who have hearts void of guile	154
As you mean to set sail for the land of delight	216
As Jamie Gay ga'd blithe his way	232
As down on Banna's banks I stray'd	259
As Dermot toil'd one summer's day	334
At the sign of the horse old Spintext	60
Away to the field	78

B.

Believe my sighs, my tears, my dear	442
Beneath a green shade a lovely young swain	178
Blow high, blow low	464
Blyth, blyth, blyth was she	410
Bright Phœbus has mounted the chariot of day	348
Busk ye, busk ye, my bonny bride	134
By Pinkie house oft let me walk	174
By the gaily circling glass	204

C.

Cease, rude Boreas, blust'ring railer	
Club your firelocks, my lads	
Come gi's a sang, the lady cry'd	20
Come rouse, brother sportsmen	74
Come on, my brave tars	142
Come, come, my jolly lads	196
Come, now, all ye social pow'rs	278
Come, come, my good shepherds	296
Contented I am, and contented I'll be	346
Curtis was old Hodge's wife	430

D.

	Page.
Dear Kathleen, you no doubt	211
Dear Tom, this brown jug	282
Dear Roger, if your Jenny geck	405
De'il tak' the war	460
Diogenes furly and proud	137
Do you hear, brother fportfman	104
Dumbarton's drums beat bonny, O	164

E.

Ev'ry man take his glafs in his hand	86

F.

Farewell to the park and the play	314
Farewell to Lochaber	434
Fill your glaffes, banifh grief	240
Fine fongfters apologies too often ufe	220
For me my fair a wreath has wove	194
Four and twenty fidlers all on a row	148
Free from the buftle, care, and ftrife	56
From the eaft breaks the morn	230
From Roflin caftle's echoing walls	426
From the court to the cottage convey me away	471

G.

Gallant failor, oft you've told me	130
Gay Bacchus, liking Eftcourt's wine	468

H.

Had I a heart for falfehood fram'd	417
Had Neptune, when firft he took charge of the fea	18
Hark, the horn from the valley	70
Hark! hark! the joy infpiring horn	198
Hark! hark! jolly fportfmen a while to my tale	302
Hear me, ye nymphs, and ev'ry fwain	423
Here awa, there awa	136
Hey for a lafs and a bottle to cheer	360
How fweetly fmiles the fimmer green	162
How little do the landmen know	210
How imperfect is expreffion	268
How happy a ftate does the miller poffefs	294
How ftands the glafs around	93
How happy the foldier who lives on his pay	350

I.

Ianthe the lovely, the joy of her fwain	205
If I live to grow old, as I find I go down	456
If to force me to fing it be your intention	88
I figh and lament me in vain	110

	Page.
I'll sing you a song, faith I'm singing it now here	332
I'm in love with twenty	447
I'm told by the wife ones a maid I shall die	316
In April, when primroses paint the sweet plain	156
In good king Charles's golden days	284
In the merry month of May	309
In vain the ills of life assail	339
In the forest here hard by	354
In London my life is a ring of delight	380
In winter when the rain rain'd cauld	412
In the garb of old Gaul	418, 420
In love shou'd there meet a fond pair	33
Its open the door some pity to show	23

J.

Jack Ratlin was the ablest seaman	390
Jove in his chair	8

K.

Kilkenny is a handsome place	384

L.

Leave, neighbours, your work	66
Let a set of sober asses	160
Let gay ones and great	427
Let the Sultan's wanton care	374
Let's be jovial, fill our glasses	274
Let's seek the bow'r of Robin Hood	326
Life is checquer'd, toil and pleasure	206
Like my dear swain no youth you'd see	362
Lock'd in my chest I've fifty pound	373
London town is just like a barber's shop	392
Lord ! Lord ! without victuals and drink	336
Lord ! what care I for mam or dad	440
Lovely goddess, sprightly May	34
Love's goddess in a myrtle grove	172

M.

Ma chere amie, my charming fair	400
Man may escape from rope or gun	53
Margaritta first possest	328
My Patie is a lover gay	4
My temples with clusters of grapes I'll entwine	12
My love was once a bonny lad	28
My laddie is gone far away o'er the plain	186
My bonny sailor won my mind	262
My name's honest Harry, O	324

INDEX.

	Page.
My daddy is a canker'd carle	345
My mind to me a kingdom is	457
My sheep I've forsaken	462

N.
Nansy's to the greenwood gane	2
Now Phœbus gilds the orient skies	54
No more my song shall be, ye swains	108
No glory I covet, no riches I want	299
No hurry I'm in to be marry'd	382

O.
O Bessy Bell and Mary Gray	46
O sweet Sir, for your courtesy	14
O thou lov'd country	112
O see that form that faintly gleams	113
O saw ye my father	121
O greedy Midas I've been told	124
O I ha'e lost a silken snood	129
O Sandy why leaves thou thy Nelly to mourn	182
O what pleasures will abound	212
O what had I ado for to marry	414
O send Lewis Gordon hame	416
Old women we are, and as wise in the chair	218
Once more I'll tune the vocal shell	166
One morning very early	261
One day I heard Mary say	42
On Ettrick banks in a summer's night	50
On a bank of flow'rs in a summer day	254

P.
Pho! pox of this nonsense, I prithee give o'er	276

R.
Rail no more, ye learned asses	236

S.
Says Plato, why should man be vain	238
Says Colin to me, I've a thought in my head	298
See the course throng'd with gazers	388
Shall I, wasting in despair	394
Shepherds, I have lost my love	1
Since there's so small difference	103
Since you mean to hire for service	202
Some talk of Alexander	184
Some say women are like the seas	306
Songs of shepherds in rustical roundelays	101
Such beauties in view	444

vi   I N D E X.

	Page.
Sweet Annie frae the fea-beach came	38
Sweet engager of my heart	63

T.

The charge is prepar'd	9
The moon had climb'd the higheſt hill	16
The topfails fhiver in the wind	40
The laſt time I came o'er the muir	44
The wealthy fool, with gold in ſtore	52
The lafs of Patie's mill	76
The blufh of Aurora now tinges the morn	80
The fun juſt glancing thro' the trees	84
The meal was dear fhort fyne	118
The pawky auld carle came o'er the lee	126
The lawland lads think they are fine	144
The fmiling morn, the breathing fpring	152
The man that's contented is void of all care	168
The fweet rofy morning peeps over the hills	171
The morn was fair	190
The fields were green, the hills were gay	222
The whiſtling plowman hails the bluſhing dawn	234
The echoing horn calls the fportfmen abroad	246
The dufky night rides down the fky	250
The moment Aurora peep'd into my room	262
The women all tell me I'm falfe to my lafs	287
The filver moon's enamour'd beams	312
The laffes are mad, the archers are mad	325
The prado I reforted	356
The fummer was fmiling, all nature round look'd gay	370
The Britiſh lion is my fign	378
The night her filent fable wore	432
The filver moon that fhines fo bright	439
The wand'ring failor ploughs the main	448
The world, my dear Myra, is full of deceit	450
Then farewell, my trim-built wherry	264
There lived a man in Balenocrazy	158
There was a jolly miller once liv'd on the river Dee	245
Tho' late I was plump, round, and jolly	200
Tho' the fate of battle on to-morrow wait	350
Tho' Leixlip is proud of its clofe fhady bowers,	366
Tho' Bacchus may boaſt of his care-killing bowl	320
Thou foft flowing Avon	300
Thurfday in the morn	24
To fpeer my love, wi' glances fair	376

INDEX.

	Page.
To fair Fidele's graffy tomb	94
To Anacreon in Heaven, where he fat in full glee	5
Tol, lol, de rol lol, my tolly, my tol	386
'Twas in that feafon of the year	425
'Twas within a mile of Edinburgh town	26
'Twas fummer and foftly the breezes were blowing	98
'Twas I learnt a pretty fong in France	106
Two goffips they merrily met	289

U.

Up amang yon cliffy rocks	352

W.

Well met, pretty nymph, fays a jolly young fwain	310
We're gaily yet	466
Welcome, welcome, brother debtor	441
What woman can do I have try'd to be free	406
What is't to us who guides the ftate	421
What Cato advifes moft certainly wife is	280
What man in his wits had not rather be poor	305
What beauties does Flora difclofe	180
When the men a-courting came	322
When ruddy Aurora awakens the day	330
When firft I began, Sir, to ogle the ladies	338
When up to London firft I came	342
When brother Bobby came firft to town	364
When the fheep are in the fauld	368
When firft I ken'd young Sandy's face	402
When I have a faxpence under my thumb	428
When Britain firft, at Heav'n's command	436
When the chill Sirocco blows	452
When daifies pied, and violets blue	454
When Orpheus went down to the regions below	292
When war's alarms entic'd my Willy from me	244
When I was a young one, what girl was like me	242
When I was in my fe'enteen years	226
When abfent from the nymph I love	176
When trees did bud and fields were green	10
When innocent paftime our pleafures did crown	140
When my locks are grown hoary	58
When morn her fweets fhall firft unfold	68
When I think on this warld's pelf	83
When merry hearts were gay	96
When firft I came to be a man	114
When once the gods, like us below	122

	Page.
Whence comes it, neighbour Dick	90
Wherever I'm going, and all the day long	258
Where's my fwain fo blithe and clever	214
While mifers all night	36
While grave divines preach up dull rules	446
Why heaves my fond bofom	213
Why hangs that cloud upon thy brow	188
Will ye go to the ew-bughts, Marion	48
Willy was a wanton wag	132
With women and wine I defy ev'ry care	308
With an honeft old friend and a merry old fong	275

Y.

Ye belles and ye flirts, and ye pert little things	252
Ye lads of true fpirit pay courtfhip to claret	272
Ye fportfmen draw near	146
Ye fylvan pow'rs that rule the plain	192
You the point may carry	208
You know I'm your prieft, and your confcience is mine	256
Young Damon was whiftling brifk and gay	318
Young Roger the ploughman, who wanted a mate	340

CALLIOPE:
OR THE
VOCAL ENCHANTRESS.

SONG I.
BANKS OF BANNA.

Shepherds, I have lost my love, have you seen my Anna?
pride of every shady grove, upon the banks of Banna.
I for her my home forsook, near yon misty mountain, left my
flock, my pipe, my crook, greenwood shade and fountain.

 Never shall I see them more
  Until her returning;
 All the joys of life are o'er,
  From gladness chang'd to mourning.
 Whither is my charmer flown?
  Shepherds, tell me whither?
 Ah, woe for me, perhaps she's gone
  For ever and for ever.

SONG II.
NANSY'S TO THE GREEN WOOD GANE.

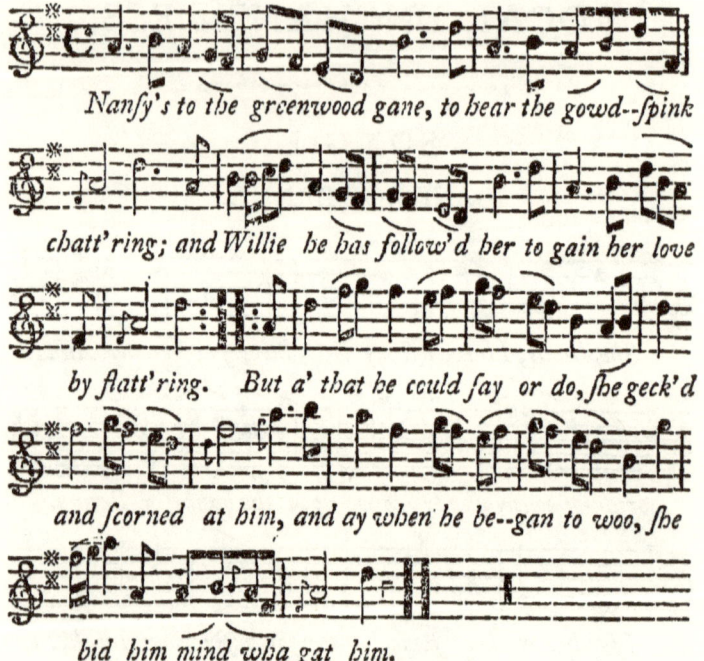

Nansy's to the greenwood gane, to hear the gowd-spink chatt'ring; and Willie he has follow'd her to gain her love by flatt'ring. But a' that he could say or do, she geck'd and scorned at him, and ay when he be--gan to woo, she bid him mind wha gat him.

What ails ye at my dad, quoth he,
   My minny, or my aunty?
Wi' croudy-mowdy they fed me,
   Lang-kail and ranty-tanty:
And bannocks of good barley-meal,
   Of thae there was right plenty.
Wi' chapped stocks, fu' butter'd weil,
   And was na' that right dainty?

Altho' my father was nae laird,
   'Tis daffin to be vaunty,
He keepit ay a good kail-yard,
   A ha' house, and a pantry:

A good blue bonnet on his head,
   An o'erlay 'bout his craigy,
And ay until the day he died,
   He rade on good fhanks naigy.

Now wae and wonder on your fnout,
   Wad ye hae bonny Nanfy?
Wad ye compare yourfelf to me,
   A docken till a tanfy?
I ha'e a wooer o' my ain,
   They ca' him fouple Sandy,
And well I wat his bonny mou'
   Is fweet like fugar-candy.

Wow, Nanfy, what needs a' this din,
   Do I na' ken this Sandy?
I'm fure the chief of a' his kin
   Was Rab the beggar randy:
His minny Meg upo' her back
   Bare baith him and his billy;
Will ye compare a nafty pack
   To me your winfome Willy?

My gutcher left a good braid fword,
   Tho' it be auld and rufty,
Yet ye may tak' it on my word,
   It is baith ftout and trufty;
And if I can but get it drawn,
   Which will be right uncafy,
I fhall lay baith my lugs in pawn,
   That he fhall get a hezzy.

Then Nancy turn'd her round about,
   And faid, Did Sandy hear ye,
Ye wadna mifs to get a clout,
   I ken he difna' fear ye:
Sae had your tongue, and fay nae mair,
   Set fomewhere elfe your fancy;
For as lang's Sandy's to the fore,
   Ye never fhall get Nanfy.

SONG III.
CORN RIGS.

My Patie is a lo--ver gay, his mind is ne—ver

muddy, his breath is sweeter than new hay, his face

is fair and rud—dy. His shape is handsome, middle

size, he's comely in his wa'k-ing, the shining of his een

surprise, 'tis heaven to hear him ta'king.

Last night I met him on a bawk,
  Where yellow corn was growing:
There mony a kindly word he spake,
  That set my heart a-glowing.
He kiss'd, and vow'd he wad be mine,
  And loo'd me best of ony;
That gars me like to sing sinsyne,
  O corn-rigs are bonny.

A good blue bonnet on his head,
  An o'erlay 'bout his craigy,
And ay until the day he died,
  He rade on good fhanks naigy.

Now wae and wonder on your fnout,
  Wad ye hae bonny Nanfy?
Wad ye compare yourfelf to me,
  A docken till a tanfy?
I ha'e a wooer o' my ain,
  They ca' him fouple Sandy,
And well I wat his bonny mou'
  Is fweet like fugar-candy.

Wow, Nanfy, what needs a' this din,
  Do I na' ken this Sandy?
I'm fure the chief of a' his kin
  Was Rab the beggar randy:
His minny Meg upo' her back
  Bare baith him and his billy;
Will ye compare a nafty pack
  To me your winfome Willy?

My gutcher left a good braid fword,
  Tho' it be auld and rufty,
Yet ye may tak' it on my word,
  It is baith ftout and trufty;
And if I can but get it drawn,
  Which will be right uneafy,
I fhall lay baith my lugs in pawn,
  That he fhall get a hezzy.

Then Nancy turn'd her round about,
  And faid, Did Sandy hear ye,
Ye wadna mifs to get a clout,
  I ken he difna' fear ye:
Sae had your tongue, and fay nae mair,
  Set fomewhere elfe your fancy;
For as lang's Sandy's to the fore,
  Ye never fhall get Nanfy.

SONG III.
CORN RIGS.

My Patie is a lo--ver gay, his mind is ne—ver

muddy, his breath is sweeter than new hay, his face

is fair and rud—dy. His shape is handsome, middle

size, he's comely in his wa'k-ing, the shining of his een

surprise, 'tis heaven to hear him ta'king.

Last night I met him on a bawk,
  Where yellow corn was growing:
There mony a kindly word he spake,
  That set my heart a-glowing.
He kiss'd, and vow'd he wad be mine,
  And loo'd me best of ony;
That gars me like to sing sinsyne,
  O corn-rigs are bonny.

VOCAL ENCHANTRESS. 5

Let lasses of a silly mind
  Refuse what maist they're wanting!
Since we for yeilding were design'd,
  We chastly should be granting.
Then I'll comply, and marry PATE;
  And fyne my cockernony
He's free to touzel air or late,
  Where corn-rigs are bonny.

SONG IV.
TO ANACREON IN HEAVEN.

To Anacreon in heaven, where he sat in full glee, a few

sons of harmony sent a petition, that he their inspirer and

patron would be; when this answer arriv'd from the jolly

old Grecian—Voice, fiddle, and flute, no longer be mute,

I'll lend you my name, and inspire you to boot; and besides,

I'll instruct you like me to entwine the myrtle of Venus with

Bacchus's vine. And besides I'll instruct you like me to en-

twine the myrtle of Venus with Bacchus's vine.

The news through Olympus immediately flew;
　When Old Thunder pretended to give himself airs—
" If these mortals are suffer'd their scheme to pursue,
" The devil a Goddess will stay above stairs.
　　" Hark! already they cry,
　　" In transports of joy,
　" Away to the sons of Anacreon we'll fly,
" And there with good fellows, we'll learn to entwine
" The myrtle of Venus with Bacchus's vine.
　　　And there with good fellows, &c.

" The yellow-hair'd God, and his nine fusty maids,
" From Helicon's Banks will incontinent flee,
" Idalia will boast but of tenantless shades,
" And the bi-forked hill a mere desart will be.
　　" My thunder, no fear on't,
　　" Shall soon do it's errand,
　" And dam'me! I'll swinge the ringleaders, I warrant,
" I'll trim the young dogs for thus daring to twine
" The myrtle of Venus with Bacchus's vine."
　　　I'll trim the young dogs, &c.

Apollo rose up; and said, " Pr'ythee ne'er quarrel,
" Good king of the Gods, with my vot'ries below:
" Your thunder is useless"—then, shewing his laurel,
　Cry'd, " *Sic evitable fulmen,* you know!
　　" Then over each head
　　" My laurels I'll spread;
" So my sons from your crackers no mischief shall dread,

" Whilſt ſnug in their club room they jovially twine
" The myrtle of Venus with Bacchus's vine.
   Whilſt ſnug in their club-room, &c.

Next Momus got up with his riſible phiz,
 And ſwore with Apollo he'd chearfully join—
" The tide of full harmony ſtill ſhall be his,
 " But the ſong, and the catch, and the laugh ſhall be mine.
  " Then Jove, be not jealous
  " Of theſe honeſt fellows."
Cry'd Jove, "We relent, ſince the truth now you tell us;
" And ſwear, by Old Styx, that they long ſhall entwine
" The myrtle of Venus with Bacchus's vine."
   And ſwear, by Old Styx, &c.

Ye ſons of Anacreon, then, join hand in hand:
 Preſerve unanimity, friendſhip, and love;
'Tis your's to ſupport what's ſo happily plann'd:
 You've the ſanction of Gods, and the fiat of Jove.
  While thus we agree,
  Our toaſt let it be,
May our club flouriſh happy, united and free!
And long may the ſons of Anacreon entwine
The myrtle of Venus with Bacchus's vine.
 And long may the ſons of Anacreon entwine
 The myrtle of Venus with Bacchus's vine.

SONG V.
JOVE IN HIS CHAIR.

Jove in his chair of the sky lord mayor, with his nods men and gods keep in awe; when he winks heaven shrinks, when he speaks hell squeaks, earth's globe is but his tawe. Cock of the school, he bears despotic rule, his word tho' absurd must be law; even Fate, tho' so great, must not prate his bauld pate, Jove would cuff, he's so bluff, for a straw; cow'd de—i--ties, like mites in cheese, to stir must cease or gnaw.

SONG VI.
THE CHARGE IS PREPAR'D.

The charge is prepar'd, the lawyers are met, the judges all rang'd, a terrible show, I go undismay'd, for death is a debt, a debt on demand, so take what I owe. Then farewell my love, dear charmers, adieu! contented I die, 'tis the better for you. Here ends all dispute the rest of our lives, for this way at once I please all my wives.

SONG VII.
DOWN THE BURN DAVIE.

When trees did bud, and fields were green, and broom bloom'd fair to see, when Mary was complete fifteen, and love laugh'd in her e'e: blyth Davie's blinks her heart did move to speak her mind thus free; gang down the burn Davie love, and I will fol—low thee.

Now Davie did each lad surpass
 That dwelt on this burn side;
And Mary was the bonniest lass,
 Just meet to be a bride.
  Blyth Davie's blinks, &c.

Her cheeks were rosy, red and white,
 Her e'en were bonny blue,
Her looks were like Aurora bright,
 Her lips like droping dew.
  Blyth Davie's blinks, &c.

What pafs'd, I guefs, was harmlefs play,
   And nothing, fure, unmeet;
For, ganging hame, I heard them fay,
   They lik'd a walk fo fweet.
     Blyth Davie's blinks, &c.

His cheeks to her's he fondly laid;
   She cry'd, " Sweet love be true;
" And when a wife, as now a maid,
" To death I'll follow you."
     Blyth Davie's blinks, &c.

As fate had dealt to him a routh,
   Straight to the kirk he led her;
There plighted her his faith and truth,
   And a bonny bride he made her.
No more afham'd to own her love,
   Or fpeak her mind thus free;
" Gang down the burn, Davie, love,
" And I will follow thee."

SONG VIII.

MY TEMPLES WITH CLUSTERS.

My temples with clusters of grapes I'll entwine, and barter all joys for a goblet of wine, and barter all joys for a goblet of wine. In search of a Venus no longer I'll run, but stop and forget her at Bacchus's tun; no longer I'll run, but stop and forget her at Bacchus's tun.

Yet why thus resolve to relinquish the fair?
'Tis folly with spirits like mine to despair;
For what mighty charms can be found in a glass,
If not fill'd to the health of some favourite lass?

THE VOCAL ENCHANTRESS.

'Tis woman whofe charms every rapture impart,
And lend a new fpring to the pulfe of the heart;
The mifer himfelf, fo fupreme is her fway,
Grows a convert to love, and refigns her the key.

At the found of her voice forrow lifts up her head,
And poverty liftens, well pleas'd, from her fhed;
While age, in an ecftacy, hob'ling along,
Beats time, with his crutch, to the tune of her fong.

Then bring me a goblet from Bacchus's hoard,
The largeft and deepeft that ftands on his board;
I'll fill up a brimmer, and drink to the fair;
'Tis the thirft of a lover—and pledge me who dare.

SONG IX.
MY JO JANET.

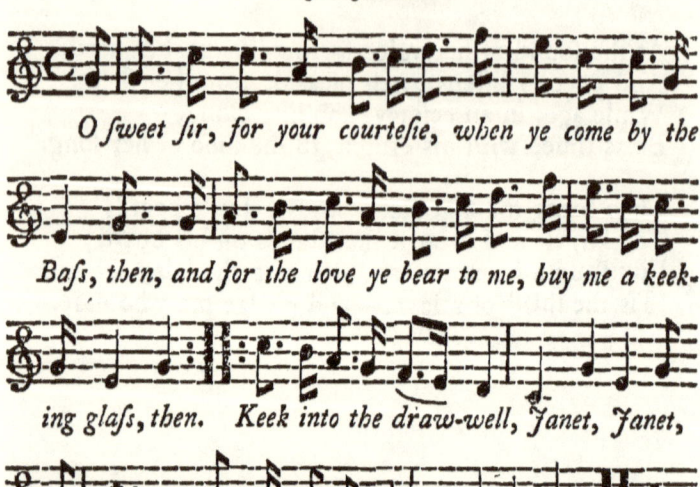

O sweet sir, for your courtesie, when ye come by the Bass, then, and for the love ye bear to me, buy me a keeking glass, then. Keek into the draw-well, Janet, Janet, and there ye'll see your bonny sell, my jo Janet.

    Keeking in the draw-well clear,
        What if I shou'd fa' in, Sir?
    Syne a' my kin will say and swear,
        I drown'd myself for sin, Sir.
    Had the better be the brae,
        Janet, Janet;
    Had the better be the brae,
        My jo Janet.

    Good Sir, for your courtesie,
        Coming through Aberdeen, then,
    For the love ye bear to me,
        Buy me a pair of sheen, then.
    Clout the auld, the new are dear,
        Janet, Janet,

Ae pair may gain ye ha'f a year,
  My jo Janet.

But what if dancing on the green,
  And skipping like a mawkin,
If they should see my clouted sheen,
  O' me they will be tawkin,
Dance ay laigh, and late at e'en,
      Janet, Janet,
Syne a' their fauts will no be seen,
  My jo Janet.

Kind Sir, for your courtesie,
  When ye gae to the crofs, then,
For the love ye bear to me,
  Buy me a pacing horse, then.
Pace upo' your spinning wheel,
      Janet, Janet,
Pace upo' your spinning wheel,
  My jo Janet.

SONG X.
MARY's DREAM.

The moon had climb'd the high-eft hill which rifes o'er the fource of Dee, and from the eaftern fum-mit fhed her fil-ver light on tow'r and tree; when Mary laid her down to fleep, her thoughts on Sandy far at fea; when foft and low a voice was heard fay Mary, weep no more for me.

    She from her pillow gently rais'd
      Her head to afk, who there might be.
    She faw young Sandy fhiv'ring ftand,
      With vifage pale and hollow eye;

" O Mary dear, cold is my clay,
  " It lies beneath a stormy sea,
" Far, far from thee, I sleep in death,
  " So Mary, weep no more for me.

" Three stormy nights and stormy days
  " We tofs'd upon the raging main:
" And long we strove our bark to save,
  " But all our striving was in vain.
" Ev'n then, when horror chill'd my blood,
  " My heart was fill'd with love for thee:
" The storm is past, and I at rest,
  " So Mary, weep no more for me.

" O maiden dear, thyself prepare,
  " We soon shall meet upon that shore,
" Where love is free from doubt and care,
  " And thou and I shall part no more."
Loud crow'd the cock; the shadow fled,
  No more of Sandy could she see;
But soft the passing spirit said,
  " Sweet Mary, weep no more for me."

C

SONG XI.
HAD NEPTUNE.

Had Neptune, when first he took charge of the sea, been as wife, or at least been as merry as we, he'd have thought better on't, and instead of the brine, would have fill'd the vast ocean with generous wine. — — — — — — — — — — — — — would have fill'd the vast ocean with generous wine.

What trafficking then would have been on the main,
For the sake of good liquor, as well as for gain,
No fear then of tempest, or danger of sinking,
The fishes ne'er drown that are always a-drinking.

The hot thirſty ſun would drive with more haſte,
Secure in the evening of ſuch a repaſt;
And when he'd got tipſey, wou'd have taken his nap,
With double the pleaſure in Thetis's lap.

By the force of his rays, and thus heated with wine,
Conſider how gloriouſly Phœbus would ſhine,
What vaſt exhalations he'd draw up on high,
To relieve the poor earth as it wanted ſupply.

How happy us mortals, when bleſt with ſuch rain,
To fill all our veſſels, and fill 'em again,
Nay even the beggar that has ne'er a diſh,
Might jump in the river and drink like a fiſh.

What mirth and contentment, on every one's brow,
Hob as great as a prince, dancing after his plough
The birbs in the air as they play on the wing,
Altho' they but ſip would eternally ſing.

The ſtars, who I think, don't to drinking incline,
Would friſk and rejoice at the fume of the wine;
And merrily twinkling would ſoon let us know,
That they were as happy as mortals below.

Had this been the caſe, what had we enjoy'd,
Our ſpirits ſtill riſing our fancy ne'er cloy'd;
A pox then on Neptune, when 'twas in his pow'r,
To ſlip like a fool, ſuch a fortunate hour.

C ij

20   CALLIOPE: OR THE

SONG XII.
TULLOCHGORUM.

Fiddlers, your pins in temper fix,
And roset weel your fiddle-sticks;
But banish vile Italian tricks
  Frae out your quorum:
Nor *fortes* wi' *pianos* mix,
  Gie's *Tullochgorum*.
                    FERGUSSON.

Come gie's a sang the lady cry'd, and lay your disputes all aside, what nonsense is't for folk to chide for what's been done before them. Let whig and tory all agree, whig and tory, whig and tory, whig and tory all agree, to drop their whig-megmorum, Let whig and tory all agree, to spend the night wi' mirth and glee, and chearfu' sing alang wi' me, the reel of Tullochgorum.

Tullochgorum's my delight,
It gars us a' in ane unite,
And ony fumph that keeps up fpite;
    In confcience I abhor him,
Blithe and merry we's be a',
Blithe and merry, blithe and merry,
Blithe and merry we's be a',
    To make a chearfu' quorum.
Blithe and merry we's be a',
As lang's we ha'e a breath to draw,
And dance till we be like to fa',
    The reel of Tullochgorum.

There needs na' be fo great a phrafe
Wi' dringing dull Italian lays
I wadna gi'e our ain Strathfpeys
    For half a hundred fcore o'm.
They're dowff and dowie at the beft,
Dowff and dowie, dowff and dowie,
They're dowff and dowie at the beft,
    Wi' a' there variorum.
They're dowff and dowie at the beft,
Their allegro's, and a' the reft,
They cannot pleafe a Highland tafte,
    Compar'd wi' Tullochgorum.

Let warldly minds themfelves opprefs
Wi' fear of want, and double cefs,
And filly fauls themfelves diftrefs
    Wi' keeping up decorum.
Shall we fae four and fulky fit,
Sour and fulky, four and fulky,
Shall we fae four and fulky fit,
    Like auld Philofophorum?
Shall we fae four and fulky fit,
Wi' neither fenfe, nor mirth, nor wit,
And canna rife to fhake a fit
    At the reel of Tullochgorum?

May choiceſt bleſſings ſtill attend
Each honeſt-hearted open friend,
And calm and quiet be his end,
 Be a' that's good before him!
May peace and plenty be his lot,
Peace and plenty, peace and plenty,
May peace and plenty be his lot,
 And dainties a great ſtore o'm!
May peace and plenty be his lot,
Unſtain'd by any vicious blot?
And may he never want a groat
 That's fond of Tullochgorum.

But for the diſcontented fool,
Who wants to be oppreſſion's tool,
May envy gnaw his rotten ſoul,
 And blackeſt fiends devour him!
My dole and ſorrow be his chance,
Dole and ſorrow, dole and ſorrow,
May dole and ſorrow be his chance,
 And honeſt ſouls abhor him!
May dole and ſorrow be his chance,
And a' the ills that come frae France
Whoe'er he be that winna dance
 The reel of Tullochgorum.

SONG XIII.

OPEN THE DOOR TO ME, OH.

It's open the door some pity to show, it's open the door

to me, Oh! Tho' you have been false, I'll always

prove true, So open the door to me, oh!

Cold is the blast upon my pale cheek,
But colder your love unto me, Oh!
    Though you have, &c.

She's open'd the door, she's open'd it wide,
She sees his pale corps on the ground, Oh!
    Though you have, &c.

My true love, she cry'd, then fell down by his side,
Never, never to shut again, Oh!
    Though you have, &c.

SONG XIV.
RUSSEL's TRIUMPH.

Thurſday in the morn, the nineteenth of May, recorded

for ever the famous ninety two, brave Ruſſel did diſcern

by break of day the lofty ſails of France advancing too. All

hands aloft, they cry, let Britiſh valour ſhine, let fly a cul-

verine, the ſignal of the line, let ev'ry man ſupply his gun,

follow me, you ſhall ſee, that the battle it will ſoon be

won, follow me, you ſhall ſee, that the battle it will ſoon

be won.

Tourville on the main triumphant rowl'd,
  To meet the gallant Ruffel in combat on the deep;
He led a noble train of heroes bold.
  To sink the English Admiral at his feet.
Now every valiant mind to victory doth aspire,
The bloody fight's begun, the sea is all on fire;
  And mighty fate stood looking on,
    Whilst a flood all of blood,
  Fill'd the scuppers of the rising sun.

Sulphur, smoak, and fire, disturbing the air,
  With thunder and wonder affright the Gallic shore;
Their regulated bands stood trembling near,
To see the lofty streamers now no more:
At six o'clock, the red, the smiling victors led.
  To give a second blow, the fatal overthrow:
    Now death and horror equal reign,
      Now they cry, run and die,
  British colours ride the vanquish'd main.

See they fly, amaz'd, thro' rocks and sands,
  One danger they grasp at to shun the greater fate,
In vain they cry for aid to weeping lands,
  The nymphs and sea-gods mourn their lost estate.
For evermore adieu, thou dazzling rising sun,
From thy untimely end thy master's fate begun:
  Enough, thou mighty god of war:
    Now we sing, bless the King!
  Let us drink to every British Tar.

D

SONG XV.
'TWAS WITHIN A MILE OF EDINBURGH.

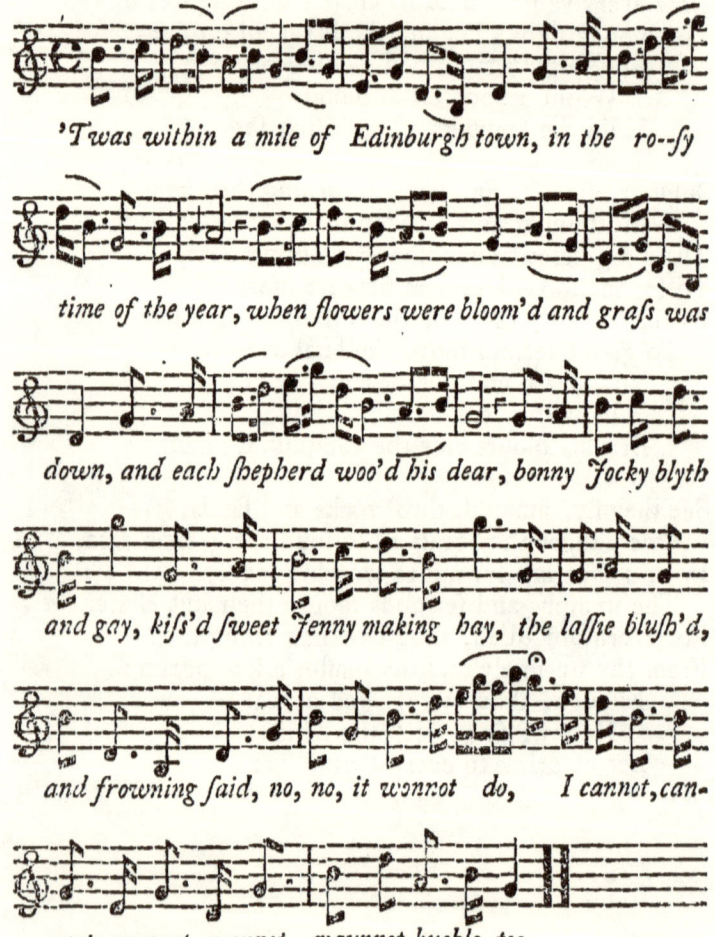

'Twas within a mile of Edinburgh town, in the ro--sy time of the year, when flowers were bloom'd and grass was down, and each shepherd woo'd his dear, bonny Jocky blyth and gay, kiss'd sweet Jenny making hay, the lassie blush'd, and frowning said, no, no, it wonnot do, I cannot, cannot, wonnot, wonnot, maunnot buckle too.

O Jocky was a wag, that never wou'd wed,
Though long he had followed the lafs,
Contented fhe work'd, and eat her brown bread,
And merrily turn'd up the grafs.
 Bonny Jocky blyth and gay,
 Won' her heart right merrily,
 But ftill fhe blufh'd and frowning faid,
  I cannot, &c.

But when that he vow'd he wou'd make her his bride,
Tho' his herds and his flocks were not few,
She gave him her hand and a kifs befides,
And vow'd fhe'd for ever be true.
 Bonny Jocky blyth and gay,
 Won her heart right merrily,
 At church fhe no more frowning faid,
  I cannot, &c.

SONG XVI.
THE FLOWERS OF EDINBURGH.

My love was once a bonny lad, he was the flow'r of all his kin, the absence of his bon-ny face, has rent my tender heart in twain. I day nor night find no delight, in fi---lent tears I still complain, and exclaim 'gainst those my ri---val foes, that hae ta'en from me my darling swain.

  Despair and anguish fills my breast,
   Since I have lost my blooming rose;
  I sigh and moan while others rest,
   His absence yields me no repose.

To seek my love I'll range and rove,
   Thro' ev'ry grove and distant plain;
Thus I'll ne'er cease, but spend my days,
   T' hear tidings from my darling swain.

There's nothing strange in nature's change,
   Since parents shew such cruelty;
They caus'd my love from me to range,
   And knows not to what destiny.
The pretty kids and tender lambs
   May cease to sport upon the plain;
But I'll mourn and lament, in deep discontent,
   For the absence of my darling swain.

Kind Neptune, let me thee intreat,
   To send a fair and pleasant gale;
Ye dolphins sweet, upon me wait,
   And do convey me on your tail.
Heav'ns bless my voyage with success,
   While crossing of the raging main,
And send me safe o'er to that distant shore,
   To meet my lovely darling swain.

All joy and mirth at our return
   Shall then abound from Tweed to Tay;
The bells shall ring, and sweet birds sing,
   To grace and crown our nuptial day.
Thus bless'd with charms in my love's arms,
   My heart once more I will regain,
Then I'll range no more to a distant shore,
   But in love will enjoy my darling swain.

SONG XVII.
THE STORM.

Ceaſe rude Boreas, bluſt'ring railer, liſt, ye landſmen

all to me, meſſmates, hear a brother ſailor ſing the dan-

gers of the ſea, from bounding billows firſt in motion, when

the diſtant whirlwinds riſe; to the tempeſt troubled o-

cean, where the ſeas contend with ſkies.

Lively.
Hark! the boatſwain hoarſely bawling,—
   By topſail ſheets, and haulyards ſtand!
Down top-gallants quick be hauling!
   Down your ſtay-ſails, hand, boys, hand!
Now it freſhens, ſet the braces;
   Quick the topſail ſheets let go;
Luff, boys, luff, don't make wry faces!
   Up your topſails nimbly clew!

Slow.
Now all you on down-beds sporting,
    Fondly lock'd in beauty's arms,
Fresh enjoyments wanton courting,
    Free from all but love's alarms,—
Round us roar the tempest louder;
    Think what fear our mind enthrals:
Harder yet, it yet blows harder;
    Now again the boatswain calls:

Quick.
The topsail-yards point to the wind, boys!
    See all clear to reef each course!
Let the fore-sheets go; don't mind, boys,
    Though the weather should be worse.
Fore and aft the sprit-sail yard get;
    Reef the mizen; see all clear:
Hand up! each preventer-brace set;
    Man the fore-yard; cheer, lads, cheer!

Slow.
Now the dreadful thunder's roaring!
    Peals on peals contending clash!
On our heads fierce rain falls pouring!
    In our eyes blue lightnings flash!
One wide water all around us,
    All above us one black sky!
Diff'rent deaths at once surround us.
    Hark! what means that dreadful cry?

Quick.
The foremast's gone, cries every tongue out,
    O'er the lee, twelve feet 'bove deck.
A leak beneath the chest-tree's sprung out;
    Call all hands to clear the wreck.
Quick the lanyards cut to pieces!
    Come, my hearts be stout, and bold!
Plumb the well, the lake increases;
    Four feet water in the hold!

Slow.
While o'er the ſhip wild waves are beating,
　We for wives or children mourn;
Alas! from hence there's no retreating;
　Alas! from hence there's no return.
Still the lake is gaining on us;
　Both chain pumps are choak'd below,
Heav'n have mercy here upon us!
　For only that can ſave us now!

Quick.
O'er the lee-beam is the land boys;
　Let the guns o'er-board be thrown;
To the pump come every hand, boys;
　See our mizen-maſt is gone,
The leak we've found; it cannot pour faſt:
　We've lighten'd her a foot or more;
Up, and rig a jury fore-maſt;
　She rights, ſhe rights, boys! wear off ſhore.

Now once more on joys we're thinking,
　Since kind fortune ſpar'd our lives;
Come the cann, boys, let's be drinking
　To our ſweethearts and our wives.
Fill it up, about ſhip wheel it;
　Cloſe to th' lips a brimmer join.
Where's the tempeſt now; who feels it?
　None! our danger's drown'd in wine!

SONG XVIII.
IN LOVE SHOULD THERE MEET.

In love should there meet a fond pair, untutor'd by fa-
shion or art, whose wishes are warm, are warm and sincere, whose words are th' excess of the heart, - - - - -
- whose words are th' excess of the heart: If ought
of substantial de--light on this side the stars can be found,
'tis sure when this couple u—nite, and Cupid by Hymen
is crown'd - - - - - - and Cupid by Hymen is crown'd.

SONG XIX.
LOVELY GODDESS.

Hear the birds around thee sing,
In the gardens of the spring;
Ev'ry bush and ev'ry tree
Warbles forth it's joy to thee.
Nature's songsters all are gay
At the lov'd approach of May:

All, great Queen, thy praises sing,
Thine, great Empress of the spring.

Goddess, in thy vest of green;
Goddess, with thy youthful mein;
Haste and bring thy mines of wealth,
Gladness, and her parent, health;
Bring with thee thy chearful train,
Chacing care, and chacing pain,
See, the lovely graces, all
Throng obedient to thy call.

Goddess, haste, and bring with thee
Virtue's child, fair liberty;
For, if liberty's away,
Who can taste the month of May?
Here he comes, I hear the sound
Of the merry songsters round:
Here he comes all fresh and gay,
Paying homage to thee, May.

Goddess, who perfum'st the air,
Who hast deck'd the earth so fair;
Thou, with gladness by thy side
Still'st the raging of the tide;
Bid'st the winds forbear to roar,
And stern winter seen no more;
Meads and groves their echos ring,
Love himself is on the wing.

Lovely nymph, divinest May,
Thou to whom this verse I pay:
O! thy healing warmth impart
To the mistress of my heart;
Ev'ry day with gladness crown,
By her health, preserve my own:
Blooming nymph, of heavenly birth,
Goddess, thou, of health and mirth.

SONG XX.
WHILE MISERS ALL NIGHT.

While misers all night still are watching their stores, and

all day sternly drive the distress'd from their doors, while

courtiers each other subvert in the state, and obstinate

churchmen new maxims create, we are frugally gen'rous,

nor each other wrong, but enjoy us at night, then conclude

with a song, but enjoy us at night then conclude with a

song.

Let sharpers attempt by false arts to ensnare,
Till at length they receive their long merited fare,
Let spendthrifts consume till too late they repent,
The loss of their riches so lavishly spent,
    While with honest industry we live the day long,
    And enjoy us at night, then conclude with a song.

Tho' drunkards in claret such rapture express,
They'd find it more sov'reign, were they to drink less:
Tho' rakes say in women is center'd our bliss,
They've reason sometimes to regret a close kiss.
    Such diff'rent extremes then to us don't belong,
    And yet women and wine are the life of our song.

Yet topers and rakes, would ye lead happy lives,
Be mod'rate in drinking and chuse modest wives,
Let churchmen with churchmen, and courtiers be friends,
For on friendship all earthly enjoyment depends.
    And when ye're united thus lasting and strong,
    Like us you'll be jovial, and end with a song.

SONG XXI.
SWEET ANNIE.

Sweet Annie frae the sea-beach came, where Jocky speel'd the vessel's side, ah! wha can keep their heart at hame, when Jocky's tost aboon the tide. Far aff to distant realms he gangs, yet I'll prove true as he has been; and when ilk lass a—bout him thrangs, he'll think on Annie, his faithful ane.

I met our wealthy laird yestreen,
  Wi' gou'd in hand he tempted me,
He prais'd my brow, my rolling een,
  And made a brag of what he'd gi'e.

What tho' my Jocky's far away,
   Toſt up and down the anſome main,
I'll keep my heart anither day,
   Since Jocky may return again.

Nae mair, falſe Jamie, ſing nae mair,
   And fairly caſt your pipe away;
My Jocky wad be troubled fair,
   To ſee his friend his love betray:
For a' your ſongs and verſe are vain,
   While Jocky's notes do faithful flow;
My heart to him ſhall true remain,
   I'll keep it for my conſtant jo.

Blaw ſaft, ye gales, round Jocky's head,
   And gar your waves be calm and ſtill;
His hameward ſail with breezes ſpeed,
   And dinna a' my pleaſure ſpill.
What tho' my Jocky's far away,
   Yet he will braw in filler ſhine;
I'll keep my heart anither day,
   Since Jocky may again be mine.

SONG XXII.
TOPSAILS SHIVER IN THE WIND.

The topsails shi--ver in the wind, the ship she casts to

sea; but yet my soul, my heart, my mind, are, Mary,

moor'd with thee. For, tho' thy sailor's bound a--far, still

love shall be his leading star; for tho' thy sailor's bound a-

far, still love shall be his lead--ing star.

Should landmen flatter when we're sail'd,
   O doubt their artful tales;
No gallant sailor ever fail'd,
   If love breath'd constant gales;
Thou art the compass of my soul
Which steers my heart from pole to pole.

Sirens in every port we meet,
  More fell than rocks or waves
But fuch as grace the Britifh fleet,
  Are lovers and not flaves :
No foes our courage fhall fubdue,
Altho' we've left our hearts with you.

Thefe are our cares, but if you're kind,
  We'll fcorn the dafhing main,
The rocks, the billows, and the wind,
  The pow'r of France and Spain :
Now England's glory refts with you,
Our fails are full, fweet girls, Adieu!

F

SONG XXIII.
I'LL NEVER LEAVE THEE.

One day I heard Mary say, how shall I leave thee?

stay, dearest A--donis, stay, why wilt thou grieve me?

Alas, my fond heart will break, if thou should leave me,

I'll live and die for thy sake, yet never leave thee,

Say, lovely Adonis, say,
    Has Mary deceiv'd thee?
Did e'er her young heart betray
    New love to grieve thee?
My constant mind ne'er shall stray,
    Thou may believe me;
I'll love thee, lad, night and day,
    And never leave thee.

Adonis, my charming youth,
    What can relieve thee?
Can Mary thy anguish soothe,
    This breast shall receive thee.

My paſſion can ne'er decay,
   Never deceive thee:
Delight ſhall drive pain away,
   Pleaſure revive thee.

But leave thee, lad, leave thee, lad,
   How ſhall I leave thee?
O! that thought makes me ſad;
   I'll never leave thee.
Where would my Adonis fly?
   Why does he grieve me?
Alas! my poor heart will die,
   If I ſhould leave thee.

SONG XXIV.

THE LAST TIME I CAME O'ER THE MUIR.

The laſt time I came o'er the muir, I left my love be-

hind me; ye pow'rs, what pain do I endure, when ſoft

i—de-as mind me. Soon as the ruddy morn diſplay'd,

the beaming day enſuing, I met betimes my love-ly maid,

in fit re--treats for wooing.

  Beneath the cooling ſhade we lay,
    Gazing and chaſtely ſporting;
  We kiſs'd and promis'd time away,
    'Till night ſpread her black curtain.
  I pitied all beneath the ſkies,
    Even kings when ſhe was nigh me;
  In raptures I beheld her eyes,
    Which could but ill deny me.

Should I be call'd where cannons roar,
　Where mortal steel may wound me;
Or cast upon some foreign shore,
　Where dangers may surround me;
Yet hopes again to see my love,
　To feast on glowing kisses,
Shall make my care at distance move,
　In prospect of such blisses.

In all my soul there's not one place
　To let a rival enter;
Since she excels in every grace,
　In her my love shall center.
Sooner the seas shall cease to flow,
　Their waves the Alps to cover;
On Greenland's ice shall roses grow,
　Before I cease to love her.

The next time I gang o'er the muir,
　She shall a lover find me;
And that my faith is firm and pure,
　Tho' I left her behind me.
Then Hymen's sacred bonds shall chain
　My heart to her fair bosom;
There, while my being does remain,
　My love more fresh shall blossom.

SONG XXV.
BESSEY BELL AND MARY GRAY.

O Beſſy Bell and Mary Gray they were twa bonny laſſes, they bigg'd a bow'r on yon burn brae, and theek'd it o'er wi' raſhes. Fair Beſſey Bell I loo'd ye-ſtreen, and thought I ne'er cou'd alter; but Mary Gray's twa pawky een they gar my fancy faulter.

Now Beſſey's hair's like a lint-tap;
  She ſmiles like a May morning,
When Phœbus ſtarts frae Thetis' lap,
  The hills with rays adorning:
White is her neck, ſaft is her hand,
  Her waiſt and feet's fu' genty;
With ilka grace ſhe can command;
  Her lips, O vow! they're dainty.

And Mary's locks are like a craw,
  Her een like diamonds glances:
She's ay fay clean, redd up, and braw,
  She kills whene'er she dances:
Blyth as a kid, with wit at will,
  She blooming, tight, and tall is;
And guides her airs fae gracefu' still,
  O Jove! she's like thy Pallas.

Dear Bessey Bell and Mary Gray,
  Ye unco fair opprefs us;
Our fancies jee between you tway,
  Ye are fic bonny laffes:
Waes me; for baith I canna get,
  To ane by law we're stented;
Then I'll draw cuts and tak my fate,
  And be with ane contented.

SONG XXVI.
EWE-BUGHTS MARION.

Will ye go to the ewe-bughts Marion, and wear in the

sheep wi' me? The sun shines sweet my Marion, but nae half

sae sweet as thee. The sun shines sweet my Marion, but nae

half sae sweet as thee.

O Marion's a bonny lafs,
   And the blyth blinks in her ee';
And fain wad I marry Marion,
   Gin Marion wad marry me.

There's goud in your garters, Marion,
   And filk on your white haufs-bane;
Fu' fain wad I kifs my Marion,
   At e'en when I come hame.

I've nine milk ewes, my Marion;
   A cow and a brawny quey,
I'll gi'e them a' to my Marion,
   Juft on her bridal day.

And ye's get a green fey apron,
　　And waftecoat of the London brown,
And vow but ye will be vap'ring,
　　Whene'er ye gang to the town.

I'm young and ftout, my Marion;
　　Nane dances like me on the green;
And gin ye forfake me Marion,
　　I'll e'en draw up wi' Jean.

Sae put on your pearlins, Marion,
　　And kyrtle of the cramafie!
And foon as my chin has nae hair on,
　　I fhall come weft, and fee ye.

G

SONG XXVII.
ETRICK BANKS.

On Etrick banks, ae summer's night, at gloming when the sheep drave hame, I met my lassie braw and tight, came wading barefoot a' her lane; my heart grew light, I ran, I flang my arms about her li--ly neck, and kiss'd and clapp'd her there fu' lang, my words they were na many feck.

  I said, My lassie, will ye go
   To the Highland hills, the Earse to learn,
  I'll baith gi'e thee a cow and ew,
   When ye come to the brigg of Earn.

At Leith auld meal comes in, ne'er faſh,
  And herring at the Broomielaw;
Chear up your heart, my bonny laſs,
  There's gear to win wé never ſaw.

All day when we have wrought enough,
  When winter, froſt and ſnaw begin,
Soon as the ſun gaes weſt the loch,
  At night when ye ſit down to ſpin,
I'll ſcrew my pipes and play a ſpring:
  And thus the weary night we'll end,
Till the tender kid and lamb-time bring
  Our pleaſant ſummer back again.

Syne when the trees are in their bloom,
  And gowans glent o'er ilka field,
I'll meet my laſs amang the broom,
  And lead you to my ſummer ſhield.
Then far frae a' their ſcornfu' din,
  That make the kindly hearts their ſport,
We'll laugh and kiſs, and dance and ſing,
  And gar the langeſt day ſeem ſhort.

SONG XXVIII.
FRIEND AND PITCHER.

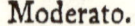

The wealthy fool with gold in store, will still desire to

grow richer, give me but these, I ask no more, my charm-
Chorus.

ing girl, my friend, and pitcher. My friend so rare, my

girl so fair, with such what mortal can be richer; give

me but these, a fig for care, with my sweet girl, my

friend and pitcher.

From morning sun I'd never grieve
   To toil a hedger or a ditcher,
If that when I come home at eve,
   I might enjoy my friend and pitcher.
      My friend so rare, &c.

Tho' fortune ever shuns my door,
I know not what can bewitch her;
With all my heart can I be poor,
With my sweet girl, my friend, and pitcher.
My friend so rare, &c.

SONG XXIX.
MAN MAY ESCAPE.

Man may escape from rope or gun, nay some have out-liv'd the doctor's pill; who takes a woman must be un-done, that ba--si--lisk is sure to kill. The fly that sips treacle is lost in the sweets, so he that tastes woman, wo-man, woman, he that tastes woman ruin meets.

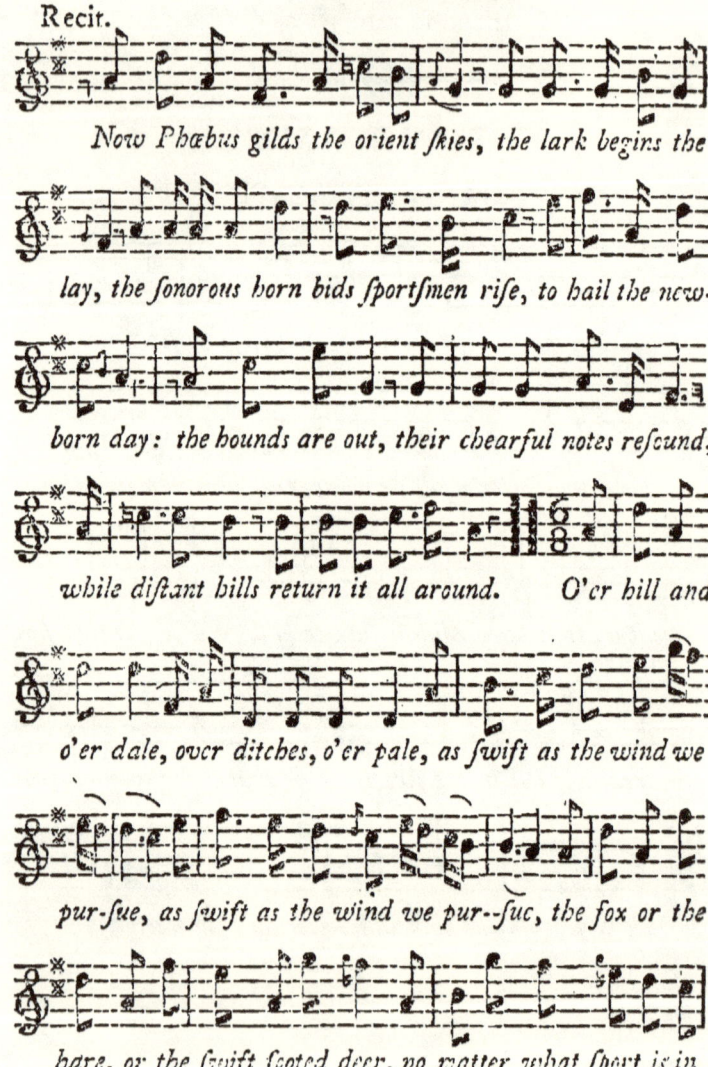

view, - - - - - - - - - - - - - - - - *no mat-
ter what sport is in view.*

Health waits on the chace,
Paints with blushes the face,
Spleen and vapours are left in the rear.
The brooks and the floods,
And the deep embrown'd woods,
Delightful around us appear.

To the sports of the field
All others must yield,
For hunting's of ancient renown;
Kings and princes, of old,
Have this pastime extoll'd,
Royal hunters have sat on the throne.

Hills and vallies o'erpast,
Now homeward we haste,
And our mistresses hearty embrace:
New strength we obtain,
By our sports on the plain,
For strength still attends on the chace.

Now the bowl comes in view,
Which with glee we pursue,
And thus happily finish the day:
To the huntress divine,
To Diana we join,
While each chorus loudly huzza.

SONG XXXI.
THE YOUNG MAN's WISH.

Free from the buſtle care and ſtrife, of this ſhort va-

rie--ga--ted life, O let me ſpend my days in rural ſweetneſs,

with a friend, to whom my mind I may unbend, nor cen-

ſure heed or praiſe, nor cenſure heed or praiſe.

  Riches bring cares—I aſk not wealth,
  Let me enjoy but peace and health,
   I envy not the great:
  'Tis theſe alone can make me bleſt;
  The riches take of eaſt and weſt,
   I claim not theſe or ſtate.

  Tho' not extravagant nor near,
  But through the well ſpent checker'd year,
   I'd have enough to live;
  To drink a bottle with a friend,
  Aſſiſt him in diſtreſs, ne'er lend,
   But rather freely give.

VOCAL ENCHANTRESS.

I too would wiſh, to ſweeten life,
A gentle, kind, good natur'd wife,
   Young, ſenſible and fair:
One who could love but me alone,
Prefer my cot to e'er a throne,
   And ſoothe my every care.

Thus happy with my wife and friend,
My life I chearfully would ſpend,
   With no vain thoughts oppreſt;
If heav'n has bliſs for me in ſtore,
O grant me this, I aſk no more,
   And I am truly bleſt.

H

SONG XXXII.
THE MATRON's WISH.

When my locks are grown hoary, and my visage looks pale, when my forehead has wrinkles, and mine eye-sight does fail, may my words and mine actions be free from all harm, may
Chorus.
I have a good husband to keep my back warm. O the plea-sures of youth, they are flow'rs but of May, our life's but a vapour, our bodies but clay, yet let me live well, tho' I live but a day.

With a sermon on Sunday, and a Bible of good print;
With a pot on the fire, and good viands in't;

With ale, beer, and brandy, both winter and summer,
To drink to my goffip, and be pledg'd by my cummer.
    The pleasures of, &c.

With pigs and with poultry, and some money in store
To purchase the needful, and to give to the poor;
With a bottle of Canary, to sip without sin,
And to comfort my daughter whene'er she lies in.
    The pleasures of, &c.

With a bed soft and easy to rest on at night,
With a maid in the morning to rise with the light,
To do her work neatly, and obey my desire,
To make the house clean, and blow up the fire.
    The pleasures of, &c.

With health and content, and a good easy chair;
With a thick hood and mantle, when I ride on my mare.
Let me dwell near my cupboard, and far from my foes,
With a pair of glass eyes to clap on my nose.
    The pleasures of, &c.

And when I am dead, with a sigh let them say,
Our honest old cummer's now laid in the clay:
When young, she was chearful, no scold, nor no whore;
She assisted her neighbours, and gave to the poor.
    Tho' the flow'r of her youth in her age did decay,
    Tho' her life like a vapour evanish'd away,
    She liv'd well and happy unto her last day.

SONG XXXIII.
THE VICAR AND MOSES.

At the sign of the horse, old Spintext of course, each

night took his pipe and his pot, o'er a jorum of nappy, quite

pleasant and happy, was plac'd this canoni-cal sot, Tol

de rol de rol ti dol di dol.

The evening was dark, when in came the clerk,
    With reverence due and submission;
First strok't his cravat, then twirl'd round his hat,
    And bowing, preferr'd his petition.

I'm come, Sir, says he, to beg, look d'ye see,
    Of your reverend worship and glory,
To inter a poor baby, with as much speed as may be,
    And I'll walk with the lanthorn before you.

The body we'll bury, but pray where's the hurry?
    Why Lord, Sir, the corpse it does stay:
You fool hold your peace, since miracles cease,
    A corpse, Moses, can't run away.

Then Mofes he fmil'd, faying, Sir, a fmall child
    Cannot long delay your intentions;
Why that's true, by St Paul, a child that is fmall,
    Can never enlarge it's dimenfions.

Bring Mofes fome beer, and bring me fome, d'ye hear,
    I hate to be call'd from my liquor:
Come, Mofes, the King, 'tis a fcandalous thing,
    Such a fubject fhould be but a Vicar.

Then Mofes he fpoke, Sir 'tis paft twelve o'clock,
    Befides there's a terrible fhower;
Why Mofes, you elf, fince the clock has ftruck twelve,
    I'm fure it can never ftrike more.

Befides, my dear friend, this leffon attend,
    Which to fay and to fwear I'll be bold,
That the corpfe, fnow or rain, can't endanger, that's plain;
    But perhaps you or I may take cold.

Then Mofes went on, Sir the clock has ftruck one,
    Pray Mafter look up at the hand;
Why it ne'er can ftrike lefs, 'tis a folly to prefs
    A man for to go that can't ftand.

At length, hat and cloak old Orthodox took,
    But cram'd his jaw with a quid;
Each tipt off a gill, for fear they fhould chill,
    And then ftagger'd away fide by fide.

When come to the grave, the clerk hum'd a ftave,
    Whilft the furplice was wrapt round the Prieft;
Where fo droll was the figure of Mofes and Vicar,
    That the parifh ftill talk of the jeft.

Good people, let's pray, put the corpfe t'other way,
    Or perchance I fhall over it ftumble;
'Tis beft to take care, tho' the fages declare,
    A *mortuum caput* can't tremble.

Woman that's born of a man, that's wrong, the leaf's torn;
  A man, that is born of a woman,
Can't continue an hour, but is cut down like a flow'r;
  You fee, Mofes, death fpareth no man.

Here, Mofes, do look, what a confounded book,
  Sure the letters are turn'd upfide down.
Such a fcandalous print, fure the devil is in't,
  That this Bafket fhould print for the Crown.

Prithee, Mofes, you read, for I cannot proceed,
  And bury the corpfe in my ftead.
    (Amen. Amen.)
Why, Mofes, you're wrong, pray hold ftill your tongue,
  You've taken the tail for the head.

O where's thy fting, Death! put the corpfe in the earth,
  For, believe me, 'tis terrible weather.
So the corpfe was interr'd, without praying a word,
  And away they both ftagger'd together,
    Singing *Tol de rol de rol ti dol di dol.*

SONG XXXIV.
SWEET ENGAGER.

Sweet en--ga-ger of my heart, gentle as the zephyr's

wing, Na-ture's beauty void of art, hear me

while thy praise I sing, hear me while thy praise

I sing, hear me while thy praise I sing.

 If I call the lilly fair,
  If the rose can shed perfume,
 The lillies on thy bosom are,
  And the rose is in thy bloom.

 Beauty and good-humour too,
  Sense and reason to thy aid;
 Ever kind and ever true,
  Polly is a lovely maid,

SONG XXXV.
CLUB YOUR FIRELOCKS.

Club your firelocks, my lads, let us march to the coasts,

to try whether Monsieur will stick to his boasts, for Par-

blew! he cries, me vill Britain invade, but Monsieur

deals largely, deals largely, deals largely, but Monsieur

deals largely, and fibbing's his trade, but Monsieur deals

largely, deals largely, deals largely, but Monsieur deals

largely, and fibbing's his trade.

What signifies all this confusion and pother,
Their routs and their marches from one place to to'ther,
Their transports to carry, their navies to fight
When learnt they that Frenchmen bold Britons could fright.

We'll remind them (if haply their mem'ries are bad)
What drubbings and dressings they formerly had,
When Britain's rous'd Lion stretch'd forth his strong paw,
To the Gallic Baboon he could always give law.

Can ye Frenchmen forget (still as friends we'll address ye)
The basting ye got at Poictiers and Cressy?
But should ye reject this as quite an old story,
The fall of last war is still recent before ye.

Cross quickly the channel! why all this delay,
We long to return you the visit you pay,
In us you will find of politeness no lack,
Will receive you so well that you'll never go back.

What tho' the dull Spaniard has join'd the French friskers,
His Donship will find we can pull his grave whiskers:
The Havannah we'll put in our pockets again,
And blow both the Bourbons quite out of the main.

SONG XXXVI.
RALPH AND SUE.

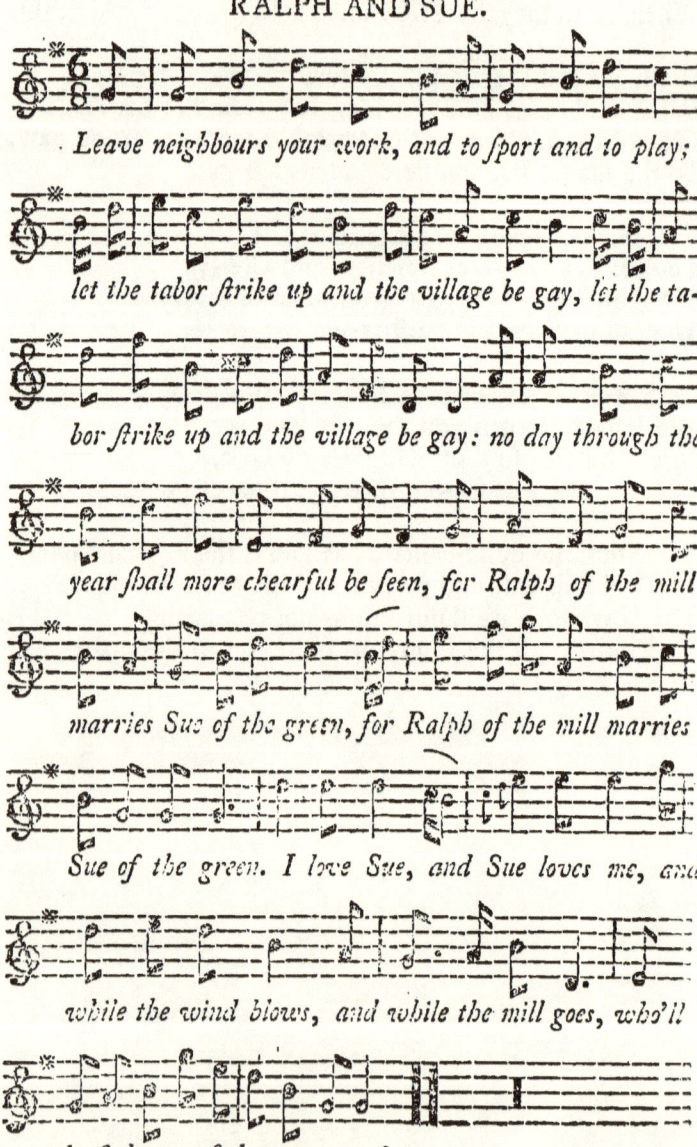

Leave neighbours your work, and to sport and to play; let the tabor strike up and the village be gay, let the tabor strike up and the village be gay: no day through the year shall more chearful be seen, for Ralph of the mill marries Sue of the green, for Ralph of the mill marries Sue of the green. I love Sue, and Sue loves me, and while the wind blows, and while the mill goes, who'll be so happy, so happy as we?

Let lords and fine folks, who for wealth take a bride,
Be marry'd to-day, and to-morrow be cloy'd:
My body is ſtout, and my heart is as found,
And my love, like my courage, will never give ground.
   I love Sue, &c.

Let ladies of faſhion the beſt jointures wed,
And prudently take the beſt bidders to bed;
Such ſigning and ſealing's no part of our bliſs,
We ſettle our hearts, and we ſeal with a kiſs.
   I love Sue, &c.

Tho' Ralph is not courtly, nor none of your beaus,
Nor bounces, nor flatters, nor wears your fine clothes,
In nothing he'll follow the folks of high life,
Nor e'er turn his back on his friend, or his wife.
   I love Ralph, &c.

While thus I am able to work at my mill,
While thus thou art kind, and thy tongue but lies ſtill,
Our joys ſhall continue, and ever be new,
And none be ſo happy as Ralph and his Sue.
   I love Sue, &c.

SONG XXXVII.
WHEN MORN HER SWEETS.

To some clear river's verdant side,
Do thou my happy footsteps guide;
In concert with the purling stream,
We'll sing, and love shall be the theme:

E'er night aſſumes her gloomy reign,
When ſhadows lengthen o'er the plain;
We'll to the myrtle grove repair,
For peace and pleaſure wait us there.

   The laughing god there keeps his court,
And little loves inceſſant ſport;
Around the winning graces wait,
And calm contentment guards the ſeat.
There loſt in extaſies of joy,
While tendereſt ſcenes our thoughts employ,
We'll bleſs the hour our loves begun,
The happy moment made us one.

SONG XXXVIII.
HARK THE HORN.

Hark the horn from the valley how lively it peals, and beats from the caverns around to the hills, how sweetly does Echo repeat her own mocks, how melting the murmur that dies in the rocks. Each note is a warning to join the career, each note is a warning to join the career, and a signal inviting the sun to appear, each note is a signal inviting the sun to appear.

Behold in the east, the clouds sever'd with light,
How glorious the prospect that bursts on the sight;
A tumult of gladness plays round the warm heart,
And the spirit of extacy throbs in each part;
The air courts the sense as it steals o'er the field,
Enrich'd with the fragrance the rose-thickets yield.

On his roost the shrill cock, early herald of morn,
Flaps his wings and proclaims the sun's welcome return.
The lark mounting sings, and the sweet-warbling thrush
Her dulcet song carols from low hawthorn bush:
For the op'ning the courses impatiently pant,
And the deep-scented hound longs the onset to chant.

But see from his covert, the fox slowly creep,
And steal leering backward along the woods steep.
That holla proclaims him discover'd! he sees
Flight's the refuge remaining, and runs with the breeze:
Away in pursuit!—we'll his vestages trace
And mix with the clamours that chorus the chace.

SONG XXXIX.
AH WHY MUST WORDS.

Ah why must words my flame reveal, what needs my
Damon bid me tell what all my actions prove, what all
my actions prove. A blush whene'er I meet his eye,
whene'er I hear his name a sigh betrays my secret love,
- - be—trays my secret love.

In all their sports upon the plain
My eyes still fix'd on him remain,
   And him alone approve;
The rest unheeded, dance or play,
He steals from all my praise away,
   And can he doubt my love.

Whene'er we meet my looks confess
The pleasures which my soul possess,
   And all it's cares remove,

Still, still too short appears his stay,
I frame excuses for delay,
   Can this be ought but love?

Does any speak in Damon's praise,
How pleas'd am I with all he says,
   And ev'ry word approve;
Is he defam'd, tho' but in jest,
I feel resentment fire my breast,
   Alas, because I love.

But O what tortures tear my heart,
When I suspect his looks impart,
   The least desire to rove.
I hate the maid who gives me pain,
Yet him I strive to hate in vain,
   For ah! that hate is love.

Then ask not words but read my eyes,
Believe my blushes, trust my sighs,
   All these my passion prove:
Words may deceive, may spring from art,
But the true language of my heart
   To Damon must be love.

K.

SONG XL.
COME ROUSE BROTHER SPORTSMAN.

Come rouse brother sportsman, the hunters all cry, we've got a strong scent and a favouring sky, we've got a strong scent, we've got a strong scent, we've got a strong scent and a favouring sky. The horn's sprightly notes, and the lark's early song will chide the dull sportsman for sleeping so long, will chide - will chide the dull sportsman for sleeping so long, will chide the dull sportsman for sleeping so long.

Bright Phœbus has shewn us the glimpse of his face,
Peep'd in at our windows, and call'd to the chace,
He soon will be up, for his dawn wears away,
And makes the fields blush with the beams of his ray.

Sweet Molly may teaze you perhaps to lie down,
And if you refuse her perhaps she may frown,
But tell her sweet love must to hunting give place,
For as well as her charms, there are charms in the chace.

Look yonder, look yonder, old Reynard I spy,
At his brush nimbly follows brisk Chanter and Fly,
They seize on their prey, see his eye-balls they roll,
We're in at the death, now return to the bowl.

There we'll fill up our glasses, and toast to the King.
From a bumper fresh loyalty ever will spring,
To George peace and glory may heaven dispense,
And fox hunters flourish a thousand years hence.

SONG XLI.
THE LASS OF PEATIE's MILL.

The lass of Peatie's mill so bonny blyth and gay, in spite of all my skill, hath stole my heart away. When tedding of the hay, bare-head-ed on the green love midst her locks did play, and wan-ton'd

in her een.

  Her arms, white, round, and smooth;
   Breasts rising in their dawn;
  To age it would give youth,
   To press them with his hand.
  Through all my spirits ran
   An extasy of bliss,
  When I such sweetness fand,
   Wrapt in a balmy kiss.

Without the help of art,
   Like flow'rs which grace the wild,
Her sweets she did impart,
   Whene'er she spoke or smil'd
Her looks, they were so mild,
   Free from affected pride,
She me to love beguil'd;
   I wish'd her for my bride.

O! had I all that wealth
   Hoptouns high mountains fill,
In sur'd long life and health,
   And pleasure at my will;
I'd promise, and fulfil,
   That none but bonny she,
The lass of Peatie's mill,
   Should share the same with me.

SONG XLII.
AWAY TO THE FIELD.

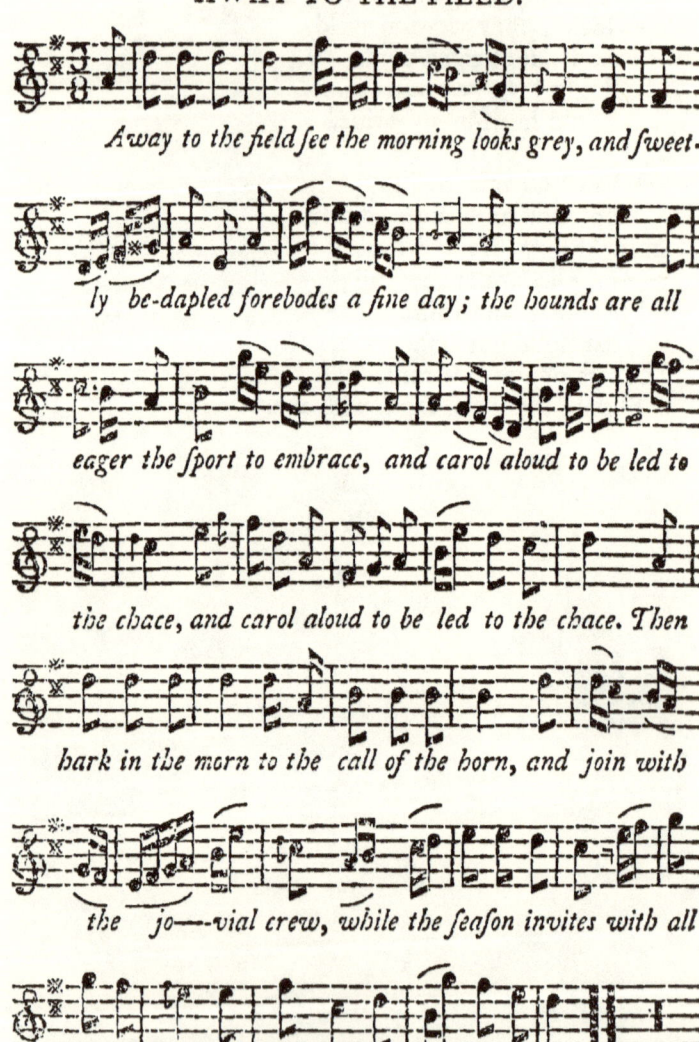

Away to the field see the morning looks grey, and sweet-

ly be-dapled forebodes a fine day; the hounds are all

eager the sport to embrace, and carol aloud to be led to

the chace, and carol aloud to be led to the chace. Then

hark in the morn to the call of the horn, and join with

the jo——vial crew, while the season invites with all

it's delights, the health-giving chace to pursue.

How charming the fight, when Aurora firft dawns,
To fee the bright beagles fpread over the lawns;
To welcome the fun, now returning from reft,
There mattins they chant as they merrily queft.
    Then hark in the morn, &c.

But oh! how each bofom with tranfport it fills,
To ftart juft as Phœbus peeps over the hills;
While joyous from valley to valley refounds
The fhouts of the hunters, and cry of the hounds.
    Then hark in the morn, &c.

See how the brave hunters with courage elate,
Fly hedges and ditches, or top the barr'd gate;
Borne by their bold courfers, no danger they fear,
And give to the winds all vexation and care.
    Then hark in the morn, &c.

Ye cits for the chace, quit the joys of the town,
And fcorn the dull pleafure of fleeping in down;
Uncertain your toil, or for honour, or wealth,
Ours ftill is repaid with contentment and health.
    Then hark in the morn, &c.

SONG XLIII.
THE BLUSH OF AURORA.

The blush of Au-ro--ra now tinges the morn, and dew-drops be-spangle the sweet scented thorn; then sound bro-ther sportsman sound, sound the gay horn, till Phœbus a-wakens the day, till Phœbus a--wakens the day: and see now he rises! in splendor how bright! IO Pœan! IO Pœan for Phœbus, for Phœbus the god of delight, all glorious in beauty now ba-nish-es night:

What raptures can equal the joys of the chace!
Health, bloom, and contentment appear in each face,
And in our swift coursers what beauty and grace,
    While we the fleet stag do pursue;
    While we, &c.
At the deep and harmonious sweet cry of the hounds,
Wing'd by terror, wing'd by terror,
Wing'd by terror, he bursts from the forest's wide bounds,
And tho' like the light'ning he darts o'er the grounds,
    Yet still, boys, we keep him in view.
We keep him in view, we keep him in view, in view,
And tho' like the light'ning, &c.

When chac'd till quite spent, he his life does resign,
Our victim we'll offer at Bacchus's shrine;
And revel in honour of Nimrod divine,
    That hunter so mighty of fame,
    That hunter, &c.
Our glasses then charge to our country and king,
Love and beauty ; love and beauty ;
Love and beauty we'll fill to, and jovially sing;
Wishing health and success, till we make the house ring,
    To all sportsmen and sons of the game.
And sons of the game ; and sons of the game ; the game ;
Wishing health and success. &c.

SONG XLIV.
THE BLATHRIE O'T.

When I think on this warld's pelf, and the little wi'

share I have o't to myself, and how the lass that wants it

is by the lads forgot, may the shame fa' the gear and the

blathrie o't.

Jockie was the laddie that held the pleugh,
But now he's got gowd and gear eneugh;
He thinks nae mair of me that wears the plaiden coat;
    May the shame, &c.

Jenny was the lassie that mucked the byre,
But now she is clad in her silken attire,
And Jockie says he loes her, and swears he's me forgot;
    May the shame, &c.

But all this shall never danton me,
Sae lang as I keep my fancy free:
For the lad that's sae inconstant, he is not worth a groat;
    May the shame, &c.

SONG XLV.
THE BRAES OF YARROW.

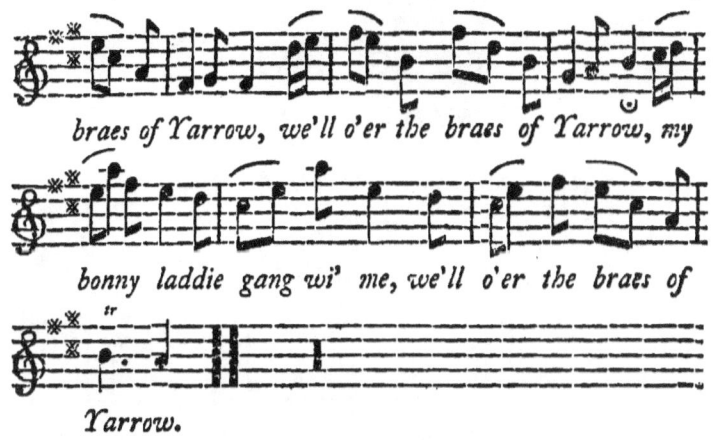

braes of Yarrow, we'll o'er the braes of Yarrow, my bonny laddie gang wi' me, we'll o'er the braes of Yarrow.

Young Sandy was the blytheſt ſwain
That ever pip'd on bonny brae;
Nae laſs could ken him free frae pain,
Sae graceful, kind, ſae fair and gay.
    And Jenny ſung, &c.

He kiſs'd and lov'd the bonny maid,
Her ſparkling een had won his heart,
No laſs the youth had e'er betray'd:
No fear had ſhe, the lad no art.
    And Jenny ſung, &c.

SONG XLVI.
EVERY MAN TAKE HIS GLASS.

Ev'ry man take his glaſs in his hand, and drink a good health to our king: many years may he rule o'er this land; may his laurels for ever freſh ſpring, let wrangling and jangling ſtraightway ceaſe; let every man ſtrive for his country's peace; neither tory nor whig, with their parties look big: here's a health to all honeſt men.

    'Tis not owning a whimſical name
      That proves a man loyal and juſt:
    Let him fight for his country's fame;
      Be impartial at home, if in truſt.

'Tis this that proves him an honest soul:
His health we'll drink in a brim-full bowl.
    Then let's leave off debate,
      No confusion create;
Here's a health to all honest men.

When a company's honestly met,
    With intent to be merry and gay,
Their drooping spirits to whet,
    And drown the fatigues of the day—
What madness is it thus to dispute,
When neither side can his man confute?
    When you've said what you dare,
      You're but just where you were.
Here's a health to all honest men.

Then agree, ye true Britons, agree,
    And ne'er quarrel about a nick-name;
Let your enemies trembling see
    That a Briton is always the same.
For our king our laws, our church, our right,
Let's lay by all feuds, and straight unite:
    Then who need care a fig
      Who's a tory or a whig?
Here's a health to all honest men.

SONG XLVII.
NOBODY.

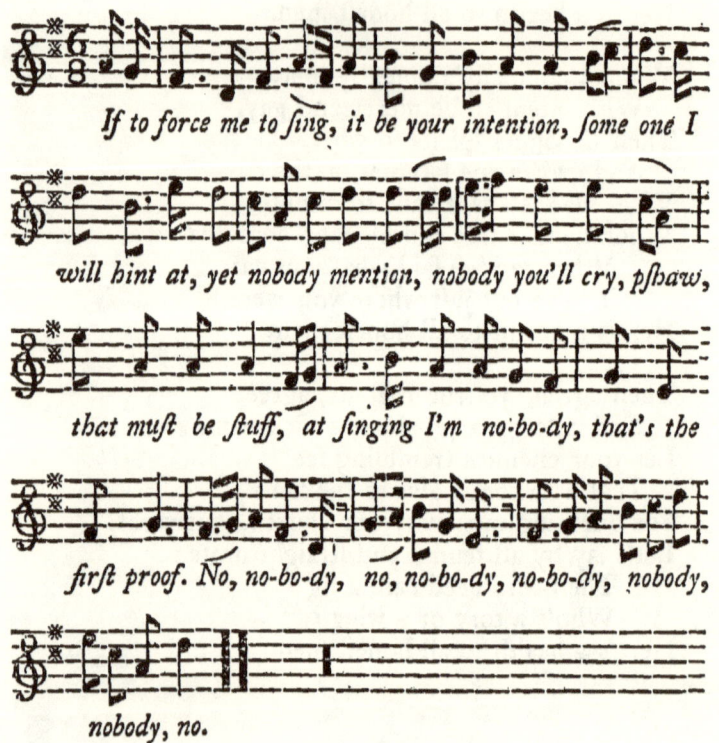

If to force me to sing, it be your intention, some one I will hint at, yet nobody mention, nobody you'll cry, pshaw, that must be stuff, at singing I'm no-bo-dy, that's the first proof. No, no-bo-dy, no, no-bo-dy, no-bo-dy, nobody, nobody, no.

Nobody's a name every body will own,
When something they ought to be asham'd of have done;
'Tis a name well applied to old maids and young beaus,
What they were intended for nobody knows.
  No, nobody, &c.

If negligent servants should china-plate crack,
The fault is still laid on poor nobody's back;
If accidents happen at home or abroad,
When nobody's blam'd for it, is not that odd?
  No, nobody, &c.

Nobody can tell you the tricks that are play'd,
When nobody's by, betwixt master and maid:
She gently crys out, Sir, there'll some body hear us,
He softly replies, my dear, no body's near us.
  No, no body, &c.

But big with child proving, she's quickly discarded,
When favours are granted, nobody's rewarded;
And when she's examined, crys, mortals, forbid it,
If I'm got with child, it was nobody did it.
  No, nobody, &c.

When by stealth, the gallant, the wanton wife leaves,
The husband's affrighten'd, and thinks it is thieves;
He rouses himself, and crys loudly Who's there?
The wife pats his cheek, and says, nobody, dear.
  No, nobody, &c.

Enough now of nobody, sure has been sung,
Since nobody's mention'd, nor nobody's wrong'd;
I hope for free speaking, I may not be blam'd,
Since nobody's injur'd, nor nobody's nam'd.
  No, nobody, &c.

     M.

SONG XLVIII.
HAPPY DICK.

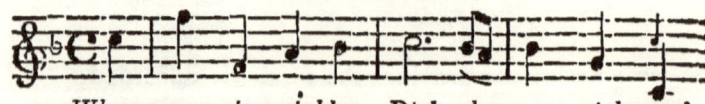

Whence comes it, neighbour Dick, that you with youth

uncommon, have ferved the girls this tri - - - - - -

- - - - - - - - - ck and weded an old wo—man,

Happy Dick!

Each belle condemns the choice
    Of a youth fo gay and fprightly;
But we, your friends, rejoice,
    That you have judg'd fo rightly:
Happy Dick!

Though odd to fome it founds,
    That on threefcore you ventur'd,
Yet in ten thoufand pounds.
    Ten thoufand charms are center'd:
Happy Dick!

Beauty, we know, will fade,
    As doth the fhort liv'd hour;

Nor can the faireſt maid
  Inſure her bloom an hour:
Happy Dick!

Then wiſely you reſign,
  For ſixty, charms ſo tranſient;
As the curious value coin
  The more for being ancient:
Happy Dick!

With joy your ſpouſe ſhall ſee
  The fading beauties round her,
And ſhe herſelf ſtill be
  The ſame that firſt you found her:
Happy Dick!

Oft is the married ſtate
  With jealouſies attended;
And hence, through foul debate,
  Are nuptial joys ſuſpended:
Happy Dick!

But you, with ſuch a wife,
  No jealous fears are under;
She's yours alone for life,
  Or much we all ſhall wonder:
Happy Dick!

Her death would grieve you ſore,
  But let not that torment you;
My life ſhe'll ſee fourſcore,
  If that will but content you:
Happy Dick!

On this you may rely,
  For the pains you took to win her,
She'll ne'er in child-bed die,
  Unleſs the d——l's in her:
Happy Dick!

Some have the name of hell
　　To matrimony given:
How falsely you can tell,
　　Who find it such a heaven :
Happy Dick!

With you each day and night
　　Is crown'd with joy and gladness;
While envious virgins bite
　　Their heated sheets for madness :
Happy Dick!

With spouse long share the bliss
　　Y'had miss'd in any other;
And when you've bury'd this,
　　May you have such another:
Happy Dick!

Observing hence, by you,
　　In marriage such decorum,
Our wiser youth shall do
　　As you have done before 'em:
Happy Dick!

SONG XLIX.

HOW STANDS THE GLASS AROUND?

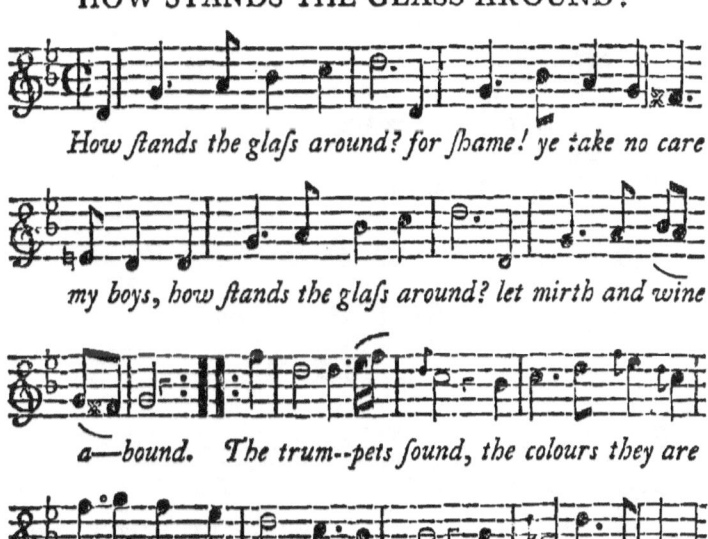

How stands the glass around? for shame! ye take no care my boys, how stands the glass around? let mirth and wine a—bound. The trum--pets sound, the colours they are

flying, boys, to fight, kill, or wound, may we still be found

content with our hard fate, my boys, on the cold ground.

  Why, soldiers, why,
Shou'd we be melancholy, boys?
  Why, soldiers, why?
 Whose business 'tis to die!
  What, sighing? fie!
Don't fear, drink on, be jolly, boys!
  'Tis he, you, or I!
 Cold, hot, wet, or dry,
We're always bound to follow, boys,
  And scorn to fly!

'Tis but in vain,—
I mean not to upbraid you, boys,—
'Tis but in vain
For foldiers to complain,
Should next campaign
Send us to him who made us, boys,
We're free from pain!
But if we remain,
A bottle and kind landlady
Cure all again.

SONG L.

FIDELE's TOMB.

To fair Fi--de--le's glaſſy tomb ſoft maids and village hinds ſhall bring each op'ning ſweet of earlieſt bloom, and ri--fle all the breath-ing ſpring.

No wailing ghoſt ſhall dare appear,
  To vex with ſhrieks this quiet grove;
But ſhepherd lads aſſemble here,
  And tender virgins own their love.

No wither'd witch ſhall here be ſeen,
  No goblins lead their nightly crew;

But female fays shall haunt the green,
　　And deck thy grave with pearly dew.

The red-breast oft at evening hours,
　　Shall kindly lend it's little aid,
With hoary mofs and gather'd flow'rs,
　　To deck the ground where thou art laid.

When howling winds and beating rain,
　　In tempeſt ſhake the Sylvian cell,
Or midſt the chace upon the plain,
　　The tender thought on thee ſhall dwell.

Each lonely ſcene ſhall thee reſtore,
　　For thee the tear be daily ſhed.
Belov'd till life could charm no more,
　　And mourn'd till pity's ſelf is dead.

SONG LI.
DONNEL AND FLORA.

When merry hearts were gay, careless of ought but play, poor Flora slipt away, sad'ning to Mora, loose flow'd her coal-black hair, quick heav'd her bosom bare, and thus to the troubled air she vented her sorrow.

"Loud howls the northern blast,
"Bleak is the dreary waste;—
"Haste then, O Donnel haste,
  "Haste to thy Flora.
"Twice twelve long months are o'er,
"Since in a foreign shore,
"You promis'd to fight no more,
  "But meet me in Mora.

"Where now is Donnel dear?
"Maids cry with taunting sneer,
"Say, is he still sincere
  To his lov'd Flora.
"Parents upbraid my moan,
"Each heart is turn'd to stone—
"Ah Flora! thou'rt now alone,
  "Friendless in Mora.

"Come, then, O come away,
"Donnel no longer stay;

" Where can my rover stray
   " From his dear Flora.
" Ah sure he ne'er could be
" False to his vows to me.
" O heav'n, is not yonder he
   " Bounding in Mora."

" Never, O wretched fair,"
(Sigh'd the sad messenger)
" Never shall Donnel mair
   " Meet his lov'd Flora.
" Cold, cold beyond the main
" Donnel thy love lies slain;
" He sent me to soothe thy pain
   " Weeping in Mora.

" Well fought our gallant men,
" Headed by brave Burgoyne;
" Our heroes were thrice led on
   " To British glory.
" But ah! tho' our foes did flee,
" Sad was the loss to thee,
" While every fresh victory
   " Drown'd us in sorrow."

" Here, take this trusty blade,"
(Donnel expiring, said)
" Give it to yon dear maid
   " Weeping in Mora.
" Tell her, O Allan, tell,
" Donnel thus bravely fell,
" And that in his last farewell,
   " He thought on his Flora."

Mute stood the trembling fair,
Speechless with wild despair,
Then striking her bosom bare,
   Sigh'd out " Poor Flora!
" Oh Donnel! O welladay!"
Was all the fond heart could say:
At length the sound died away,
   Feebly in Mora.

SONG LII.
THE BANKS OF THE DEE.

'Twas summer and softly the breezes were blowing, and sweetly the nightingale sung from the tree, at the foot of a rock where the river was flowing, I sat myself down on the banks of the Dee. Flow on lovely Dee, flow on thou sweet river, thy banks, purest stream shall be dear to me ever; for there I first gain'd the affection and favour of Jamie the glory and pride of the Dee.

But now he's gone from me, and left me thus mourning,
To quell the proud rebels for valiant is he;
And ah! there's no hopes of his speedy returning,
To wander again on the Banks of the Dee.
He's gone, hapless youth! o'er the loud roaring billows;
The kindest and sweetest of all the gay fellows;
And left me to stray 'mongst the once loved willows,
The loneliest maid on the banks of the Dee.

But time and my prayers, may perhaps yet restore him,
Blest peace may restore my dear shepherd to me;
And when he returns, with such care I'll watch o'er him;
He never shall leave the sweet Banks of the Dee.
The Dee then shall flow, all it's beauties displaying;
The lambs on it's banks shall again be seen playing;
While I, with my Jamie, am carelessly straying,
And tasting again all the sweets of the Dee.

ADDITIONS BY A LADY.

THUS sung the fair maid on the banks of the river,
And sweetly re-echo'd each neighbouring tree;
But now all these hopes must evanish for ever,
Since Jamie shall ne'er see the Banks of the Dee.
On a foreign shore the sweet youth lay dying,
In a foreign grave his body's now lying;
While friends and acquaintance in Scotland are crying
For Jamie the glory and pride of the Dee.

Mis-hap on the hand by whom he was wounded;
Mis-hap on the wars that call'd him away
From a circle of friends by which he was surrounded,
Who mourn for dear Jamie the tedious day.
Oh! poor hapless maid, who mourns discontented,
The loss of a lover so justly lamented;
By time, only time, can her grief be contented,
And all her dull hours become chearful and gay.

'Twas honour and bravery made him leave her mourning,
From unjuſt rebellion his country to free;
He left her, in hopes of his ſpeedy returning
To wander again on the Banks of the Dee.
For this he deſpiſed all dangers and perils;
'Twas thus he eſpouſed Britannia's quarrels,
That when he came home he might crown her with laurels,
The happieſt maid on the Banks of the Dee.

But fate had determin'd his fall to be glorious,
Though dreadful the thought muſt be unto me;
He fell like brave Wolf where the troops were victorious,
Sure each tender heart muſt bewail the decree:
Yet, though he is gone, the once faithful lover,
And all our fine ſchemes of true happineſs over,
No doubt he implored his pity and favour
For me he had left on the Banks of the Dee.

SONG LIII.

SONGS OF SHEPHERDS.

Songs of shepherds in rustical roundelays, form'd in fancy, and whistl'd on reeds, sung to solace young nymphs upon holidays, are too unworthy for wonderful deeds. Sottish Silenus to Phœbus the genius was sent by dame Venus, a song to prepare, in phrase nicely coin'd, and verse quite refin'd, how the states divine hunted the hare.

Stars quite tired with pastimes Olympical,
   Stars and planets that beautiful shone,
Could no longer endure that men only should
   Revel in pleasures, and they but look on.
Round about horned Lucina they swarmed,
   And quickly inform'd her how minded they were,

Each god and goddess to take human bodies,
  As lords and ladies to follow the hare.

Chaste Diana applauded the motion,
  And pale Proserpina sat down in her place,
To guide the welkin, and govern the ocean,
  While Dian conducted her nephews in chace.
By her example, their father to trample,
  The earth old and ample, they soon leave the air:
Neptune the water, and wine Liber pater,
  And Mars the slaughter, to follow the hare.

Young god Cupid was mounted on Pegasus,
  Borrow'd o' the muses with kisses and prayers;
Stern Alcides upon cloudy Caucasus
  Mounted a centaur that proudly him bears.
The postilion of the sky, light-heeled sir Mercury,
  Made his swift courser fly fleet as the air;
While tuneful Apollo the pastime did follow,
  To whoop and to hollow, boys, after the hare.

Drowned Narcissus, from his metamorphosis
  Rous'd by Echo, new manhood did take.
Snoring Somnus upstarted from Cim'rics:
  Before for a thousand years he did not wake.
There was lame club-footed Mulciber booted;
  And Pan, too, promoted on Corydon's mare.
Æolus flouted; with mirth Momus shouted;
  While wife Pallas pouted, yet follow'd the hare.

Grave Hymen ushers in lady Astrea.
  The humour took hold of Latona the cold.
Ceres the brown, too, with bright Cytherea,
  And Thetis the wanton, Bellona the bold;
Shamefac'd Aurora, with witty Pandora,
  And Maria with Flora did company bear;
But Juno was stated too high to be mated,
  Although, Sir, she hated not hunting the hare.

Three brown bowls of Olympical nectar
The Troy-born boy now presents on his knee;
Jove to Phœbus now carouses in nectar,
And Phœbus to Hermes, and Hermes to me:
Wherewith infused, I piped and mused,
In language unused, their sports to declare,
Till the vast house of Jove like the bright spheres did move,
Here's a health, then, to all that love hunting the hare.

SONG LIV.

SINCE THERE's SO SMALL DIFFERENCE.

Since there's so small diff'rence 'twixt drowning and drinking, we'll tipple and pray too, like mariners sinking. While they drink salt water, we'll pledge them in wine, and
Chorus.
pay our devotion at Bacchus's shrine. Oh! Bacchus, great Bacchus, for ever defend us, and plentiful store of good Burgundy send us,

SONG LV.
DO YOU HEAR BROTHER SPORTSMAN.

Do you hear brother sportsman, the sound of the horn, and yet the sweet pleasure decline? For shame, rouse your senses, and e'er it be morn, with me the sweet me-lo-dy join, with me the sweet me--lo--dy join. Thro' the wood and the valley, how the traitor we'll rally, nor quit him till panting he lies, nor quit him till panting he lies. While hounds in full cry, thro' hedges shall fly,

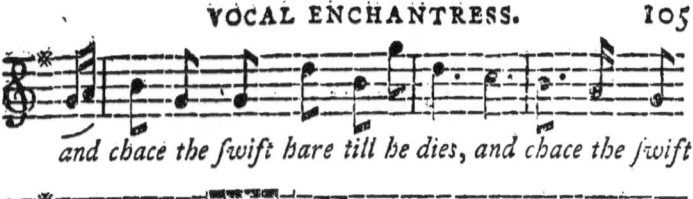

and chace the swift hare till he dies, and chace the swift

hare till he dies.

  Then saddle your steed, to the meadows and fields,
   Both willing and joyous repair;
  No pastime in life greater happiness yields,
   Than chacing the fox or the hare.
    Such comforts my friend,
    On the sportsman attend,
   No pleasure like hunting is found;
    For when it is o'er,
    As brisk as before,
  Next morning we spurn up the ground.

SONG LVI.
FAL DE RAL TIT.

'Twas I learnt a pretty song in France, and I brought it
o'er the sea by chance; and then in Wapping I did dance,
Oh the like was never seen, for I made the music loud for
to play, all for to pass the dull hours away, and when I
had nothing left for to say, then I sung Fal de ral tit, tit
fal de ral, tit fal de ray, then I sung fal de ral tit, then
we sung fal de ral tit.

As I was walking down Thames ſtreet,
A ſhip mate of mine I chanc'd for to meet,
And I was reſolv'd him for to treat,
With a cann of grog, gillio!
A cann of grog they brought us ſtrait,
All for to pleaſure my ſhip mate,
And ſatisfaction give him ſtrait,
  Then I ſung Fal de ral tit, &c.

The macaronies next came in,
All dreſt ſo neat, and look'd ſo trim,
And thinking for to ſtrike me dum,
There was half a ſcore or more.
Some was ſhort, and ſome was tall,
But 'tis very well known that I lick'd them all,
For I dous'd their heads againſt the wall,
  Then I ſung Fal de ral tit, &c.

The landlord then aloud did ſay,
As how he wiſh'd I wou'd go away;
And if I 'tempted for to ſtay,
As how he'd take the law.
Lord d——me, ſays I, you may do your worſt,
For I've not ſcarcely quench'd my thirſt,
All this I ſaid, and nothing worſe,
  Then I ſung Fal de ral tit, &c.

It's when I've croſt the raging main,
And be come back to Old England again,
Bringing home plenty of gold from Spain,
Of grog I'll dring galore;
With a pretty girl for to ſit by my ſide,
And for her coſtly robes I'll provide,
So that ſhe ſhall be ſatisfied,
  Then I'll ſing Fal de ral tit, &c.

SONG LVII.
HIGHLAND QUEEN.

No more my song shall be, ye swains, of purl-ing

streams, or flow'ry plains; more pleasing beauties now in-

spire, and Phœbus tunes the warbling lyre; divinely aid-

ed, thus I mean to ce—le—brate to ce—le—brate my

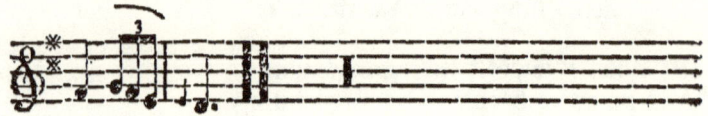

Highland Queen.

In her, sweet innocence you'll find,
With freedom, truth, and beauty join'd;
From pride and affectation free,
Alike she smiles on you and me,
The brightest nymph that trips the green,
I do pronounce my Highland Queen.

No fordid wifh, or trifling joy,
Her fettled calm of mind deftroy;
Strict honour fills her fpotlefs foul,
And adds a luftre to the whole;
A matchlefs fhape a graceful mein,
All center in my Highland Queen.

How bleft that youth, whom gentle Fate
Has deftin'd for fo fair a mate;
Has all thefe wond'rous gifts in ftore,
And each returning day brings more:
No youth fo happy can be feen,
Poffeffing thee, my Highland Queen.

SONG LVIII.
QUEEN MARY's LAMENTATION.

I sigh and lament me in vain, these walls can but e—cho my moan, a—las it increases my pain, when I think of the days that are gone, thro' the grate of my prison, I see the birds as they wanton in air, my heart how it pants to be free, my looks they are wild with de—spair.

    Above tho' opprest by my fate,
      I burn with contempt for my foes,
    Tho' fortune has alter'd my state
      She ne'er can subdue me to those;

False woman in ages to come,
　　Thy malice detested shall be
And when we are cold in the tomb
　　Some heart still will sorrow for me.

Ye roofs where cold damps and dismay,
　　With silence and solitude dwell,
How comfortless passes the day,
　　How sad tolls the evening bell;
The owls from the battlements cry,
　　Hollow wind seems to murmur around,
O Mary, prepare thee to die,
　　My blood it runs cold at the sound.

SONG LIX.
QUEEN MARY's FAREWELL TO FRANCE.

O! thou lov'd country, where my youth was spent, dear golden days all past in sweet content, where the fair morning of my clouded day shone mildly bright, and temperately gay, dear France, adieu, a long and sad farewell; no thought can image, and no tongue can tell, the pangs I feel at that drear word farewell!

The ship that wafts me from my friendly shore,
  Conveys my body, but conveys no more.
My soul is thine, that spark of heav'nly flame,
  That better portion of my mingled frame,
Is wholy thine, that part I give to thee,
  That in the temple of thy memory,
The other ever may enshrined be.

SONG LX.
OSCAR's GHOST.

O see that form that faintly gleams, 'tis Oscar come

to chear my dreams, on wings of wind he flies away, O

stay my lovely Oscar, stay.

Wake Ossian, last of Fingal's line,
And mix thy tears and sighs with mine.
Awake the Harp to doleful lays,
And soothe my soul with Oscar's praise.
The Shell is ceas'd in Oscar's Hall,
Since gloomy Kerbar wrought the fall,
The Roe on Morven lightly bounds,
Nor hears the cry of Oscar's hounds.

P

SONG LXI.
JOHN O'BADENYON.

When first I came to be a man, of twenty years or so, I thought myself a handsome youth, and fain the world would know, in best attire I stept abroad, with spirits brisk and gay, and here and there, and ev'ry where, was like a morn in May. No care I had, nor fear of want, but rambled up and down, and for a beau I might have pass'd, in country or in town; I still was pleas'd where'er I went, and

when I was alone, I tun'd my pipe, and pleas'd myſell wi'

John O' Badenyon.

Now in the days of youthful prime,
   A miſtreſs I muſt find;
For love they ſay, gives one an air,
   And even improves the mind:
On Phillis fair, above the reſt,
   Kind fortune fix'd my eyes,
Her piercing beauty ſtruck my heart,
   And ſhe became my choice:
To Cupid then, with hearty pray'r,
   I offer'd many vow,
And danc'd, and ſung, and ſigh'd and ſwore,
   As other lovers do:
But when at laſt I breath'd my flame,
   I found her cold as ſtone;
I left the girl, and tun'd my pipe
   To John of Badenyon.

When love had thus my heart beguil'd,
   With fooliſh hopes and vain,
To friendſhip's port I ſteer'd my courſe,
   And laugh'd at lovers' pain;
A friend I got by lucky chance,
   'Twas ſomething like divine;
An honeſt friend's a precious gift,
   And ſuch a gift was mine:
And now whatever might betide,
   A happy man was I,
In any ſtrait I knew to whom
   I freely might apply:

A ſtrait ſoon came, my friend I try'd,
  He laugh'd and ſpurn'd my moan:
I hy'd me home, and pleas'd myſelf
  With John of Badenyon.

I thought I ſhould be wiſer next,
  And would a patriot turn;
Began to doat on Johnny Wilkes,
  And cry up Parſon-Horne:
Their noble ſpirit I admir'd,
  And prais'd their manly zeal,
Who had with flaming tongue and pen,
  Maintain'd the public weal;
But 'ere a month or two was paſt,
  I found myſelf betray'd;
'Twas ſelf and party after all,
  For all the ſtir they made.
At laſt I ſaw theſe factious knaves
  Inſult the very throne;
I curs'd them all, and tun'd my pipe
  To John of Badenyon.

What next to do I mus'd a while,
  Still hoping to ſucceed,
I pitch'd on books for company,
  And gravely try'd to read;
I bought and borrow'd ev'ry where,
  And ſtudy'd night and day;
Nor miſt what dean or doctor wrote,
  That happen'd in my way:
Philoſophy I now eſteem'd
  The ornament of youth,
And carefully, thro' many a page,
  I hunted after truth:
A thouſand various ſchemes I try'd,
  And yet was pleas'd with none:
I threw them by, and tun'd my pipe
  To John of Badenyon.

And now, ye youngsters, every where,
  Who want to make a show,
Take heed in time, nor vainly hope
  For happiness below;
What you may fancy pleasure here,
  Is but an empty name;
For girls, and friends, and books are so,
  You'll find them all the same.
Then be advis'd, and warning take,
  From such a man as me;
I'm neither Pope nor Cardinal,
  Nor one of low degree,
You'll find displeasure ev'ry where:
  Then do as I have done,
E'en tune your pipe, and please yourself
  With John of Badenyon.

SONG LXII.
MAGGY's TOCHER.

The meal was dear short syne, we buckled us a the gither, and Maggy was just in her prime when Willy made court-ship till her. Twa pistols charg'd beguess to gie the court-ing shot, and syne came ben the lass wi' swats drawn frae the butt. He first speer'd at the guidman, and syne at Giles the mither, an ye wad gie's a bit land, wi'd buckle us e'en the gither.

My doughter ye fhall hae,
  I'll gi' you her by the hand ;
But I'll part wi' my wife by my fire,
  Or I part wi' my land.
Your tocher it fhall be good,
  There's nane fall hae it's maik,
The lafs bound in her fnood,
  And Crummie wha kens her ftake :
With an auld bedden o' claiths,
  Was left me by my mither,
They're jet black o'er wi' flaes,
  Ye may cuddle in them the gither.

Ye fpeak right well guidman,
  But ye maun mend your hand,
And think o' modefty,
  Gin ye'll not quat your land :
We are but young ye ken,
  And now we're gawn the gither :
A houfe is but and ben,
  And Crummie will want her fother.
The bairns are coming on,
  And they'll cry, O their mither !
We have nouther pat nor pan,
  But four bare legs the gither.

Your tocher's be good enough
  For that you need nae fear,
Twa good ftilts to the pleugh,
  And ye yourfell maun fteer :
Ye fhall hae twa good pocks
  That ane's were o' the tweel,
The t'ane to had the grots,
  The ither to had the meal ;
With an auld kift made of wands,
  And that fall be your coffer ;
Wi' aiken woody bands,
  And that may had your tocher.

Confider well guidman,
  We hae but borrowed gear,
The horfe that I ride on
  Is Sandy Wilfon's mare :
The faddle's nane of my ain :
  And thae's but borrow'd boots,
And when that I gae hame,
  I maun tak to my koots :
The cloak is Geordy Watt's,
  That gars me look fae croufe ;
Come fill us a cogue of fwats,
  We'll make nae mair toom rufe.

I like you well young lad,
  For telling me fae plain.
I married when little I had
  O' gear that was my ain :
But fyne that things are fae,
  The bride fhe maun come furth,
Tho' a' the gear fhe'll hae,
  It'll be but little worth.

A bargain it maun be,
  Fy cry on Giles the mither :
Content am I quo' fhe,
  E'en gar the hiffy come hither.
The bride fhe gade till her bed,
  The bridgroom he came till her ;
The fidler crap in at the fit,
  And they cuddl'd it a' the gither.

SONG LXIII.
THE GRAY COCK.

O saw ye my father, or saw ye my mother, or saw

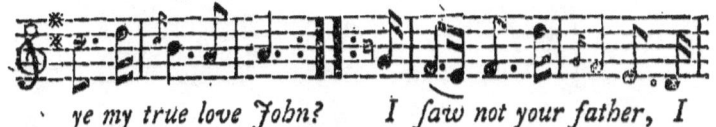

ye my true love John? I saw not your father, I

saw not your mother, but I saw your true love John.

Up Johnny rose, and to the door he goes,
    And gently tirled the pin.
The lassie taking tent, unto the door she went,
    And she open'd and let him in.

Flee up, flee up, my bonny gray cock,
    And craw when it is day;
Your neck shall be like the bonny beaten gold,
    And your wings of the silver gray.

The cock prov'd false, and untrue he was,
    For he crew an hour o'er soon.
The lassie thought it day when she sent her love away,
    And it was but a blink of the moon.

SONG LXIV.
WHEN ONCE THE GODS.

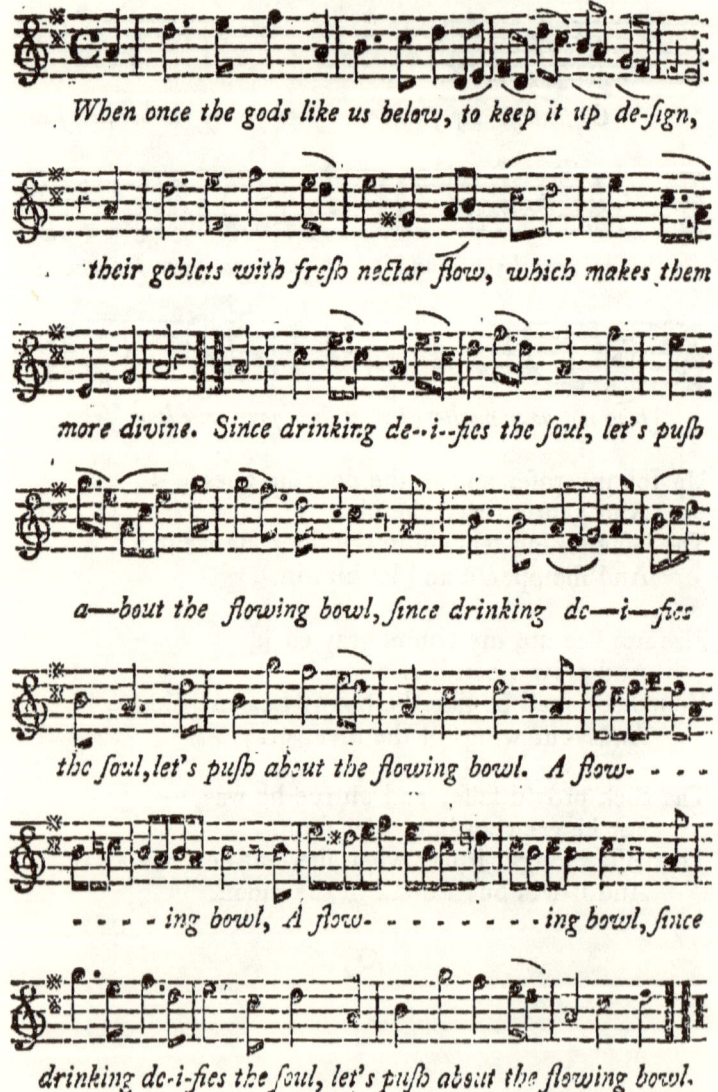

When once the gods like us below, to keep it up de-sign, their goblets with fresh nectar flow, which makes them more divine. Since drinking de-i-fies the soul, let's push a—bout the flowing bowl, since drinking de—i—fies the soul, let's push about the flowing bowl. A flow- - - - - - ing bowl, A flow- - - - - - - - - ing bowl, since drinking de-i-fies the soul, let's push about the flowing bowl.

The glittering ftar and ribbon blue,
　　That deck the courtier's breaſt,
May hide a heart of blackeſt hue,
　　Though by the king careſs'd.
Let him in pride and ſplendor roll;
We'er happier o'er a flowing bowl.
　　A flowing bowl, &c.

For liberty let patriots rave,
　　And damn the courtly crew,
Becauſe, like them, they want to have
　　The loaves and fiſhes too.
I care not who divides the cole,
So I can ſhare a flowing bowl.
　　A flowing bowl, &c.

Let Mansfield Lord-chief-juſtice be,
　　Sir Fletcher ſpeaker ſtill;
At home let Rodney rule the ſea,
　　And Pitt the treaſury ſtill:
No place I want, throughout the whole,
I want an ever-flowing, bowl.
　　A flowing bowl, &c.

The ſon wants ſquare-toes at old Nick,
　　And miſs is mad to wed;
The doctor wants us to be ſick;
　　The undertaker dead.
All have their wants from pole to pole;
I want an ever-flowing bowl.
　　A flowing bowl, &c.

SONG LXV.
O GREEDY MIDAS.

O greedy Midas, I've been told, that what you touch you turn to gold, that what you touch you turn to gold. O had I but a pow'r like thine, O had I but a pow'r like thine, I'd tu- - - - - - - - - - - - - - - - - - - rn, I'd turn whate'er I touch to wine. I'd turn whate'er I touch to wine.

Each purling stream shou'd feel my force,
Each fish my fatal power mourn,
    Each fish, &c.
And wond'ring at the mighty change,
    And wond'ring, &c.
Shou'd in their native regions burn,
    Shou'd in, &c.

Nor shou'd there any dare t' approach
Unto my mantling sparkling shrine,
    Unto my, &c.
But first shou'd pay their vows to me,
    But first, &c.
And stile me only god of wine,
    And style, &c.

SONG LXVI.
THE GABERLUNZIE MAN.

The pawky auld carle came o'er the lee, wi' mony good-eens and days to me, saying goodwife, for your courtesie, will ye lodge a sil--ly, silly poor man? The night was cauld, the carle was wat, and down ayont the ingle he sat; my daughter's shoulders he gan to clap, and cadgily cadgi-ly ranted and sang.

O vow! quo' he, were I as free,
As first when I saw this country,
How blyth and merry wad I be!
    And I wad never think lang.
He grew canty, and she grew fain;
But little did her auld minny ken
What thir slee twa together were say'ng,
    When wooing they were sae thrang.

And O! quo' he, ann ye were as black
As e'er the crown of my dady's hat,
'Tis I wad lay thee by my back,
    And awa' wi' me thou shou'd gang.
And O! quo' she, ann I were as white,
As e'er the snaw lay on the dike,
I'd clead me braw and lady-like,
    And awa' wi' thee I would gang.

Between the twa was made a plot;
They raise a wee before the cock,
And wilily they shot the lock,
    And fast to the bent are they gane.
Up in the morn the auld wife raise,
And at her leisure put on her claise;
Syne to the servants bed she gaes,
    To speer for the silly poor man.

She gaed to the bed where the beggar lay,
The strae was cauld, he was away,
She calpt her hands, cry'd, walladay!
    For some of our gear will be gane.
Some ran to coffers, and some to kists,
But nought was stown that cou'd be mist,
She danc'd her lane, cry'd praise be blest!
    I have lodg'd a leal poor man.

Since naething's awa', as we can learn,
The kirn's to kirn, and milk to earn,
Gae butt the house, lass, and waken my bairn,
    And bid her come quickly ben.

The fervant gade where the daughter lay,
The sheets was cauld, she was away,
And faft to her goodwife did fay,
   She's aff wi the gaberlunzie-man.

O fy gar ride and fy gar rin,
And hafte ye find thefe traytors again;
For fhe's be burnt, and he's be flain,
   The wearifu' gaberlunzie-man.
Some rade upo' horfe, fome ran a foot,
The wife was wood, and out o' her wit;
She cou'd na gang, nor yet cou'd fhe fit,
   But ay fhe curs'd and fhe bann'd.

Mean time far hind out o'er the lee,
Fu' fnug in a glen where nane could fee,
The twa with kindly fport and glee,
   Cut fra a new cheefe a whang:
The priving was good, it pleas'd them baith,
To lo'e her for ay, he gae her his aith,
Quo' fhe to leave thee I will be laith,
   My winfom gaberlunzie-man.

O kend my minny I were wi' you,
Ill-fardly wad fhe crook her mou',
Sic a poor man fhe'd never trow,
   After the gaberlunzie-man.
My dear, quo' he, ye're yet o'er young,
And ha' nae learn'd the beggars tongue,
To follow me frae town to town,
   And carry the gaberlunzie on.

Wi' cauk and keel I'll win your bread,
And fpindles and whorles for them wha need,
Whilk is a gentle trade indeed,
   To carry the gaberlunzie on.
I'll bow my leg, and crook my knee,
And draw a black clout o'er my eye,
A cripple or blind they will ca' me,
   While we fhall be merry and fing.

SONG LXVII.
TWINE WEEL THE PLAIDEN.

He prais'd my e'en fae bonny blue,
  Sae lilly white my fkin, O,
And fyne he prie'd my bonny mou',
  And fwore it was nae fin, O.
And twine it weel, my bonny dow,
  And twine it weel the plaiden;
The laffie loft her filken fnood,
  In pu'ing of the bracken.

R

But he has left the lafs he loo'd,
  His ain true love forfaken,
Which gars me fair to greet the fnood,
  I loft among the bracken,
And twine it weel, my bonny dow,
  And twine it weel the plaiden;
The laffie loft her filken fnood,
  In pu'ing of the bracken.

SONG LXVIII.

GALLANT SAILOR.

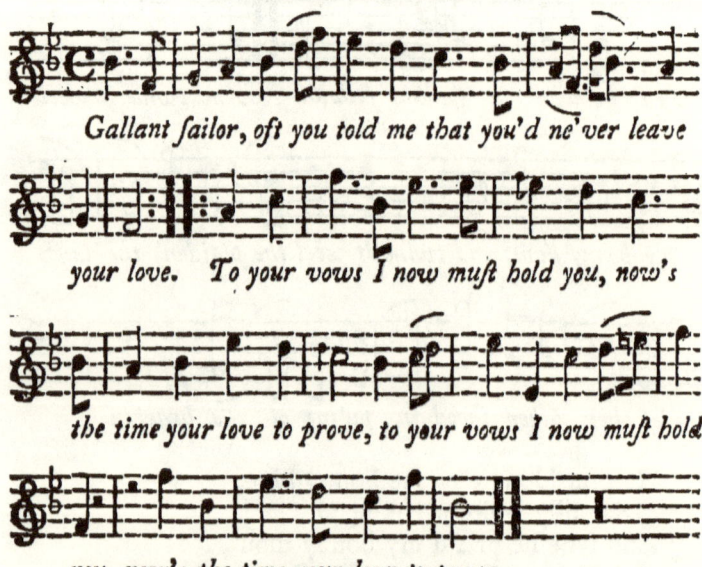

Gallant failor, oft you told me that you'd ne'ver leave your love. To your vows I now muft hold you, now's the time your love to prove, to your vows I now muft hold you, now's the time your love to prove.

SAILOR.

Is not Britain's flag degraded,
Have not Frenchmen brav'd our fleet?
How can failors live upbraided,
While the Frenchmen dare to meet;

How can sailors live upbraided,
While the Frenchmen dare to meet.

N A N.
Hear me, gallant sailor, hear me,
While your country has a foe,
He is mine too, never fear me,
I may weep but you must go ;
I may weep, I may weep,
I may weep, but you shall go.

S A I L O R.
Though this flow'ry season woes you
To the peaceful sports of May,
And love sighs so long to loose you,
Love to glory shall give way ;
Love to glory, love to glory,
Love to glory, must give way.

Can the sons of Britain fail her,
While her daughters are so true ;
Your soft courage must avail her,
We love honour loving you ;
We love honour, we love honour,
We love honour loving you.

B O A T S W A I N.
War and danger now invite us,
Blow ye winds, auspicious blow ;
Ev'ry gale will most delight us,
That can waft us to the foe ;
Ev'ry gale will most delight us,
That can waft us to the foe.

SONG LXIX.
WILLY WAS A WANTON WAG.

Willy was a wanton wag, the blytheſt lad that e'er I

ſaw, at bridals ſtill he bore the brag, and carried ay the

gree awa. His doublet was of Zetland ſhag, and vow!

but Willy he was braw; at his ſhoulder hang a tag that

2d Ver.

pleas'd the laſſes beſt of a'. He was a man

He was a man without a clag,
  His heart was frank without a flaw:
And ay whatever Willy ſaid,
  It was ſtill hadden as a law.
His boots they were made of the jag,
  When he went to the weapon-ſhaw;
Upon the green nane durſt him brag
  The fiend a ane amang them a'.

And was not Willy well worth gowd,
  He wan the love of great and fma';
For after he the bride had kifs'd,
  He kifs'd the laffes hale-fale a'.
Sae merrily round the ring they row'd,
  When by the hand he led them a',
And fmack on fmack on them beftow'd,
  By virtue of a ftanding law.

And was na Willy a great lown,
  As fhyre a lick as e'er was feen?
When he danc'd with the laffes round,
  The bridegroom fpeer'd where he had been.
Quoth Willy, I've been at the ring,
  With bobbing, faith, my fhanks are fair.
Gae ca' your bride and maidens in,
  For Willy he dow do na mair.

Then reft ye, Willy, I'll gae out,
  And for a wee fill up the ring;
But fhame light on his fouple fnout,
  He wanted Willy's wanton fling.
Then ftraight he to the bride did fare,
  Says, well's me on your bonny face;
With bobbing, Willy's fhanks are fair,
  And I'm come out to fill his place.

Bridegroom, fhe fays, you'll fpoil the dance,
  And at the ring you'll ay be lag,
Unlefs, like Willy, ye advance;
  (O! Willy has a wanton wag:)
For wi't he learns us a' to fteer,
  And foremoft ay bears up the ring;
We will find nae fick dancing here,
  If we want Willy's wanton fling.

SONG LXX.
BUSK YE, BUSK YE.

Busk ye, busk ye, my bonny bride, busk ye busk ye my winsome marrow, busk ye, busk ye my bonny bride, and let us to the braes of Yarrow. There will we sport and gather dew, dancing while lav'rocks sing in the morning: there learn frae turtles to prove true, O Bell ne'er vex me with thy scorning.

To westlin breezes Flora yields,
   And when the beams are kindly warning,
Blythness appears o'er all the fields,
   And nature looks mair fresh and charming.
Learn frae the burns that trace the mead,
   Tho' on their banks the roses blossom,
Yet hastylie they flow to Tweed,
   And pour their sweetness in his bosom.

Haste ye, haste ye, my bonny Bell,
   Haste to my arms, and there I'll guard thee;
With free consent my fears repel;
   I'll with my love and care reward thee.
Thus sang I saftly to my fair,
   Wha rais'd my hopes with kind relenting,
O queen of smiles, I ask nae mair
   Since now my bonny Bell's consenting.

SONG LXXI.

HERE AWA, THERE AWA.

Plaintive.

Here awa, there awa, here awa Willy, here awa, there

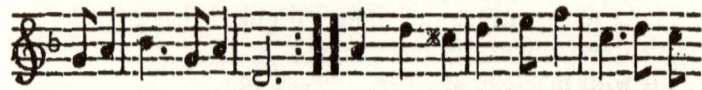

awa, here awa, hame. Lang have I fought thee, dear have

I bought thee, now I have gotten my Willy again.

Through the lang muir I follow'd my Willy,
Through the lang muir I follow'd him hame,
Whate'er betide us, nought fhall divide us;
Love now rewards all my forrow and pain.

Here awa, there awa, here awa, Willy:
Here awa, there awa, here awa hame;
Come love, believe me, naething can grieve me,
Ilka thing pleafes while Willy's at hame.

SONG LXXII.

DIOGENES SURLY AND PROUD.

Di-o-ge-nes surly and proud, who snarl'd at the Macedon youth, delighted in wine that was good, because in good wine there is truth; but growing as poor as a Job, and un-a-ble to purchase a flask, he chose for his mansion a tub, and liv'd by the scent of the cask, and liv'd by the scent of the cask.

Heraclitus would never deny
   A bumper to cherish his heart;
And, when he was maudlin, would cry,
   Because he had empty'd his quart:

Though some were so foolish to think
  He wept at men's folly and vice,
When 'twas only his custom to drink
  'Till the liquor ran out at his eyes.

Democritus always was glad
  To tipple and cherish his soul;
Would laugh like a man that was mad,
  When over a jolly full bowl:
While his cellar with wine was well stor'd,
  His liquor he'd merrily quaff;
And, when he was drunk as a lord,
  At those that were sober he'd laugh.

Copernicus, too, like the rest,
  Believ'd there was wisdom in wine;
And knew that a cup of the best
  Made reason the brighter to shine:
With wine he replenish'd his veins,
  And made his philosophy reel:
Then fancy'd the world, as his brains,
  Turn'd round like a chariot wheel.

Aristotle, that master of arts,
  Had been but a dunce without wine;
For what we ascribe to his parts,
  Is due to the juice of the vine;
His belly, some authors agree,
  Was as big as a watering-trough:
He therefore leap'd into the sea,
  Because he'd have liquor enough.

When Pyrrho had taken a glass,
  He saw that no object appear'd
Exactly the same as it was
  Before he had liquor'd his beard;
For things running round in his drink,
  Which sober he motionless found,

Occasion'd the sceptic to think
  There was nothing of truth to be found.

Old Plato was reckon'd divine,
  Who wisely to virtue was prone;
But, had it not been for good wine,
  His merit had never been known:
By wine we are generous made;
  It furnishes fancy with wings;
Without it we ne'er should have had
  Philosophers, poets, or kings.

Does the death of a lintwhite give Anny the spleen?
  Can tyning of trifles be uneasy to thee?
Can lap-dogs, or monkies, draw tears from these een,
  That look with indiff'rence on poor dying me!
Rouse up thy reason, my beautiful Anny,
  And dinna prefer a paroquet to me:
O! as thou art bonny, be prudent and canny,
  And think upon Jamie wha doats upon thee.

Ah! should a new mantua, or Flanders-lace head,
  Or yet a wee cotty, tho' never sae fine,
Gar thee grow forgetful, or let his heart bleed,
  That anes had some hope of purchasing thine?
Rouse up thy reason, my beautiful Anny,
  And dinna prefer your fleegaries to me:
O! as thou art bonny, be solid and canny,
  And tent a true lover that doats upon thee.

Shall a Paris-edition of new-fangled Sawny,
  Tho' gilt o'er wi' laces and fringes he be,
By adoring himself he admir'd by fair Anny,
  And aim at those bennisons promis'd to me:
Rouse up thy reason, my beautiful Anny,
  And never prefer a light dancer to me:
O! as thou art bonny, be constant and canny,
  Love only thy Jamie wha doats upon thee

O think, my dear charmer, on ilka sweet hour,
  That slade awa' saftly between thee and me,
'Ere squirrels, or beaux, or fopp'ry, had pow'r
  To rival my love, or impose upon thee.
Rouse up thy reason, my beautiful Anny,
  And let thy desires be a' center'd in me:
O! as thou art bonny, be faithfu' and canny,
  And love him wha's langing to center in thee.

SONG LXXIV.
COME ON MY BRAVE TARS.

Come on my brave tars, let's away to the wars, to ho-

nour and glory advance; for now we've beat Spain, let

us try this campaign, to humble the pride of old France,

my brave boys, to humble the pride of old France.

  See William, brave prince,
  A true blue ev'ry inch,
Who will honour th' illustrious name:
  May he conqueror be
  O'er our empire the sea,
And transmit British laurels to fame,
  My brave boys, &c.

  There heroes combin'd,
  When the Dons they could find,
Vied who should be foremost in battle;
  By no lee shore affrighted,
  Altho' they're benighted,
They made British thunder to rattle.
  Brave boys, &c.

See Dalrymple, Prevoſt,
  Gallant Barrington too,
And Farmer who glorioufly fell :
  With brave Pearſon, all knew
  That the hearts of true blue,
Once rous'd, not the world could excel,
  My brave boys, &c.

With ſuch heroes as thoſe,
  Tho' we've numberleſs foes,
Britiſh valour reſplendant ſhall ſhine :
  And we ſtill hope to ſhow
  That their pride will be low,
In eighty, as fam'd fifty-nine,
  My brave boys, &c.

Then brave lads enter here,
  And partake of our cheer,
You ſhall feaſt and be merry and ſing :
  With the grog at your noſe,
  Drink ſucceſs to true blues,
Huzza ! and ſay God ſave the king,
  My brave boys, &c.

SONG LXXV.
THE HIGHLAND LADDIE.

The lawland lads think they are fine, but oh they're vain

and i—dly gawdy; how much unlike the gracefu' mein,

and manly looks of my Highland laddie. O my bonny High-

land laddie, my handsome smiling Highland laddie, may

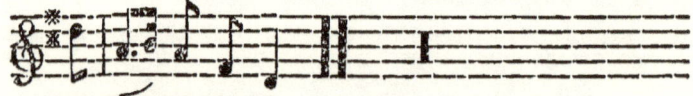

heaven still guard, and love reward, the lawland lass and

her Highland laddie.

  If I were free at will to chuse
   To be the wealthiest lawland lady,
  I'd take young Donald without trews,
   With bonnet blue, and belted plaidy.
    O my bonny, &c.

The braweft beau in borough's-town,
   In a' his airs, with art made ready,
Compar'd to him, he's but a clown;
   He's finer far in's belted plaidy.
      O my bonny, &c.

O'er benty hills with him I'll run,
   And leave my lawland kin and daddy;
Frae winter's cauld and fummer's fun,
   He'll fcreen me with his Highland plaidy.
      O my bonny, &c.

A painted room, and filken bed,
   May pleafe a lawland laird and lady;
But I can kifs, and be as glad,
   Behind a bufh in's Highland plaidy.
      O my bonny, &c.

Few compliments between us pafs,
   I ca' him my dear Highland laddie,
And he ca's me his lawland lafs,
   Syne rows me in beneath his plaidy.
      O my bonny, &c.

Nae greater joy I'll e'er pretend,
   Than that his love prove true and fteady,
Like mine to him, which ne'er fhall end,
   While heaven preferves my Highland laddie.
      O my bonny, &c.

T.

CALLIOPE: OR THE

SONG LXXVI.
YE SPORTSMEN DRAW NEAR.

Ye sportsmen draw near, and ye sportswomen too, who delight in the joys of the field, who delight in the joys of the field. Mankind, tho' they blame, are all eager as you, and no one the contest will yield, - - - and no one the contest will yield. His lordship, his worship, his honour, his grace, a hunting con——ti-nual--ly go, all ranks and degrees are engag'd in the chace, with hark forward, huz-

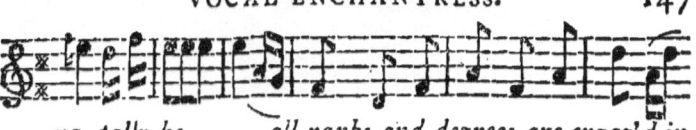

za, tally ho, - - - all ranks and degrees are engag'd in

the chace, hark forward, huzza, tally ho, - - - tally ho,

tally ho, tally ho, tally ho, tally ho, tally ho, tally ho, - -

- hark forward, huzza, tally ho - - -.

The lawyer will rife with the firſt of the morn
  To hunt for a mortgage or deed;
The huſband gets up at the ſound of the horn
  And rides to the commons full ſpeed;
The patriot is thrown in purſuit of the game;
  The poet too often lays low,
Who, mounted on Pegaſus, flies after fame,
  With hark forward, huzza, tally ho.

While fearleſs o'er hills and o'er woodlands we ſweep
  Tho' prudes on our paſtime may frown,
How oft do they Decency's bounds overleap
  And the fences of Virtue break down?
Thus public, or private, for penſion, for place,
  For amuſement, for paſſion, for ſhew,
All ranks and degrees are engag'd in the chace,
  With hark forward, huzza, tally ho.

T ij

SONG LXXVII.
FOUR AND TWENTY FIDDLERS.

Four and twenty fiddlers all on a row, four and twenty

fiddlers all on a row, there was fiddle faddle fiddle, and my

double damme semi quibble, down below. It is my la-

dy's holiday, therefore let us be merry.

2 Four and twenty drummers all on a row, there was hey rub a dub, ho rub a dub, fiddle faddle, &c.

3 Four and twenty trumpeters all on a row, there was tantara rara, tantara rera, hey rub a dub, &c.

4 Four and twenty coblers all on a row, there was ſtab awl and cobler, and cobler and ſtab awl, tantara rera, &c.

5 Four and twenty fencing maſters all on a row, there was puſh carte and tierce, down at heel, cut him acroſs, ſtab awl and cobler, &c.

6 Four and twenty captains all on a row, there was Oh! d—n me, kick him down ſtairs, puſh carte and tierce, &c.

7 Four and twenty parſons all on a row, there was Lord have mercy upon us! O! d—n me, kick him down ſtairs, &c.

8 Four and twenty taylors all on a row, one caught a loufe, another let it loofe, and another cried knock him down with the goofe, Lord have mercy upon us, &c.

9 Four and twenty barbers all on a row, there was bag whigs, fhort bobs, toupees, long ques, fhave for a penny, Oh d—n'd hard times two ruffles and ne'er a fhirt, one caught a loufe, &c.

10 Four and twenty quakers all on a row, there was Abraham begat Ifaac, and Ifaac begat Jacob, and Jacob peopled the twelve tribes of Ifrael, with bag wigs, fhort bobs, toupees, long quees, fhave for a penny, Oh d—n'd hard times two ruffles and ne'er a fhirt, one caught a loufe, another let it loofe, and another cried knock him down with the goofe, Lord have mercy upon us, Oh d—n me kick him down ftairs, pufh carte and tierce, down at heel, cut him acrofs, ftab awl and cobler, and cobler ftab awl, tantara rara, tantara rera, hey rub a dub, ho rub a dub, fiddle faddle fiddle and my double damme femi quibble down below, It is my lady's holiday therefore let us be merry.

SONG LXXIX.
WINTER.

A-dieu, ye groves, adieu ye plains, all nature mourn-ing lies. See gloomy clouds, and thick'ning rains ob-scure the lab'ring skies. See, see, from a-far, th' im-pend--ing storm with sullen haste ap—pear, see win-ter comes a dreary form, to rule - - the falling year.

No more the lambs with gamesome bound,
    Rejoice the gladen'd sight:
No more the gay enamell'd ground,
    Or Silvan scenes delight.
Thus lovely Nancy, much lov'd maid,
    Thy early charms must fail;
Thy rose must droop the lilly fade,
    And winter soon prevail.

Again the lark, sweet bird of day,
  May rise on active wing,
Again the sportive herds may play,
  And hail reviving spring.
But youth, my fair, sees no return,
  The pleasing bubble's o'er,
In vain it's fleeting joys you mourn,
  They fall to bloom no more.

Haste, then, dear girl, the time improve,
  Which art can ne'er regain,
In blissful scenes of mutual love,
  With some distinguish'd swain;
So shall life's spring, like jocund May,
  Pass smiling and serene;
Thus summer, autumn, glide away,
  And winter soon prevail.

SONG LXXIX.
BIRKS OF INVERMAY.

For soon the winter of the year,
And age, life's winter, will appear;
At this thy living bloom will fade,
As that will strip the verdant shade:

Our taste of pleasure then is o'er,
The feather'd songsters are no more;
And when they droop, and we decay,
Adieu the birks of Invermay.

Behold the hills and vales around,
With lowing herds and flocks abound;
'The wanton kids, and frisking lambs,
Gambol and dance about their dams;
The busy bees with humming noise,
And all the reptile kind rejoice;
Let us like them, then sing and play
About the birks of Invermay.

Hark, how the waters as they fall,
Loudly my love to gladness call;
The wanton waves sport in the beams,
And fishes play throughout the streams;
The circling sun does now advance,
And all the planets round him dance:
Let us as jovial be as they
Among the birks of Invermay.

SONG LXXX.
ONE BOTTLE MORE.

Assist me, ye lads who have hearts void of guile, to sing

in the praises of old Ireland's isle. Where true ho-spi-ta-

li—ty o--pens the door, and friendship detains us for

one bottle more, one bottle more, arra, one bottle more,

and friendship detains us for one bottle more.

Old England, your taunts on our country forbear;
With our bulls, and our brogues, we are true and sincere,
For if but one bottle remain'd in our store,
We have generous hearts, to give that bottle more.-

In Candy's, in Church-street, I'll sing of a sett
Of six Irish blades who together had met;

Four bottles a piece made us call for our score,
And nothing remained but one bottle more.

Our bill being paid, we were loath to depart,
For friendship had grappled each man by the heart;
Where the least touch you know makes an Irishman roar
And the whack from shilella, brought six bottles more.

Slow Phœbus had shone thro' our window so bright,
Quite happy to view his blest children of light.
So we parted, with hearts neither sorry nor sore,
Resolving next night to drink twelve bottles more.

SONG LXXXI.
THE YELLOW-HAIR'D LADDIE.

In April, when Primroses paint the sweet plain, and summer approaching rejoiceth the swain. joiceth the swain, the yellow-haird laddie would of-ten--times go, to wilds and deep glens where the hawthorn trees grow. hawthorn trees grow.

There, under the shade of an old sacred thorn,
With freedom, he sung his loves, evening and morn.
He sang with so soft and inchanting a sound;
That Sylvans and Fairies, unseen, danc'd around.

The shepherd thus sung: tho' young Maddie be fair,
Her beauty is dash'd with a scornful, proud air:
But Susie was handsome, and sweetly could sing;
Her breath, like the breezes, perfum'd in the spring.

That Maddie, in all the gay bloom of her youth,
Like the moon, was inconstant, and never spoke truth:
But Susie was faithful, good humour'd, and free,
And fair as the goddess that sprung from the sea.

That mamma's fine daughter, with all her great dow'r,
Was aukwardly airy, and frequently sour:
Then, sighing, he wish'd, would parents agree,
The witty, sweet Susie, his mistress might be.

SONG LXXXII.
ALLY CROAKER.

This artlefs young man, juft come from his fchoolery,
A novice in love, and all it's foolery;
Too dull for a wit, too grave for a joker,
And thus the gentle youth befpoke her,
    Will your marry, &c.

He drank with the father, he talk'd with the mother,
He rompt with the fifter, he gam'd with the brother;

He gam'd till he pawn'd his coat to the broker,
Which loſt him the heart of his dear Ally Croaker,
    Oh! the fickle, fickle Ally Croaker,
    Oh! the fickle Ally, Ally Croaker.

To all ye young men who are fond of gaming,
Who are ſpending your money, whilſt others are ſaving,
Fortune's a jilt, the de'il may choke her,
A jilt more inconſtant than dear Ally Croaker,
    Oh! the inconſtant Ally Croaker,
    Oh! the inconſtant Ally, Ally Croaker.

SONG LXXXIII.

LET A SET OF SOBER ASSES.

Let a set of sober asses, rail against the joys of drinking,

while water, tea, and milk agree to set cold brains a-think-

ing. Power, and wealth, beauty, health, wit, and mirth in

wine are crown'd. Joys abound, pleasure's found only where

the glass goes round.

   The ancient sects on happiness
    All differ'd in opinion;
     But wiser rules
     Of modern schools
   In wine fix her dominion.
    Power and wealth, &c.

  Wine gives the lover vigour,
   Makes glow the cheeks of beauty;

Makes poets write,
And soldiers fight,
And friendship do it's duty.
  Power and wealth, &c.

Wine was the only Helicon
Whence poets are long-liv'd so;
'Twas no other main
Than brisk champaign
Whence Venus was deriv'd too.
  Power and wealth, &c.

When heaven in Pandora's box
All kinds of ill had sent us,
In a merry mood
A bottle of good
Was cork'd up to content us.
  Power and wealth, &c.

All virtues wine is nurse to,
Of ev'ry vice destroyer;
Gives dullards wit,
Makes just the cit,
Truth forces from the lawyer.
  Power and wealth, &c.

Wine sets our joys a-flowing,
Our care and sorrow drowning,
Who rails at the bowl,
Is a Turk in's soul,
And a Christian ne'er should own him.
  Power and wealth, &c.

SONG LXXXIV.
BONNY CHRISTY.

How sweetly smells the simmer green! sweet tastes the

peach and cherry: painting and order please our een, and

claret makes us merry; but finest colours, fruits and flow-

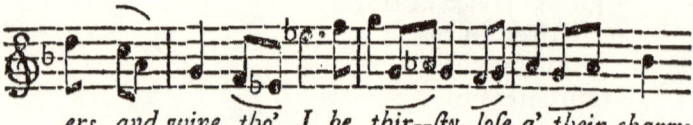
ers, and wine, tho' I be thir--sty, lose a' their charms

and weaker powers, compar'd with those of Christy.

When wand'ring o'er the flow'ry park,
   No nat'ral beauty wanting,
How lightsome is't to hear the lark,
   And birds in concert chanting!
But if my Christy tunes her voice,
   I'm rapt in admiration;
My thoughts with ecstasies rejoice,
   And drap the haill creation.

Whene'er she smiles a kindly glance,
　I take the happy omen,
And aften mint to make advance,
　Hoping she'll prove a woman:
But, dubious of my ain desert,
　My sentiments I smother;
With secret sighs I vex my heart,
　For fear she love another.

Thus sang blate Edie by a burn,
　His Christy did o'erhear him;
She doughtna let her lover mourn,
　But e'er he wist drew near him.
She spake her favour with a look,
　Which left nae room to doubt her:
He wisely this white minute took,
　And flang his arms about her.

My Christy!——witness, bonny stream,
　Sic joys frae tears arising,
I wish this mayna be a dream;
　O love the maist surprising!
Time was too precious now for talk;
　This point of a' his wishes
He wadna with set speeches bauk,
　But war'd it a' on kisses.

CALLIOPE: OR THE

SONG LXXXV.
DUMBARTON'S DRUMS.

Dumbarton's drums beat bonny O, when they mind me of my dear Jonny O, how happy am I when my Soldier is by, while he kisses and blesses his Annie O. 'Tis a Soldier alone can delight me, O, for his graceful looks do invite me, O: whilst guarded in his arms, I'll fear no war's alarms, neither danger, nor death shall e'er fright me, O.

My love is a handsome laddie, O,
Genteel, but ne'er foppish nor gaudy, O :
   Tho' commissions are dear,
     Yet I'll buy him one this year,
For he shall serve no longer a cadie, O.
A soldier has honour and bravery, O,
Unacquainted with rogues and their knavery, O :
   He minds no other thing,
     But the Ladies or the King ;
For every other care is but slavery O.

   Then I'll be the Captain's Lady, O,
Farewell all my friends and my Daddy, O ;
   I'll wait no more at home,
     But I'll follow with the drum,
And whene'er that beats, I'll be ready, O.
Dumbarton's drums sound bonny, O ;
They are sprightly, like my dear Jonny, O.
   How happy shall I be,
     When on my soldier's knee,
And he kisses and blesses his Annie, O.

SONG LXXXVI.
ONCE MORE I'LL TUNE.

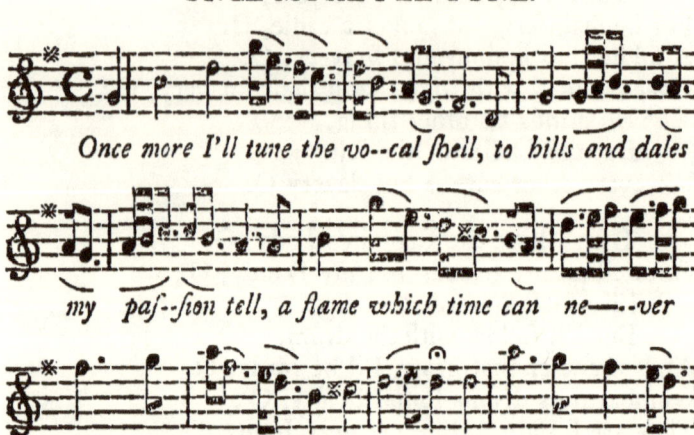

Once more I'll tune the vo--cal shell, to hills and dales my paf--sion tell, a flame which time can ne----ver quell, that burns for lovely Peggy. Ye greater bards the

lyre should hit, for say what subject is more fit, than to

record the sparkling wit and bloom of lovely Peggy.

The sun first rising in the morn,
That paints the dew-bespangled thorn,
Does not so much the day adorn,
    As does my lovely Peggy.
And when in Thetis lap to rest,
He streaks with gold the ruddy west,
He's not so beauteous, as undress'd
    Appears my lovely Peggy.

Were she array'd in rustic weed,
With her the bleating flocks I'd feed,
And pipe upon mine oaten reed,
   To please my lovely Peggy.
With her a cottage would delight,
All's happy when she's in my sight,
But when she's gone it's endless night,
   All's dark without my Peggy.

The zephyr's air the violet blows,
Or breath upon the damask rose,
He does not half the sweets disclose,
   That does my lovely Peggy.
I stole a kiss the other day,
And trust me, nought but truth I say,
The fragrant breath of blooming May,
   Was not so sweet as Peggy.

While bees from flow'r to flow'r shall rove,
And linnets warble thro' the grove,
Or stately swans the waters love,
   So long shall I love Peggy.
And when Death with his pointed dart,
Shall strike the blow that rives my heart,
My word shall be when I depart,
   Adieu! my lovely Peggy.

SONG LXXXVII.
THE CONTENTED MAN.

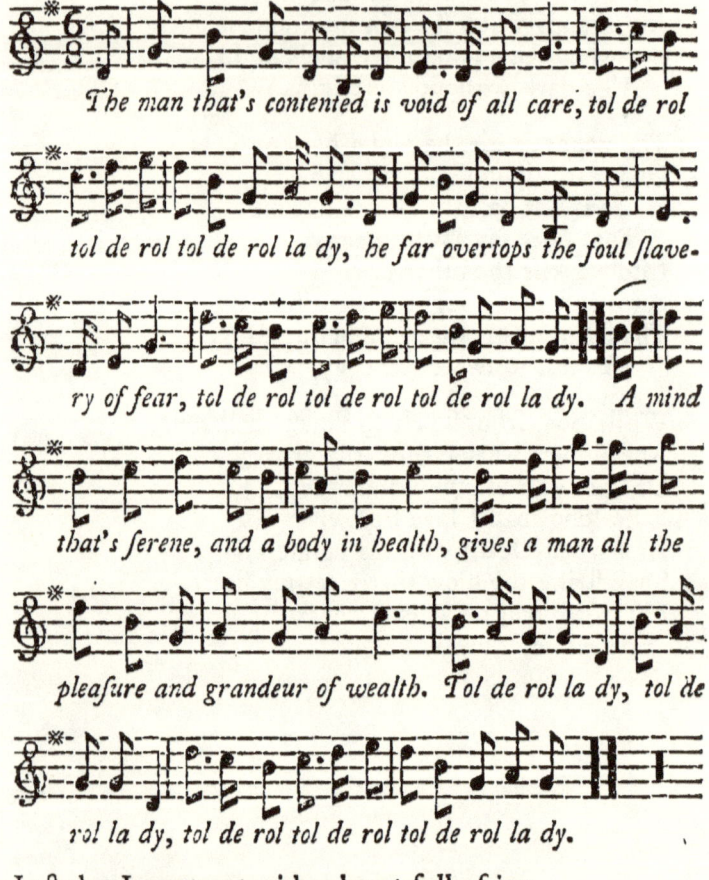

The man that's contented is void of all care, tol de rol tol de rol tol de rol la dy, he far overtops the foul slavery of fear, tol de rol tol de rol tol de rol la dy. A mind that's serene, and a body in health, gives a man all the pleasure and grandeur of wealth. Tol de rol la dy, tol de rol la dy, tol de rol tol de rol tol de rol la dy.

Last day I went out with a heart full of joy.
    Tol de rol, &c.
Which nothing but vice or sharp pain could annoy;
    Tol de rol, &c.
The first that I meet was a miser, whose gloom
Shew'd a soul that was muddy, and straiten'd in room.
    Tol de rol, &c.

In Britain's fair island there's none to be seen
    Tol de rol, &c.
Of more sullen, selfish, and sordid a mein;
    Tol de rol, &c.
Regardless of honour, a slave to his gold,
Despis'd of the young, and contemn'd of the old,
    Tol de rol, &c.

The next that I met was a profligate ass,
    Tol de rol, &c.
Whose brains were of cork, and his forehead of brass;
    Tol de rol, &c.
By game he was galloping thro' his estate,
And mis'ry attended his sad sinking fate.

O place me, kind heav'n! in what station you please,
    Tol de rol, &c.
So my body's in health, and my soul be at ease;
    Tol de rol, &c.
By command of myself, independent and free,
Contentment shall still be a pleasure to me.
    Tol de rol, &c.

O rather in a cottage may I be fed
    Tol de rol, &c.
With roots the most common, and coarsest brown bread,
    Tol de rol, &c.
Than to riot with luxury, fopp'ry, and vice,
They're the loss of contentment, too precious a price.
    Tol de rol, &c.

Let rakes ramble after their harlots and wine,
    Tol de rol, &c.
'Till with poxes and palsies their carcases dwine;
    Tol de rol, &c.
Grow old while they're young, and have wasted their store,
While the vot'ries of virtue are blithe at fourscore.
    Tol de rol, &c.

The thunder may roar, and the hurricanes make
    Tol de rol, &c.
The ocean to boil, and the forests to shake;
    Tol de rol, &c.
The light'ning may flash, and the rocks may be rent,
But nothing can ruffle the mind that's content.

This world's well freighted with wonders in store,
    Tol de rol, &c.
And we're sent into it to think and explore;
    Tol de rol, &c.
And when the due summons shall call us away,
No more's to be said, but contented obey.
    Tol de rol, &c.

SONG LXXXVIII.
THE SWEET ROSY MORNING.

The sweet rosy morning peeps o-ver the hills, with blush-es adorning the meadows and fields. The merry, merry merry horn calls come, come, come away, awake from your slumbers, and hail the new day.

  The stag rous'd before us,
   Away seems to fly,
  And pants to the chorus,
   Of hounds in full cry.
Cho. Then follow follow follow follow,
   The musical chace,
  Where pleasure and vigour,
   And health all embrace.

  The day's sport when over,
   Makes blood circle right,
  And gives the brisk lover,
   Fresh charms for the night.
Cho. Then let us, let us now enjoy
   All we can while we may;
  Let love crown the night,
   As our sports crown the day.

SONG LXXXIX.
BONNY JEAN.

Love's goddess in a myrtle grove, said, Cupid, bend thy bow with speed, nor let the shaft at random rove, for Jen--ny's haughty heart must bleed. - The smil-ing boy with di-vine art from Paphos shoot an arrow keen, which flew unerring to the heart, and kill'd the pride of bonny Jean.

No more the nymph, with haughty air,
Refuses Willy's kind address;
Her yielding blushes shew no care,
But too much fondness to suppress.

No more the youth is fullen now,
But looks the gayeſt on the green,
Whilſt every day he ſpies ſome new
Surprizing charms in bonny Jean.

A thouſand tranſports crowd his breaſt,
He moves as light as fleeting wind ;
His former ſorrows ſeem a jeſt
Now when his Jenny is turn'd kind.
Riches he looks on with diſdain,
The glorious fields of war look mean ;
The chearful hound and horn gives pain ;
If abſent from his bonny Jean.

The day he ſpends in am'rous gaze,
Which ev'n in ſummer ſhort'ned ſeems ;
When ſunk in downs, with glad amaze,
He wonders at her in his dreams.
All charms diſclos'd, ſhe looks more bright
Than Troy's prize, the Spartan Queen.
With breaking day, he lifts his ſight,
And pants to be with bonny Jean.

SONG XC.
PINKY HOUSE.

By Pin-kie house oft let me walk, while cir-cled in my arms I hear my Nelly sweetly talk, and gaze o'er all her charms. O let me ever fond be-hold those gra-ces void of art, those chearful smiles that sweetly hold in will--ing chains my heart.

 O come, my love! and bring a-new
  That gentle turn of mind;
 That gracefulness of air, in you,
  By nature's hand defign'd;
 That beauty like the blushing rofe,
  First lighted up this flame;
 Which, like the sun, for ever glows
  Within my breast the same.

VOCAL ENCHANTRESS.

Ye light coquets! ye airy things!
   How vain is all your art!
How feldom it a lover brings!
   How rarely keeps a heart!
O gather from my Nelly's charms,
   That fweet, that graceful eafe;
That blufhing modefty that warms;
   That native art to pleafe!

Come then, my love! O come along,
   And feed me with thy charms;
Come, fair infpirer of my fong,
   O fill my longing arms.
A flame like mine can never die,
   While charms, fo bright as thine,
So heav'nly fair, both pleafe the eye,
   And fill the foul divine!

SONG XCI.
WHEN ABSENT FROM THE NYMPH.

All day I wander through the groves,
    And, fighing, hear from ev'ry tree,
The happy birds chirping their loves;
    Happy, compar'd with lonely me.
When gently fleep with balmy wings,
    To reft fans ev'ry weary'd wight,
A thoufand fears my fancy brings,
    That keep me watching all the night.

Sleep flies, while like the goddess fair,
   And all the graces in her train,
With melting smiles and killing air,
   Appears the cause of all my pain.
A while my mind delighted flies
   O'er all her sweets with thrilling joy;
Whilst want of worth makes doubts arise,
   That all my trembling hopes destroy.

Thus, while my thoughts are fix'd on her,
   I'm all o'er transport and desire;
My pulse beats high, my cheeks appear
   All roses, and mine eyes all fire.
When to myself I turn my view,
   My veins grow chill, my cheeks looks wan:
Thus, whilst my fears my pains renew,
   I scarcely look, or love a man.

Z.

SONG XCII.
BRAES OF BALLENDEAN.

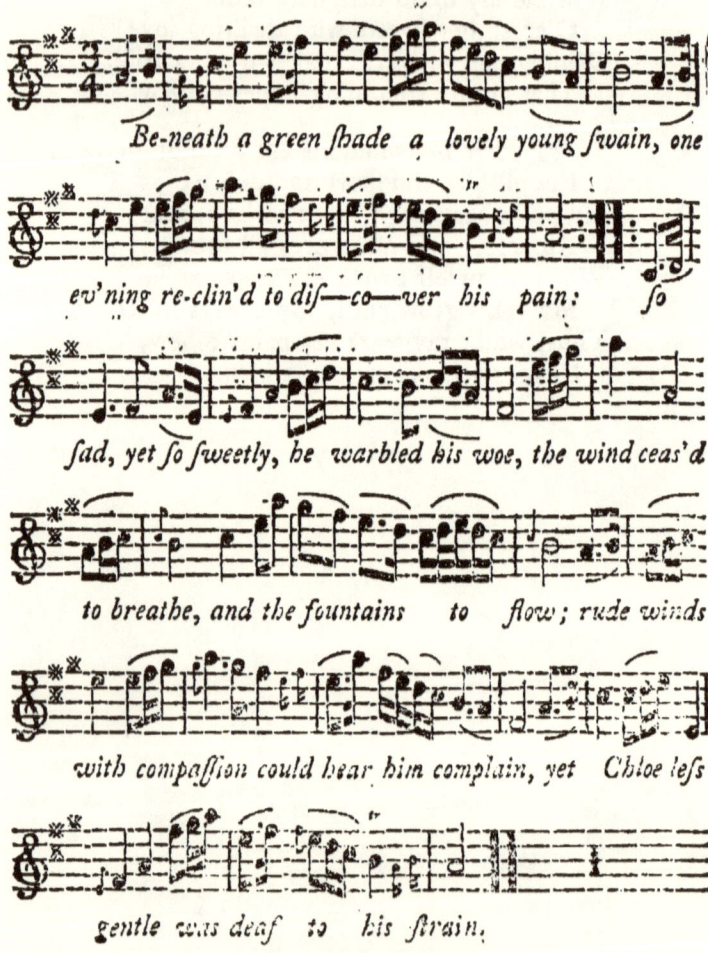

How happy he cry'd, my moments once flew,
E'er Chloe's bright charms first flash'd in my view!
Those eyes, then, with pleasure, the dawn could survey;
Nor smil'd the fair morning more chearful than they.

Now, scenes of diftrefs pleafe only my fight:
I ficken in pleafure, and languifh in light.

   Thro' changes, in vain, relief I purfue:
All, all, but confpire, my griefs to renew:
From funfhine, to zephyrs and fhades, we repair;
To funfhine we fly from too piercing an air:
But love's ardent fever burns always the fame!
No winter can cool it, no fummer inflame.

   But, fee! the pale moon, all clouded, retires!
The breezes grow cool, not Strephon's defires!
I fly from the dangers of tempeft and wind:
Yet nourifh the madnefs that preys on my mind.
Ah, wretch! how can life be worthy thy care,
Since length'ning it's moments but lengthens defpair?

SONG XCIII.
TWEED-SIDE.

What beauties does Flora disclose, how sweet are her

smiles u--pon Tweed, yet Mary's still sweeter than those,

both nature and fancy exceed.   No dai-sy, nor sweet

blushing rose, nor all the gay flow'rs of the field, nor

Tweed gliding gent-ly thro' those such beau-ty and plea-

sure does yield.

  The warblers are heard in the grove.
   The linnet, the lark, and the thrush,
  The blackbird and sweet cooing dove,
   With music enchant every bush.

Come, let us go forth to the mead,
   Let us see how the primroses spring;
We'll lodge in some village on Tweed,
   And love while the feather'd folks sing,

How does my love pass the lang day?
   Does Mary not tend a few sheep?
Do they never carelessly stray,
   While happily she lies asleep?
Tweed's murmurs should lull her to rest;
   Kind nature indulging my bliss,
To relieve the saft pains of my breast,
   I'd steal an ambrosial kiss.

'Tis she does the virgins excel,
   No beauty with her may compare;
Love's graces around her do dwell:
   She's fairest where thousands are fair.
Say, charmer, where do thy flocks stray,
   Oh! tell me at noon where they feed;
Shall I seek them on sweet winding Tay,
   Or pleasanter banks of the Tweed.

SONG XCIV.
THRO' THE WOOD LADDIE.

O Sandy, why leaves thou thy Nelly to mourn, thy presence could ease me, when naithing can please me, now dowie I sigh on the banks of the burn, or thro' the wood laddie, un--til thou return. Tho' woods now are gay, and mornings so clear, while lavrocks are singing, and prim--ro-ses springing: yet none of them please my eye or my ear; when thro' the wood laddie ye dinna

ap--pear.

That I am forsaken, some spare na to tell:
    I'm fash'd wi' their scorning,
    Baith evening and morning;
Their jeering gaes aft to my heart wi' a knell,
When thro' the wood, laddie, I wander mysell.

Then stay, my dear Sandy, nae langer away,
    But quick as an arrow,
    Haste here to thy marrow;
Wha's living in langour, till that happy day,
When thro' the wood, laddie, we'll dance, sing and play.

SONG XCV.
BRITISH GRENADIERS.

Some talk of A-lexander, and some of Hercu--les, of

Conon, and Lysander, and some Milti--a--des; but of all

the world's brave heroes there's none that can compare,

with a tow, row, row, row, row, to the British gre-na-

diers. But of all the world's brave heroes, there's none

that can compare, with a tow, row, row, row, row, to

the British grena--diers.

None of thofe ancient heroes e'er faw a cannon ball,
Or knew the force of powder to flay their foes withal;
But our brave boys do know it, and banifh all their fears,
With a tow, row, row, row, row, the Britifh Grenadiers.
  But our brave boys, &c.

Whene'er we are commanded to ftorm the Palifades,
Our leaders march with fufees, and we with hand granades,
We throw them from the glacis about our enemies ears,
With a tow, row, row, row, row, the Britifh Grenadiers.
  We throw them, &c.

The god of war was pleafed, and great Bellona fmiles,
To fee thefe noble heroes, of our Britifh Ifles;
And all the gods celeftial, defcended from their fpheres,
Beheld with admiration the Britifh Grenadiers.
  And all the gods celeftial, &c.

Then let us crown a bumper, and drink a health to thofe
Who carry caps and pouches that wear the looped clothes.
May they and their commanders, live happy all their years,
With a tow, row, row, row, row, the Britifh Grenadiers.
  May they and their commanders, &c.

A 2

haſte, haſte my dear Jockey, to me back again.

When lads, and their laſſes, are on the green met;
They dance, and they ſing; and they laugh, and they chat;
Contented and happy, with hearts full of glee:
I can't without envy, their merriment ſee.
Thoſe paſtimes offend me; my ſhepherd's not there:
No pleaſure I reliſh, that Jockey don't ſhare.
It makes me to ſigh; I from tears ſcarce refrain,
   I wiſh my dear Jockey,
   I wiſh my dear Jockey,
   I wiſh my dear Jockey return'd back again.

But hope ſhall ſuſtain me; nor will I deſpair:
He promis'd he would in a fortnight be here.
On fond expectation my wiſhes I'll feaſt;
For love my dear Jockey to Jenny will haſte.
Then, farewell, each care: and, adieu, each vain ſigh:
Who'll then be ſo bleſt, or ſo happy, as I?
I'll ſing on the meadows, and alter my ſtrain.
   When Jockey returns,
   When Jockey returns,
   When Jockey returns to my arms back again.

A a i!

SONG XCVII.
WHY HANGS THAT CLOUD.

Why hangs that cloud u-pon thy brow, that beauteous heaven e'er while serene, whence do these storms and tempests flow, or what this gust of passion mean: and must then mankind lose that light, which in thine eyes was wont to shine, and ly obscur'd in endless night, for each poor sil--ly speech of mine.

Dear child, how can I wrong thy name,
  Since 'tis acknowledged at all hands,
That could ill tongues abuse thy fame,
  Thy beauty can make large amends;

Or if I durst profanely try
   Thy beauty's pow'rful charms t' upbraid,
Thy virtue well might give the lie,
   Nor call thy beauty to it's aid.

For Venus every heart t' ensnare,
   With all her charms has deck'd thy face,
And Pallas with unusual care,
   Bids wisdom heighten every grace.
Who can the double pain endure!
   Or who must not resign the field
To thee, celestial maid, secure
   With Cupid's bow, and Pallas' shield?

If then to thee such pow'r is given,
   Let not a wretch in torment live,
But smile, and learn to copy Heaven,
   Since we must sin ere it forgive.
Yet pitying Heaven not only does
   Forgive th' offender and th' offence,
But even itself appeas'd bestows,
   As the reward of penitence.

SONG XCVIII.
LEADER-HAUGHS AND YARROW.

The morn was fair, saft was the air, all nature's sweets

were springing. The buds did bow with silver dew, ten

thousand birds were singing; when on the bent with blyth

content, young Jamie sang his marrow, nae bonnier lass

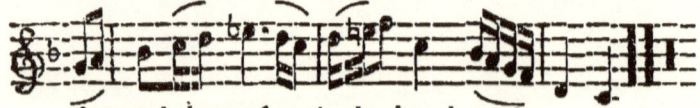

e'er trod the grass on leader-haughs and yarrow.

How sweet her face, where ev'ry grace
    In heavenly beauty's planted!
Her smiling een, and comely mein,
    That nae perfection wanted.
I'll never fret, nor ban my fate,
    But bless my bonny marrow:
If her dear smile my doubts beguile,
    My mind shall ken nae sorrow.

Yet tho' she's fair, and has full share
   Of ev'ry charm inchanting,
Each good turns ill, and soon will kill
   Poor me, if love be wanting.
O bonny lass! have but the grace
   To think ere ye gae further,
Your joys maun flit, if you commit
   The crying sin of murder.

My wand'ring ghaist will ne'er get rest,
   And day and night affright ye;
But if ye're kind, and joyful mind,
   I'll study to delight ye.
Our years around with love thus crown'd,
   From all things joy shall borrow:
Thus none shall be more blest than we,
   On Leader-haughs and Yarrow.

O sweetest Sue! 'tis only you
   Can make life worth my wishes,
If equal love your mind can move
   To grant this best of blisses.
Thou art my sun, and thy least frown
   Would blast me in the blossom:
But if thou shine, and make me thine,
   I'll flourish in thy bosom.

SONG XCIX.
THE BANKS OF FORTH.

Oft in the thick embow'ring groves,
   Where birds their music chirp aloud,
Alternately we sing our loves,
   And Fortha's fair meanders view'd.

The meadows wore a gen'ral smile,
Love was our banquet all the while;
The lovely prospect charm'd the eye,
To where the ocean met the sky.

Once on the grassy bank reclin'd,
　　Where Forth ran by in murmurs deep,
It was my happy chance to find
　　The charming Mary lull'd asleep.
My heart then leap'd with inward bliss,
I softly stoop'd and stole a kiss;
She wak'd, she blush'd, and gently blam'd,
Why, Damon! are you not asham'd?

Ye Sylvan Pow'rs, ye Rural Gods,
　　To whom we swains our cares impart,
Restore me to these bless'd abodes,
　　And ease, oh! ease my love-sick heart:
These happy days again restore,
When Mall and I shall part no more;
When she shall fill these longing arms,
And crown my bliss with all her charms.

B b

SONG C.

FOR ME MY FAIR.

For me my fair a wreath has wove, where rival flow'rs in union meet, where rival flow'rs in union meet: As oft she kiss'd this gift of love, her breath gave sweetness to the sweet; as oft she kiss'd this gift of love, her breath gave sweetness to the sweet, her breath gave sweetness to the sweet.

A bee within a damaſk roſe
    Had crept, the nectar'd dew to ſip;
But leſſer ſweets the thief forgoes,
    And fixes on Louiſa's lip.

There, taſting all the bloom of ſpring,
    Wak'd by the rip'ning breath of May,
Th' ungrateful ſpoiler left his ſting,
    And with the honey fled away.

Tho' to the Spanish coast
  We're bound to steer,
We'll still our rights maintain ;
Then bear a hand, be steady boys,
  ' Soon we'll see
Old England once again :
  From shore to shore,
  While cannons roar,
Our tars shall show
The haughty foe
  Britannia rules the main.

Then fling the flowing bowl ;
  Fond hopes arise,
  The girls we prize
Shall bless each jovial soul :
  The cann, boys, bring,
  We'll drink and sing,
While foaming billows roll.

Cho. Then fling the, &c.

SONG CII.
HARK! HARK!

Hark! hark! the joy in-spi-ring horn, Sa-lutes the

ro-sy ri-sing morn, And e-choes thro' the dale ---

And e-choes thro' the dale: With clam'rous peals the

hills resound, The hounds quick scent-ed scow'r the

ground, And snuff the fragrant gale --- And snuff

the fragrant gale.

Nor gates nor hedges can impede
The brisk high-mettl'd starting steed,
   The jovial pack pursue;
Like light'ning darting o'er the plains,
The distant hills with speed he gains,
   And sees the game in view.

Her path the timid hare forsakes,
And to the copse for shelter makes,
   There pants a while for breath;
When now the noise alarms her ear,
Her haunt's descry'd, her fate is near,
   She sees approaching death.

Directed by the well-known breeze,
The hounds their trembling victim seize;
   She faints, she falls, she dies:
The distant coursers now come in,
And join the loud triumphant din,
   Till echo rend the skies.

SONG CIII.

THO' LATE I WAS PLUMP.

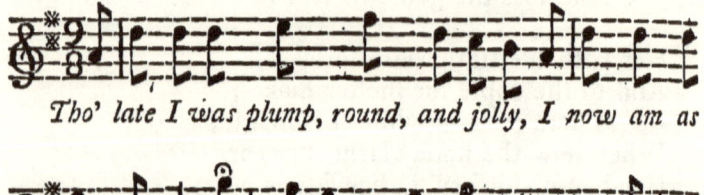

Tho' late I was plump, round, and jolly, I now am as

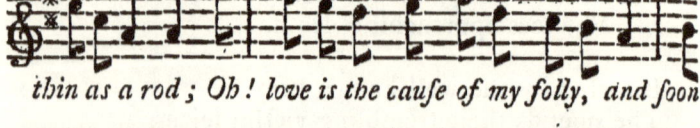

thin as a rod; Oh! love is the cauſe of my folly, and ſoon

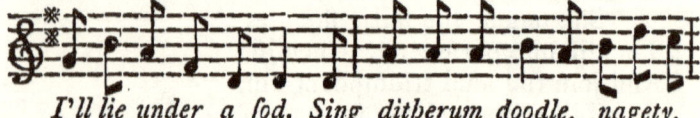

I'll lie under a ſod. Sing ditherum doodle, nagety,

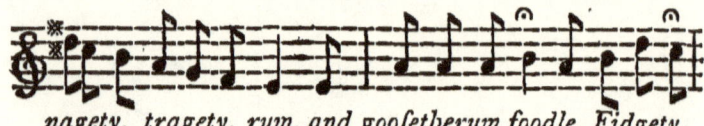

nagety, tragety, rum, and gooſetherum foodle, Fidgety,

fidgety, nidgety, mum.

Dear Kathleen, then why did you flout me,
 A lad that's ſo coſey and warm?
Oh! ev'ry thing's handſome about me,
 My cabin and ſnug little farm.
  Sing ditherum, &c.

What tho' I have scrap'd up no money?
　No duns at my chamber attend;
On Sunday I ride on my poney,
　And still have a bit for a friend.
　　Sing ditherum, &c.

The cock courts his hens all around me,
　The sparrow, the pigeon, and dove;
Oh! how all this courting confounds me,
　When I look and think of my love.
　　Sing ditherum, &c.

SONG CIV.
SINCE YOU MEAN

With three crowns, your ſtanding wages,
　　You ſhall daintily be fed;
Bacon, beans, ſalt-beef, and cabbage,
　　Butter-milk, and oaten bread.
　　　　Farra diddle, &c.

Come, ſtrike hands, you'll live in clover
   When we get you once at home;
And when daily labour's over
   We'll all dance to your ſtrum ſtrum.
     Farra diddle, &c.

Done; ſtrike hands, I take your offer;
   Farther on I may fare worſe;
Zooks! I can no longer ſuffer
   Hungry guts and empty purſe.
     Farra diddle, &c.

SONG CV.
BY THE GAILY

By the gaily circling glafs, We can fee how minutes pafs; By the hollow cafk we're told How the waning night grows old, How the waning night grows old.

Soon, too foon, the bu-fy day drives us from our fport a-way. What have we with day to do? Sons of Care, 'twas made for you! Sons of Care, 'twas made for you!

 By the filence of the owl,
  By the chirping on the thorn,
 By the butts that empty roll,
  We foretel th' approach of morn.
 Fill, then, fill the vacant glafs,
  Let no precious moment flip;
 Flout the moralizing afs;
  Joys find entrance at the lip.

SONG CVI.

IANTHE THE LOVELY.

I-an-the the lovely, the joy of her swain, by Iphis was lov'd, and lov'd Iphis again. She liv'd in the youth, and the youth in the fair; their pleasure was equal, and equal their care: No delight, no enjoyment, their dotage withdrew; but the longer they liv'd still the fonder they grew. No delight, no enjoyment, their dotage withdrew; but the longer they liv'd still the fonder they grew.

A paffion fo happy alarm'd all the plain:
Some envy'd the nymph; but more envy'd the fwain:
Some fwore 'twou'd be pity their loves to invade,
That the lovers alone for each other were made.
But all, all confented, that none ever knew
A nymph be more kind, or a fhepherd fo true.

Love faw them with pleafure, and vow'd to take care
Of the faithful, the tender, the innocent pair;
What either might want he bid either to move;
But they wanted nothing but ever to love.
He faid all to blefs them his godhead cou'd do,
That they still fhou'd be kind and they fhou'd be true.

SONG CVII.
LIFE IS CHECQUER'D.

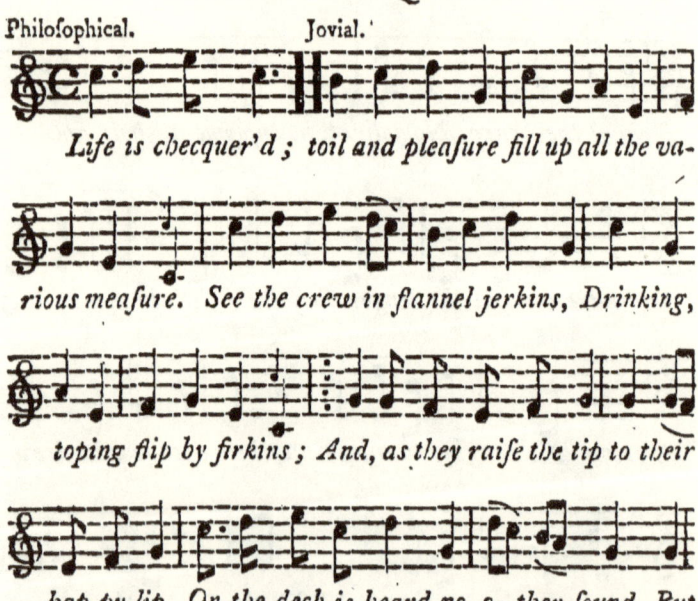

Life is checquer'd; toil and pleafure fill up all the various meafure. See the crew in flannel jerkins, Drinking,
toping flip by firkins; And, as they raife the tip to their
hap-py lip, On the deck is heard no o-ther found, But

prithee, Jack, prithee, Dick, prithee, Sam, prithee, Tom,

Let the cann go round. Then hark to the boatſwain's

whiſtle! whiſtle! Then hark to the boatſwain's whiſtle!

whiſtle! Buſtle, buſtle, buſtle, my boy: Let us ſtir,

let us toil, but let's drink all the while; For labour's the

price of our joy, For labour's the price of our joy.

  Life is checquer'd; toil and pleaſure
  Fill up all the various meaſure.
  Hark! the crew, with ſun-burnt faces,
  Chanting black-ey'd Suſan's graces:
   And, as they raiſe their notes
   Thro' their ruſty throats,
  On the deck is heard no other ſound, &c. &c.

Life is checquer'd; toil and pleasure
Fill up all the various measure.
Hark! the crew their cares discarding
With hustle-cap, or with chuck-farthing?
   Still in a merry pin,
    Let them lose or win,
On the deck is heard no other sound, &c. &c.

SONG CVIII.
YOU THE POINT MAY CARRY.

You the point may carry, If a while you tarry;—But

for you, I tell you true, no, you I'll never marry.

You the point may carry, If a while you tarry;—But for

you, I tell you true, no, you I'll never marry.

Care our fouls difowning,
Punch our forrows drowning,
    Laugh and love,
    And ever prove
Joys our wifhes crowning.
  Care our, &c.

To the church I'll hand her.
Then thro' the world I'll wander:
    I'll fob and figh
    Until I die
A poor forfaken gander.
  To the church, &c.

Each pious prieft fince Mofes
One mighty truth difclofes;
    You're never vex't
    If this his text,
Go fuddle all your nofes.
  Each pious, &c.

Dd

SONG CIX.

HOW LITTLE DO THE LANDMEN KNOW.

How little do the landmen know Of what we sailors

feel, When waves do mount and winds do blow; But we

have hearts of steel.   No danger can af-fright us,

No enemy shall flout; We'll make the monsieurs right

us: So tofs the cann about.

  Stick ſtout to orders, meſſmates;
   We'll plunder, burn, and ſink.
  Then, France, have at your firſt-rates:
   For Britons never ſhrink.
  We'll rummage all we fancy;
   We'll bring them in by ſcores:
  And Moll and Kate and Nancy
   Shall roll in Louis d'ors.

VOCAL ENCHANTRESS.

While here at Deal we're lying
    With our noble commodore,
We'll fpend our wages freely, boys,
    And then to fea for more.
In peace we'll drink and fing, boys;
    In war we'll never fly.
Here's a health to George our king, boys,
    And the royal family.

SONG CX.

GOOD MORROW TO YOUR NIGHT-CAP.

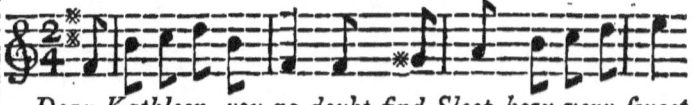
Dear Kathleen, you no doubt find Sleep how very fweet

'tis; Dogs bark and cocks have crow'd out; You never

dream how late 'tis. This morning gay I poft away,

to have with you a bit of play; on two legs rid along

to bid Good morrow to your night-cap.

Last night a little bousy
With whisky, ale, and cyder,
I ask'd young Betty Blousy
To let me sit beside her.
  Her anger rose;
  And, sour as sloes,
The little gipsey cock'd her nose.
Yet here I've rid along to bid
Good morrow to your night-cap.

SONG CXI.

WHEN MY WIFE IS LAID IN GROUND.

O what pleasures will abound When my wife is

laid in ground! Let earth cover her, we'll dance

over her, When my wife is laid in ground.

Oh how happy shou'd I be
Would little Nysa pig with me!
How I'd mumble her, touze and tumble her,
Wou'd little Nysa pig with me!

SONG CXII.

WHY HEAVES.

Why heaves my fond bo-fom? Ah! what can it mean?

Why flut-ters my heart which was once so se-rene?

Why this sigh-ing and trembling when Daphne is near?

Or why, when she's ab-sent, this sor-row and fear?

Or why, when she's absent, this sor-row and fear?

For ever, methinks, I with wonder could trace
The thousand soft charms that embellish thy face.
Each moment I view thee, new beauties I find:
With thy face I am charm'd; but enslav'd by thy mind.

Untainted with folly; unsullied by pride:
There native good humour and virtue reside.
Pray Heaven that virtue thy soul may supply
With compassion for him who without thee must die.

SONG CXIII.
WHERE'S MY SWAIN.

Where's my swain so blithe and clever? Why d'ye leave

me all in sorrow? Three whole days are gone for ever

Since you said you'd come to-morrow. If you lov'd but

half as I do, You'd been here with looks so bonny;

Love has fly-ing wings I well know, Not for ling'ring

la-zy Johnny. Love has flying wings I well know,

Not for ling'ring la-zy Johnny.

What can he be now a-doing?
  Is he with the laſſes Maying?
He had better here be wooing
  Than with others fondly playing.
Tell me truly where he's roving,
  That I may no longer ſorrow.
If he's weary grown of loving,
  Let him tell me ſo to-morrow.

Does ſome fav'rite rival hide thee?
  Let her be the happy creature:
I'll not plague myſelf to chide thee,
  Nor diſpute with her a feature.
But I can't and will not tarry,
  Nor will kill myſelf with ſorrow:
I may loſe the time to marry
  If I wait beyond to-morrow.

Think not, ſhepherd, thus to brave me:
  If I'm yours, pray wait no longer:
If you won't, another 'll have me.
  I may cool but not grow fonder.
If your lovers, girls, forſake ye,
  Whine not in deſpair and ſorrow;
Bleſt another lad may make ye.
  Stay for none beyond to-morrow.

SONG CXIV.
THE LAND OF DELIGHT.

As you mean to set sail for the land of delight,

And in wedlock's soft hammock to swing ev'ry night;

If you hope that your voyage suc-cess-ful shou'd prove,

Fill your sails with affection, your cabins with love.

If you hope that your voyage successful shou'd prove,

Fill your sails with affection, your cabins with love.

Fill your sails with affection, your ca-bins with love.

Let your heart, like the main-maſt, be ever upright,
And the union you boaſt, like our tackle, be tight;
Of the ſhoals of indiff'rence be ſure to keep clear,
And the quickſands of jealouſy never come near.

But if vapours and whims, like ſea-ſickneſs, prevail,
You muſt ſpread all your canvas and catch the freſh gale:
For if briſk blows the wind and there comes a rough
    ſea,
You muſt lower your top-ſail and ſcud under lee.

If huſbands e'er hope to live peaceable lives,
They muſt reckon themſelves, give the helm to their
    wives:
For the ſmoother we ſail, boys, we're ſafeſt from harm,
And on ſhipboard the head is ſtill rul'd by the helm.

Then liſt to your pilot, my boys, and be wiſe;
If my precepts you ſcorn and my maxims deſpiſe,
A brace of proud antlers your brows may adorn;
And a hundred to one but you double Cape Horn.

SONG CXV.

THE OLD WOMAN's SONG.

Old women we are, and as wife in the chair, and as fit for the quorum as men. We can fcold on the bench, and ex - amine a wench; and like them, and like them, and like them can be wrong now and then, now and then, now and then; and like them can be wrong now

Chorus.

and then. For look the world thro', and you'll find,

nine in ten, Old women can do, Old women can do,

Old women can do as much as old men.

We can hear a sad case with a no-meaning face,
   And tho' shallow yet seem to be deep:
Leave all to the clerk; and when matters grow dark,
   Their worships had better go sleep.
     For look, &c.

When our wisdom is task'd, and hard questions are ask'd,
   We answer them best with a snore;
We can mump a tit bit, and can joke without wit:
   And what can their worships do more?
     For look, &c.

SONG CXVI.
THE THING.

Fine songsters a-po-lo-gies too often use: When call'd

on I'm ready to sing. With hums or with haws ne'er

attempt to refuse: And egad, Sirs, I'll give you the

thing; the thing; and egad, Sirs, I'll give you the thing.

Conceited our beaux arm in arm walk the street;
   In idleness take their full swing:
Each levels his glass when a lady they meet;
   And if handsome, they swear—she's the thing.

Thus at Smithfield the jockey his nag will commend :
   What a shape! why, he's fit for the king!
He's found wind and limb, on the word of a friend ;
   And for spirits—he's really the thing.

With smile of self-interest the landlord imparts,
   Butt-entire I always do bring :
Old stingo I draw that will cherish your hearts ;'
   And in flavour indeed—'tis the thing.

See Jenny with Jocky to playhouse repair
  Miss Brent to hear warble and sing;
Pretenders to music, they praise ev'ry air
  With I vow and protest—she's the thing.

The sportsman with joy views the hare in full speed,
  In ecstasy hears the sky ring;
With cry of the hounds, and of each neighing steed,
  And in transport he cries—'tis the thing.

The prude her own person consults in the glass,
  Admiring her finger and ring;
Then concludes that her beauty all others surpass,
  And that man must confess—she's the thing.

Jack Tar, full of glee, to the garden will stroll,
  In search, Sirs, of something like l—g;
There boards on Moll Jenkins, and swears by his soul
  She's rigg'd, fore and aft—quite the thing.

The parson, well pleas'd, trims the smoaking Sir Loin,
  And slyly leers at the pudding;
Lord bless me, he cries, how nobly I dine!
  O pudding and beef is—the thing!

But, clasp'd in the arms of a good-natur'd pair,
  With mutual embraces we cling;
That enjoyment alone dispels ev'ry care,
  Which you all must allow is—the thing.

SONG CXVII.

HE STOLE MY TENDER HEART AWAY.

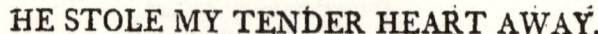

The fields were green, the hills were gay, And birds

were singing on each spray, When Colin met me in the

grove, And told me tender tales of love. Was ever swain

so blithe as he? So kind, so faithful, and so free? In

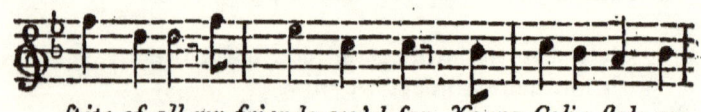

spite of all my friends cou'd say, Young Colin stole my

heart away. In spite of all my friends cou'd say, Young

Colin stole my heart away.

Whene'er he trips the meads along
He sweetly joins the woodlark's song;
And when he dances on the green
There's none so blithe as Colin seen.
If he's but by I nothing fear;
For I alone am all his care:
Then, spite of all my friends can say,
He's stole my tender heart away.

My mother chides whene'er I roam,
And seems surpris'd I quit my home:
But she'd not wonder that I rove,
Did she but feel how much I love.
Full well I know the gen'rous swain
Will never give my bosom pain:
Then, spite of all my friends can say,
He's stole my tender heart away.

SONG CXVIII.
COME ON, MY BRAVE TARS.

Come on, my brave tars, Let's away to the wars, To

honour and glory advance: For now we've beat

Spain, Let us try this campaign To humble the pride

of old France, my brave boys; to humble the pride of

old France.

  See William, brave prince,
  A true blue ev'ry inch,
Who will honour th' illuftrious name.
  May he conqueror be
  O'er our empire the fea,
And tranfmit Britifh laurels to fame,
   My brave boys, &c.

Three heroes combin'd,
When the Dons they cou'd find,
Vied who ſhou'd be foremoſt in battle:
By no lee-ſhore affrighted,
Altho' they're benighted,
They made Britiſh thunder to rattle,
    Brave boys, &c.

See Dalrymple, Prevoſt,
Gallant Barrington too,
And Farmer who glorioufly fell;
With brave Pearſon: all knew
That the hearts of true blue,
Once rouz'd, not the world cou'd excel,
    My brave boys, &c.

With ſuch heroes as thoſe,
Tho' we've numberleſs foes,
Britiſh valour reſplendent ſhall ſhine:
And we ſtill hope to ſhow
That their pride will be low
In eighty, as fam'd fifty-nine,
    My brave boys, &c.

Then, brave lads, enter here,
And partake of our cheer;
You ſhall feaſt and be merry and ſing.
With the grog at your noſe
Drink ſucceſs to true blues:
Huzza! and ſay God ſave the King!
    My brave boys, &c.

SONG CXIX.
JOHNNY's GREY BREEKS.

When I was in my fe'enteen years, I was baith

blithe and bonny, O. The lads lo'ed me baith far and

near; But I lo'ed nane but Johnny, O. He gain'd

my heart in twa three weeks, He fpak' fae blithe and

kindly, O; And I made him new grey breeks That fitted

him moft finely, O. He gain'd my heart in twa three

weeks, He spak' sae blithe and kindly, O; And I made him

new grey breeks That fitted him most finely, O.

He was a handsome fellow;
   His humour was baith frank and free:
His bonny locks sae yellow,
   Like gou'd they glitter'd in my ee',
His dimpl'd chin and rosy cheeks,
   And face sae fair and ruddy, O;
And then a-days his grey breeks
   Were neither auld nor duddy, O.

But now they are thread-bare worn;
   They're wider than they wont to be;
They're tashed like and sair torn;
   And clouted sair on ilka knee.
But gin I had a summer's day,
   As I have had right mony, O,
I'll mak' a web o' new grey
   To be breeks to my Johnny, O.

For he's weel wordy o' them,
   And better gin I had to gi'e;
And I'll tak' pains upo' them;
   Frae fau'ts I'll strive to keep them free.
To clead him weel shall be my care,
   And please him a' my study, O;
But he maun wear the auld pair
   A wee, tho' they be duddy, O.

For when the lad was in his prime,
  Like him there was nae mony, O.
He ca'd me ay his bonny thing:
  Say, wha wou'd nae lo'e Johnny, O?
Sae I lo'e Johnny's grey breeks
  For a' the care they've gi'en me yet;
And gin we live anither year
  We'll keep them haill between us yet.

Now, to conclude his grey breeks;
  I'll fing them up wi' mirth and glee.
Here's luck to a' the grey fteeks
  That fhow themfelves upo' the knee:
And if wi' health I'm fpared
  A wee while, as I wifh I may,
I fhall ha'e them prepared
  As weel as ony that's o' grey.

SONG CXX.

ALL YE WHO WOU'D WISH.

All ye who wou'd wifh to fucceed with a lafs, Learn

how the affair's to be done: For if you ftand fooling

and fhy, like an afs, You'll lofe her, lofe her, You'll lofe

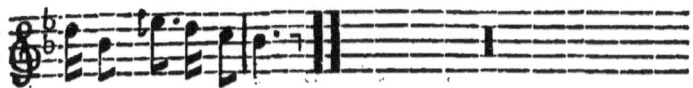

her, as sure as a gun.

With whining, and sighing, and vows, and all that,
    As far as you please you may run:
She'll hear you and jeer you, and give you a pat;
    But jilt you, jilt you,
She'll jilt you, as sure as a gun.

To worship, and call her bright goddess, is fine;
    But mark you the consequence, mum:
The baggage will think herself really divine,
    And scorn you, scorn you,
She'll scorn you, as sure as a gun.

Then be with a maiden bold, frolic, and stout,
    And no opportunity shun:
She'll tell you she hates you, and swear she'll cry out:
    But mum—mum—
But mum—she's as sure as a gun.

SONG CXXI.

FROM THE EAST BREAKS THE MORN.

From the east breaks the morn, See the sun-beam's adorn

The wild heath and the mountains so high, The wild

heath and the mountains so high. Shrilly opes the

staunch hound, The steed neighs to the sound, And the

floods and the valleys re - - - - - - - ply. And the floods

and the valleys re - ply.

Our forefathers, so good,
Prov'd their greatness of blood
By encount'ring the pard and the boar;
Ruddy health bloom'd the face,
Age and youth urg'd the chace,
And taught woodlands and forests to roar.

Hence of noble descent,
Hills and wilds we frequent,
Where the bosom of nature's reveal'd;
Tho' in life's busy day
Man of man make a prey,
Still let ours be the prey of the field.

With the chace in full sight,
Gods! how great the delight!
How our mutual sensations refine!
Where is care? where is fear?
Like the winds in the rear,
And the man's lost in something divine.

Now to horse, my brave boys:
Lo! each pants for the joys
That anon shall enliven the whole:
Then at eve we'll dismount,
Toils and pleasures recount,
And renew the chace over the bowl.

SONG CXXII.

JAMIE GAY.

Affettuoso.

As Jamie Gay gae'd blithe his way Along the banks of Tweed, A bonny lass as e-ver was came tripping o'er the mead. The hearty swain, untaught to feign, the buxom nymph survey'd; And, full of glee as lad cou'd be, Be-spoke the blooming maid.

Dear laſſie, tell, why by thyſell
  Thou lonely wander'ſt here?
My ewes, ſhe cry'd, are ſtraying wide;
  Canſt tell me, laddie, where?
To town I hie, he made reply,
  Some pleaſing ſport to ſee:
But thou'rt ſo neat, ſo trim, ſo ſweet,
  I'll ſeek thy ewes with thee.

She gave her hand, nor made a ſtand;
  But lik'd the youth's intent:
O'er hill and dale, o'er plain and vale,
  Right merrily they went.
The birds ſang ſweet, the pair to greet,
  And flow'rets bloom'd around;
And as they walk'd, of love they talk'd,
  And lovers joys when crown'd.

And now the ſun had roſe to noon,
  The zenith of his pow'r,
When to the ſhade their ſteps they made
  To paſs the mid-day hour.
The bonny lad row'd in his plaid
  The laſs, who ſcorn'd to frown:
She ſoon forgot the ewes ſhe ſought,
  And he to gang to town.

G g

SONG CXXIII.

THE WHISTLING PLOWMAN.

The whistling plowman hails the blushing dawn: The

thrush melodious drowns the rustic note: Loud sings the

blackbird thro' resounding groves: And the lark soars

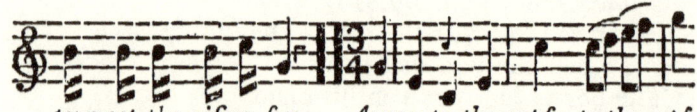
to meet the rising sun. Away to the copse, to the copse

lead away; And now, my boys, throw off the hounds.

I'll warrant he shows us, he shows us some play: See

yonder he skulks thro' the grounds - - - - - - - See

yonder he skulks thro' the grounds. Then spur your brisk

coursers, and smoke 'em, my bloods; 'tis a delicate scent-

ly-ing morn: What concert is equal to those of the

woods; betwixt echo, the hounds and the horn? The hounds

and the horn, the hounds and the horn, the hounds and

the horn, -

- betwixt echo, the hounds and the horn.

Each earth, fee, he tries at in vain,
   The cover no fafety can find;
So he breaks it and fcow'rs amain,
   And leaves us at diftance behind.
O'er rocks and o'er rivers and hedges we fly;
   All hazard and danger we fcorn.
Stout Reynard we'll follow until that he die:
   Cheer up the good dogs with the horn.

And now he fcarce creeps thro' the dale;
   All parch'd from his mouth hangs his tongue;
His fpeed can no longer prevail;
   Nor his life can his cunning prolong.
From our ftaunch and fleet pack 'twas in vain that he fled:
   See his brufh falls bemir'd forlorn!
The farmers with pleafure behold him lie dead,
   And fhout to the found of the horn.

SONG CXXIV.

RAIL NO MORE.

Rail no more, ye learned affes, 'Gainft the joys the

bowl fupplies. Sound its depth, and fill your glaffes;

Wifdom at the bottom lies. Fill them higher ftill and

higher: Shallow draughts perplex the brain: Sipping

quenches all our fire; Bumpers light it up agai ----

------------ n. Sipping quenches all our fire;

Bumpers light it up a-gain.

Draw the fcene for wit and pleafure;
    Enter jollity and joy;
We for thinking have no leifure;
    Manly mirth is our employ.
Since in life there's nothing certain,
    We'll the prefent hour engage;
And, when death fhall drop the curtain,
    With applaufe we'll quit the ftage.

SONG CXXV.
PLATO's ADVICE.

Says Pla-to, why shou'd man be vain? Since boun-

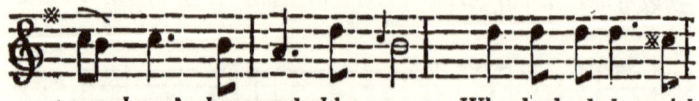

teous heav'n has made him great, Why looketh he with

insolent disdain On those undeck'd with wealth or state?

Can splendid robes, or beds of down, or costly gems

that deck the fair; Can all the glo - - - - - - - -

- - - - - - - - - - - ries of a crown, Give

health, or ease the brow of care?

The scepter'd king, the burthen'd slave,
  The humble, and the haughty, die;
The rich, the poor, the base, the brave,
  In dust, without distinction, lie.
Go search the tombs where monarchs rest,
  Who once the greatest titles bore:
The wealth and glory they possess'd,
  And all their honours, are no more.

So glides the meteor thro' the sky,
  And spreads along a gilded train;
But, when its short-liv'd beauties die,
  Dissolves to common air again.
So 'tis with us, my jovial souls!—
  Let friendship reign while here we stay;
Let's crown our joys with flowing bowls,—
  When Jove us calls we must away.

SONG CXXVI.
FILL YOUR GLASSES.

Fill your glasses, banish grief, Laugh, and worldly care

despise: Sorrow ne'er will bring relief: Joy from drink-

ing will arise. Why should we, with wrinkl'd care,

Change what nature made so fair? Drink, and set the

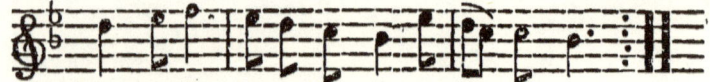

heart at rest; Of a bad market make the best.

Busy brains, we know, alas!
    With imaginations run,
Like the sands i' th' hour-glafs,
    Turn'd, and turn'd, and still run on;
Never knowing where to stay,
But uneasy ev'ry way.
Drink, and set the heart at rest;
Peace of mind is always best.

Some purſue the winged wealth;
  Some to honours high aſpire:
Give me freedom, give me health;
  There's the ſum of my deſire.
What the world can more preſent
Will not add to my content:
Drink, and ſet the heart at reſt;
Peace of mind is always beſt.

Mirth, when mingled with our wine,
  Makes the heart alert and free;
Should it ſnow, or rain, or ſhine,
  Still the ſame thing 'tis with me.
There's no fence againſt our fate;
Changes daily on us wait.
Drink, and ſet your hearts at reſt;
Of a bad market make the beſt.

SONG CXXVII.

WHEN I WAS A YOUNG ONE.

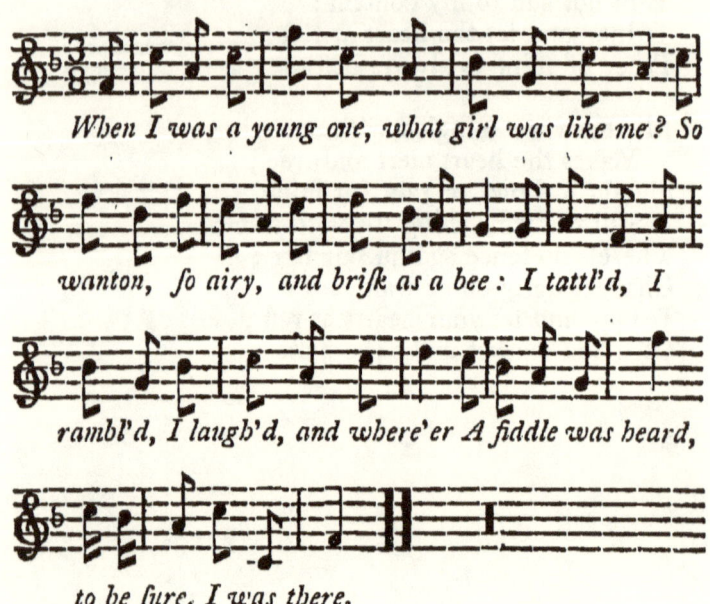

When I was a young one, what girl was like me? So wanton, so airy, and brisk as a bee: I tattl'd, I rambl'd, I laugh'd, and where'er A fiddle was heard, to be sure, I was there.

To all that came near I had something to say.
'Twas this, Sir! and that, Sir! but scarce ever nay:
And Sundays drest out in my silks and my lace:
I warrant I stood by the best in the place.

At twenty I got me a husband—poor man!
Well rest him—we all are as good as we can:
Yet he was so peevish, he'd quarrel for straws,
And jealous—tho' truly I gave him some cause.

He fnub'd me and huff'd me—but let me alone,
Egad I've a tongue—and I paid him his own:
Ye wives take the hint, and, when fpoufe is untow'rd,
Stand firm to our charter—and have the laft word.

But now I'm quite alter'd, the more to my woe,
I'm not what I was forty fummers ago:
This Time's a fore foe, there's no fhunning his dart;
However, I keep up a pretty good heart.

Grown old, yet I hate to be fitting mum chance;
I ftill love a tune, tho' unable to dance:
And, books of devotion laid by on the fhelf,
I teach that to others—I once did myfelf.

SONG CXXVIII.

WHEN WAR's ALARMS.

But I no longer, tho' a maid forsaken,
　Thus will mourn like yonder dove:
For, 'ere the lark to-morrow shall awaken
　I will seek my absent love.
　　The hostile country over
　　I'll fly to seek my lover,
Scorning ev'ry threat'ning fear;
　　Nor distant shore,
　　Nor cannon's roar,
Shall longer keep me from my dear.

SONG CXXIX.
THERE WAS A JOLLY MILLER.

There was a jolly miller once liv'd on the river Dee:
He danc'd and he sung from morn till night; no lark so blithe as he. And this the burden of his song for ever us'd to be: I care for nobody, no, not I, if no-bo-dy cares for me.

246   CALLIOPE: OR THE

I live by my mill, God blefs her! fhe's kindred, child,
    and wife;
I would not change my ftation for any other in life.
No lawyer, furgeon, or doctor, e'er had a groat from me.
I care for nobody, no, not I, if nobody cares for me.

When fpring begins its merry career, oh! how his heart
    grows gay!
No fummer's drouth alarms his fears, nor winter's fad
    decay;
No forefight mars the miller's joy, who's wont to fing
    and fay,
Let others toil from year to year, I live from day to day.

Thus, like the miller, bold and free, let us rejoice and
    fing:
The days of youth are made for glee, and time is on
    the wing.
This fong fhall pafs from me to thee, along this jovial
    ring:
Let heart and voice and all agree, to fay,—long live the
    King!

SONG CXXX.

THE ECHOING HORN.

The echoing horn calls the fportfmen abroad; To horfe,

my brave boys, and away. The morning is up, and the

cry of the hounds Upbraids our too tedious delay. What

pleasure we feel in pursuing the fox! O'er hill and o'er

valley he flies: Then follow, we'll soon overtake him,

huzza! The traitor is seiz'd on, and dies. He dies - - -

- - - - - - - - - - - The traitor is seiz'd on and dies.

Chorus.

Then follow, we'll soon overtake him, huzza! The trai-

tor is seiz'd on, and dies.

Triumphant returning at night with the spoil,
  Like Bacchanals, shouting and gay;
How sweet with a bottle and lass to refresh,
  And drown the fatigues of the day!
With sport, love, and wine, fickle fortune defy;
  Dull wisdom all happiness sours.
Since life is no more than a passage at best,
  Let's strew the way over with flow'rs.
With flow'rs; lets strew, &c.

SONG CXXXI.

A COBLER THERE WAS.

A cobler there was, and he liv'd in a stall; Which

serv'd him for parlour, for kitchen, and hall. No coin in

his pocket, no care in his pate; No ambition had he, nor

yet duns at his gate. Derry down, down, down, derry down.

Contented he work'd; and he thought himself happy
If at night he could purchase a cup of brown nappy:
He'd laugh, then, and whistle, and sing, too, most sweet;
Saying, just to a hair I've made both ends to meet.
    Derry down, &c.

But love, the disturber of high and of low,
That shoots at the peasant as well as the beau,
He shot the poor cobler quite thorough the heart.
I wish it had hit some more ignoble part.
    Derry down, &c.

It was from a cellar this archer did play,
Where a buxom young damsel continually lay:
Her eyes shone so bright, when she rose ev'ry day,
That she shot the poor cobler quite over the way.
    Derry down, &c.

He sung her love-songs as he sat at his work;
But she was as hard as a Jew or a Turk.
Whenever he spoke she would flounce and would fleer;
Which put the poor cobler quite into despair.
    Derry down, &c.

He took up his AWL that he had in the world,
And to make away with himself was resolv'd:
He pierc'd thro' his body instead of the SOLE;
So the cobler he died, and the bell it did toll.
    Derry down, &c.

And now, in good-will, I advise as a friend:
All coblers take notice of this cobler's END:
Keep your hearts out of love; for we find, by what's past,
That love brings us all to an END at the LAST.
    Derry down, down, down, derry down.

SONG CXXXII.
THE DUSKY NIGHT.

The dusky night rides down the sky, And ushers in

the morn; The hounds all join in jovial cry, The hounds

all join in jovial cry; The huntsman winds his horn,

The huntsman winds his horn. And a hunting we will

go, A hunting we will go, A hunting we will

go --- A hunting we will go. And a hunting we will

go, A hunting we will go, And hunting we will

go - - -, A hunting we will go.

The wife around her huſband throws
   Her arms to make him ſtay:
My dear, it rains, it hails, it blows,
   You cannot hunt to-day.
      Yet a hunting, &c.

Sly Reynard now like light'ning flies,
   And ſweeps acroſs the vale;
But when the hounds too near he ſpies
   He drops his buſhy tail.
      Then a hunting, &c.

Fond echo ſeems to like the ſport,
   And join the jovial cry;
The woods and hills the ſound retort,
   And muſic fills the ſky,
      When a hunting, &c.

At laſt his ſtrength to faintneſs worn,
   Poor Reynard ceaſes flight;
Then hungry homeward we return
   To feaſt away the night.
      And a drinking, &c.

Ye jovial hunters in the morn
   Prepare then for the chace;
Riſe at the ſounding of the horn,
   And health with ſport embrace,
      When a hunting, &c.

I i ij

SONG CXXXIII.

YE BELLES AND YE FLIRTS.

Ye belles and ye flirts, and ye pert little things, Who trip in this frolicsome round; Prithee tell me from whence this indecency springs, The sexes at once to confound? What means the cock'd hat and the masculine air, With each motion design'd to perplex? Bright eyes were intended to languish, not stare, And softness the test of your sex, dear girls; And softness the test of your sex.

The girl who on beauty depends for support
　May call ev'ry art to her aid;
The bofom difplay'd, and the petticoat fhort,
　Are famples fhe gives of her trade:
But you on whom fortune indulgently fmiles,
　And whom pride has preferv'd from the fnare,
Should flyly attack us with coynefs and wiles,
　Not with open and infolent airs,
　　　　　　　　Brave girls, not with, &c.

The Venus, whofe ftatue delights all mankind,
　Shrinks modeftly back from the view;
And kindly fhou'd feem by the artift defign'd
　To ferve as a model for you.
Then learn, with her beauties, to copy her air,
　Nor venture too much to reveal:
Our fancies will paint what you cover with care,
　And double each charm you conceal,
　　　　　　　　Sweet girls, and double, &c.

The blufhes of morn and the mildnefs of May
　Are charms which no art can procure.
Oh! be but yourfelves and our homage we'll pay,
　And your empire is folid and fure.
But if, Amazon-like, you attack your gallants,
　And put us in fear of our lives,
You may do very well for fifters and aunts;
　But, believe me, you'll never be wives,
　　　　　　　　Poor girls, believe me, &c.

SONG CXXXIV.

ON A BANK OF FLOW'RS.

On a bank of flow'rs, in a summer's day, inviting

and undress'd, In her bloom of years bright Celia lay,

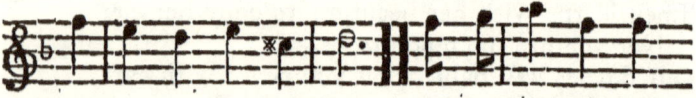

with love and sleep oppress'd; When a youthful swain,

with admiring eyes, Wish'd he durst the fair maid sur-

prise, With a fa, la, la, &c. - - - But fear'd approach-

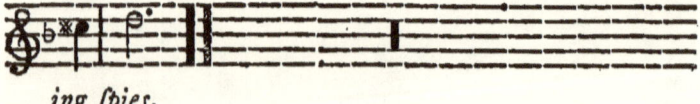

ing spies.

As he gaz'd a gentle breeze arose
    That fann'd her robes aside;
And the sleeping nymph did charms disclose
    Which, waking, she would hide;

Then his breath grew fhort, and his pulfe beat high;
He long'd to touch what he chanc'd to fpy,
   With a fa, la, la, &c.
But durft not yet draw nigh.

All amaz'd he ftood, with her beauties fir'd,
   And blefs'd the courteous wind ;
Then in whifpers figh'd, and the gods defir'd
   That Celia might be kind.
Then, with hope grown bold, he advanc'd amain :
But fhe laugh'd aloud in a dream, and again,
   With a fa, la, la, &c.
Repell'd the tim'rous fwain.

Yet, when once defire has inflam'd the foul,
   All modeft doubts withdraw;
And the god of love does each fear controul
   That would the lover awe.
Shall a prize like this, fays the vent'rous boy,
Efcape, and I not the means employ,
   With a fa, la, la, &c.
To feize the proffer'd joy?

Here the glowing youth, to relieve his pain,
   The flumb'ring maid carefs'd,
And, with trembling hands, (oh ! the fimple fwain !)
   Her glowing bofom prefs'd.
Then the virgin wak'd and affrighted flew,
Yet look'd as wifhing he would purfue,
   With a fa, la, la, &c.
But Damon mifs'd his cue.

Now, repenting that he had let her fly,
   Himfelf he thus accus'd :
What a dull and ftupid thing was I
   That fuch a chance abus'd !
To my fhame 'twill now on the plains be faid,
Damon a virgin afleep betray'd,
   With a fa, la, la, &c.
Yet let her go a maid !

SONG CXXXV.
YOU KNOW I'M YOUR PRIEST.

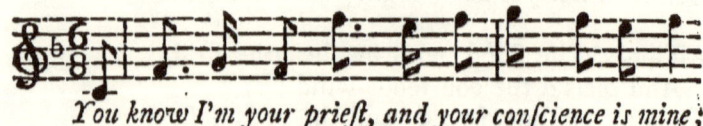

You know I'm your prieſt, and your conſcience is mine;

But if you grow wicked, 'tis not a good ſign: So leave

off your raking, and marry a wife; And then, my dear

Darby, you're ſettled for life. Sing a Ballina-mona,

o - ro, Ballina-mona, o - ro, Ballina - mona, o - ro,

A good merry wedding for me.

The banns being publifh'd, to chapel we go,
The bride and the bridegroom, in coats white as fnow;
So modeft her air, and fo fheepifh your look,
You out with your ring, and I pull out my book.
 Sing Ballinamona, &c.
 A good merry wedding for me.

I thumb out the place, and I then read away;
She blufhes at love, and fhe whifpers obey;
You take her dear hand to have and to hold;
I fhut up my book, and I pocket your gold.
 Sing Ballinamona, &c.
 That fnug little guinea for me.

The neighbours wifh joy to the bridegroom and bride;
The pipers before us, you march fide by fide;
A plentiful dinner gives mirth to each face;
The piper plays up, and myfelf I fay grace.
 Sing Ballinamona, &c.
 A good wedding-dinner for me.

The joke now goes round, and the ftocking is thrown;
The curtains are drawn, and you're both left alone;
'Tis then, my dear boy, I believe you're at home;
And hey for a chriftening at nine months to come.
 Sing Ballinamona, &c.
 A good merry chriftening for me.

SONG CXXXVI.

BALLINAMONA.

To the foregoing tune.

WHerever I'm going, and all the day long,
At home and abroad, or alone in a throng,
I find that my paſſion's ſo lively and ſtrong,
That your name, when I'm ſilent, ſtill runs in my ſong,
 Sing Ballinamona, &c.
 A kiſs of your ſweet lips for me.

Since the firſt time I ſaw you I take no repoſe;
I ſleep all the day to forget half my woes;
So hot is the flame in my ſtomach that glows,
By St Patrick! I fear it will burn thro' my clothes,
 Sing Ballinamona, &c.
 Your pretty black hair for me.

In my conſcience I fear I ſhall die in my grave,
Unleſs you comply and poor Phelim will ſave,
And grant the petition your lover does crave,
Who never was free till you made him your ſlave.
 Sing Ballinamona, &c.
 Your pretty black eyes for me.

On that happy day when I make you my bride,
With a ſwinging long ſword, how I'll ſtrut and I'll ſtride!
With coach and ſix horſes with honey I'll ride,
As before you I walk to the church by your ſide.
 Sing Ballinamona, &c.
 Your lily-white fiſt for me.

SONG CXXXVII.

GRAMACHREE MOLLY.

As down on Banna's banks I stray'd, One evening in

May, The little birds in blithest notes Made vocal ev'ry

spray: They sung their little tales of love, They sung them

o'er and o'er. Ah Gramachree, ma Colleenouge, ma

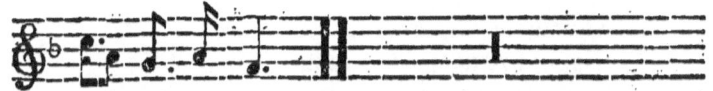

Molly Ashtore!

The daisy pied, and all the sweets
    The dawn of nature yields;
The primrose pale, the vi'let blue,
    Lay scatt'red o'er the fields:
Such fragrance in the bosom lies
    Of her whom I adore.
                Ah Gramachree, &c.

I laid me down upon a bank,
　　Bewailing my sad fate,
That doom'd me thus the slave of love
　　And cruel Molly's hate:
How can she break the honest heart
　　That wears her in its core?
　　　　　　　Ah Gramachree, &c.

You said you lov'd me, Molly dear;
　　Ah! why did I believe?
Yet, who could think such tender words
　　Were meant but to deceive?
That love was all I ask'd on earth;
　　Nay, heav'n could give no more.
　　　　　　　Ah Gramachree, &c.

Oh had I all the flocks that graze
　　On yonder yellow hill,
Or low'd for me the num'rous herds
　　That yon green pasture fill;
With her I love I'd gladly share
　　My kine and fleecy store.
　　　　　　　Ah Gramachree, &c.

Two turtle doves above my head
　　Sat courting on a bough;
I envied not their happiness,
　　To see them bill and coo:
Such fondness once for me she shew'd;
　　But now, alas! 'tis o'er.
　　　　　　　Ah Gramachree, &c.

Then fare thee well, my Molly dear,
　　Thy loss I e'er shall mourn;
Whilst life remains in Strephon's heart
　　'Twill beat for thee alone:
Tho' thou art false, may heav'n on thee
　　Its choicest blessings pour!
　　　　　　　Ah Gramachree, &c.

SONG CXXXVIII.

THE MAID IN BEDLAM.

To the foregoing tune.

ONE morning very early, one morning in the spring,
  I heard a maid in Bedlam who mournfully did sing;
Her chains she rattled on her hands, while sweetly thus
    sung she:
I love my love, because I know my love loves me.

O cruel were his parents, who sent my love to sea;
And cruel, cruel was the ship that bore my love from me:
Yet I love his parents, since they're his, altho' they've
    ruin'd me;
And I love my love, because I know my love loves me.

O should it please the pitying pow'rs to call me to the
    sky,
I'd claim a guardian angel's charge around my love to fly;
To guard him from all dangers how happy should I be!
For I love my love, because I know my love loves me.

I'll make a strawy garland, I'll make it wond'rous fine;
With roses, lilies, daisies, I'll mix the eglantine;
And I'll present it to my love when he returns from sea;
For I love my love, because I know my love loves me.

O if I were a little bird, to build upon his breast!
Or if I were a nightingale, to sing my love to rest!
To gaze upon his lovely eyes, all my reward shou'd be;
For I love my love, because I know my love loves me.

O if I were an eagle, to soar into the sky!
I'd gaze around with piercing eyes, where I my love
    might spy:
But ah! unhappy maiden! that love you ne'er shall see;
Yet I love my love, because I know my love loves me.

SONG CXXXIX.
HARK AWAY.

The moment Au-ro-ra peep'd in-to my room, I put

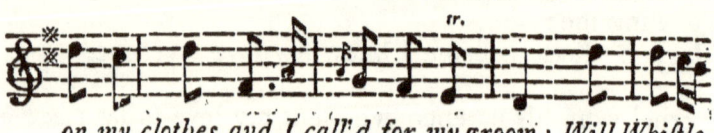

on my clothes and I call'd for my groom: Will Whiſtle,

by this, had uncoupl'd the hounds; Who lively and

mettleſome friſk'd o'er the grounds. And now we're all

ſaddl'd, fleet, dapple, and grey; Who ſeem'd longing

to hear the glad ſound hark away! Hark away!

Hark away! Who ſeem'd longing to hear the glad ſound

hark a - way!

'Twas now, by the clock, about five in the morn;
And we all gallop'd off to the found of the horn:
Jack Garter, Bill Babbler, and Dick at the goofe,
When, all of a fudden, out ſtarts Mrs Puſs :
Men, horſes, and dogs, not a moment would ſtay,
And echo was heard to cry, Hark, hark away!

The courſe was a fine one ſhe took o'er the plain;
Which ſhe doubl'd, and doubl'd, and doubl'd again;
Till at laſt ſhe to cover return'd out of breath,
Where I and Will Whiſtle were in at the death:
Then, in triumph, for you I the hare did difplay;
And cry'd to the horns, my boys, Hark, hark away!

SONG CXL.
MY TRIM-BUILT WHERRY.

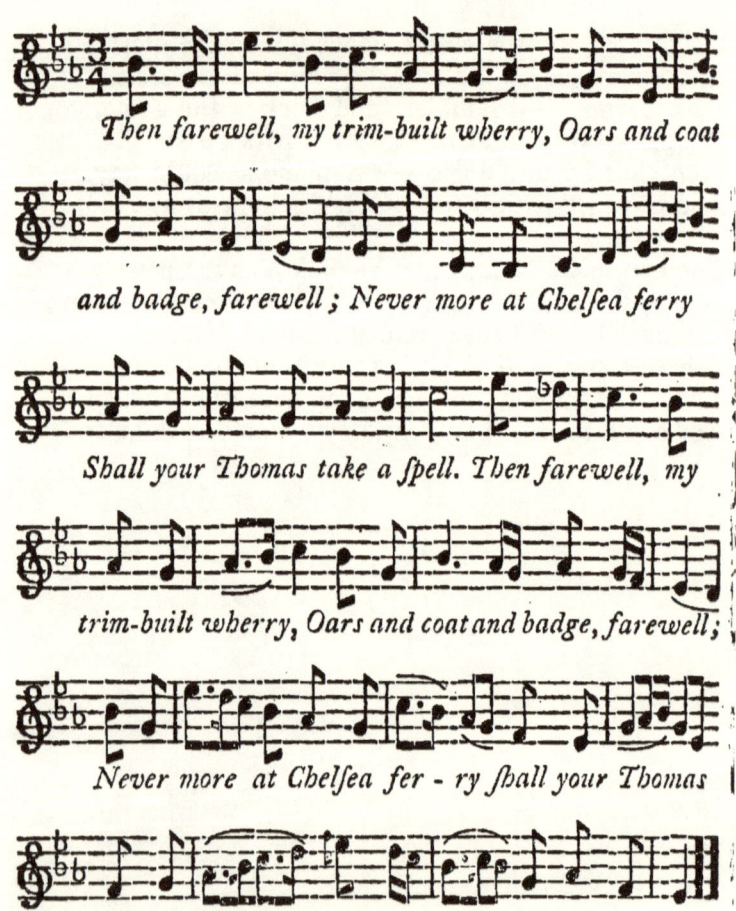

But, to hope and peace a stranger,
  In the battle's heat I go ;
Where, expos'd to ev'ry danger,
  Some friendly ball shall lay me low.

Then, mayhap, when homeward steering,
  With the news my messmates come ;
Even you, my story hearing,
  With a sigh may cry—poor Tom !

SONG CXLI.
THE BONNY SAILOR.

My bonny sailor won my mind; My heart is now

with him at sea; I hope the summer's western breeze

will bring him safe-ly back to me: I wish to hear

what glorious toils, What dangers he has un-dergone!

What forts he's storm'd! How great the spoils from France

or Spain my sailor's won! My sailor's won, my sailor's

won; From France or Spain my sailor's won.

A thoufand terrors chill'd my breaft
   When fancy brought the foe in view;
And day and night I've had no reft,
   Left ev'ry gale a tempeft blew.
Bring, gentle gales, my failor home;
   His fhip at anchor may I fee!
Three years are, fure, enough to roam;
   Too long for one who loves like me.

His face, by fultry climes, is wan;
   His eyes, by watching, fhine lefs bright;
But ftill I'll own my charming man,
   And run to meet him when in fight.
His honeft heart is what I prize;
   No weather can make that look old:
Tho' alter'd were his face and eyes
   I'll love my jolly failor bold.

SONG CXLII.
HOW IMPERFECT IS EXPRESSION.

How imperfect is expreſſion Some e-motions to

im-part! When we mean a ſoft confeſſion, and yet ſeek

to hide the heart. When our boſoms, all complying,

With de-licious tu-mults ſwell, And beat what bro-

ken, falt'ring, dying, language would, but can-not,

tell.

Deep confusion's rosy terror,
  Quite expressive paints my cheek,
Ask no more—behold your error;
  Blushes eloquently speak.
What tho' silent is my anguish,
  Or breath'd only to the air?
Mark my eyes; and, as they languish,
  Read what yours have written there.

O that you could once conceive me!
  Once my heart's strong feelings view!
Love has nought more fond, believe me;
  Friendship nothing half so true.
How imperfect is expression
  Some emotions to impart!
When we mean a soft confession,
  And yet seek to hide the heart.

SONG CXLIII.

SAE MERRY AS WE TWA HAE BEEN.

Slow.

A lafs that was laden with care fat hea-vi-ly under

yon thorn, I liften'd a while for to hear, When thus

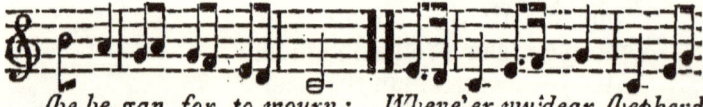

fhe be-gan for to mourn: Whene'er my dear fhepherd

was here, the birds did melodioufly fing, And cold nip-

ping winter did wear A face that refembled the

spring. Sae merry as we twa hae been; Sae merry as

we twa hae been; My heart it is like for to break

when I think on the days we have feen.

 Our flocks feeding clofe by his fide,
  He gently prefling my hand,
 I view'd the wide world in its pride,
  And laugh'd at the pomp of command!
 My dear, he wou'd oft to me fay,
  What makes you hard-hearted to me?
 Oh! why do you thus turn away
  From him who is dying for thee!
   Sae merry, &c.

 But now he is far from my fight,
  And perhaps a deceiver may prove;
 Which makes me lament day and night,
  That ever I granted my love.
 At eve, when the reft of the folk
  Are merrily feated to fpin,
 I fet myfelf under an oak,
  And heavily figh for him.
   Sae merry, &c.

SONG CXLIV.
YE LADS OF TRUE SPIRIT.

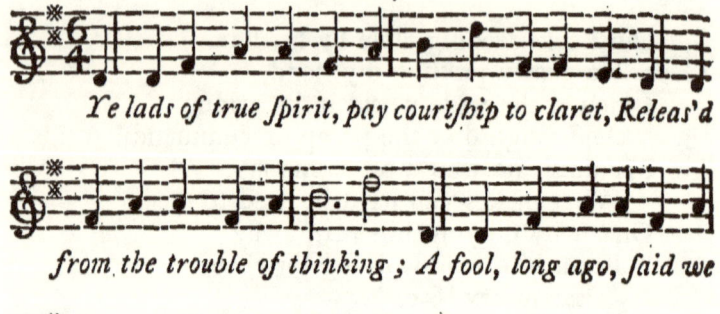

Ye lads of true spirit, pay courtship to claret, Releas'd

from the trouble of thinking; A fool, long ago, said we

nothing could know; The fellow knew nothing of drink-

ing. To pore over Plato, or practise with Cato, Dif-

passionate dunces might make us; But men, now more

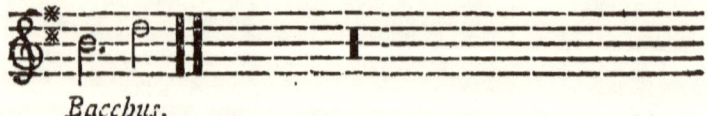

wise, self-denial despise, And live by the lessons of

Bacchus.

Big-wig'd, in fine coach, fee the doctor approach;
  He folemnly up the ftair paces;
Looks grave—fmells his cane—applies finger to vein,
  And counts the repeats with grimaces.
As he holds pen in hand, life and death are at ftand—
  A tofs up which party fhall take us.
Away with fuch cant—no prefcription we want
  But the nourifhing noftrum of Bacchus.

We jollily join in the practice of wine,
  While mifers 'midft plenty are pining;
While ladies are fcorning, and lovers are mourning,
  We laugh at wealth, wenching, and whining.
Drink, drink, now 'tis prime; tofs a bottle to Time,
  He'll not make fuch hafte to o'ertake us;
His threats we prevent, and his cracks we cement,
  By the ftyptical balfam of Bacchus.

What work is there made, by the newfpaper trade,
  Of this man's and t'other man's ftation!
The ins are all bad, and the outs are all mad;
  In and out is the cry of the nation.
The politic patter which both parties chatter,
  From bumpering freely fhan't fhake us;
With half-pints in hand, independent we'll ftand
  To defend Magna Charta of Bacchus.

Be your motions well-tim'd; be all charg'd and all prim'd;
  Have a care—right and left—and make ready.
Right hand to glafs join—at your lips reft your wine;
  Be all in your exercife fteady.
Our levels we boaft when our women we toaft;
  May gracioufly they undertake us!
No more we defire—fo drink and give fire,
  A volley to beauty and Bacchus!

M m

SONG CXLV.
LET's BE JOVIAL.

Let's be jovial, fill our glasses, Madness 'tis for us

to think, How the world is rul'd by asses, And the

wise are sway'd by chink. Never let vain cares oppress

us, Riches are to them a snare; We are all as rich as

Cræsus, While our bottle drowns our care.

Wine will make us red as roses,
    And our sorrows quite forget;
Come let's fuddle all our noses,
    Drink ourselves quite out of debt.

When grim Death comes looking for us
    We are toping off our bowls;
Bacchus joining in the chorus,
    Death begone! here's none but souls.

Godlike Bacchus thus commanding,
  Trembling Death away fhall fly;
Ever after underftanding,
  Drinking fouls can never die.

SONG CXLVI.

WITH AN HONEST OLD FRIEND.

With an honeft old friend and a merry old fong, And a

flafk of old port, let me fit the night long: And laugh

at the malice of thofe who repine That they muft fwig

porter while I can drink wine.

CALLIOPE : OR THE

I envy no mortal, though ever so great,
Nor scorn I a wretch for his lowly estate;
But what I abhor, and esteem as a curse,
Is poorness of spirit, not poorness in purse.

Then dare to be generous, dauntless, and gay;
Let's merrily pass life's remainder away:
Upheld by our friends, we our foes may despise;
For the more we are envied the higher we rise.

SONG CXLVII.

THE HONEST FELLOW.

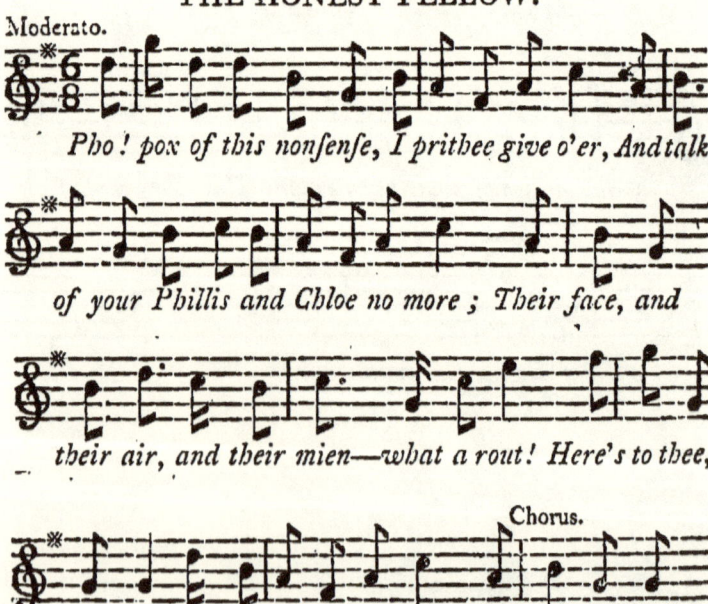

Pho! pox of this nonsense, I prithee give o'er, And talk of your Phillis and Chloe no more; Their face, and their air, and their mien—what a rout! Here's to thee, my lad, push the bottle about. Here's to thee, my

lad, to thee, my lad; Here's to thee, my lad, push

the bottle about.

Let finical fops play the fool and the ape;
They dare not confide in the juice of the grape:
But we honest fellows—'sdeath! who'd ever think
Of puling for love, while he's able to drink?

'Tis wine, only wine, that true pleasure bestows;
Our joys it increases, and lightens our woes;
Remember what topers of old us'd to sing,
The man that is drunk is as great as a king.

If Cupid assaults you, there's law for his tricks;
Anacreon's cases, see page twenty-six:
The precedent's glorious, and just, by my soul!
Lay hold on, and drown the young dog in a bowl.

What's life but a frolic, a song, and a laugh.
My toast shall be this, whilst I've liquor to quaff,
May mirth and good fellowship always abound:
Boys, fill up a bumper, and let it go round.

SONG CXLVIII.

COME, NOW, ALL YE SOCIAL POW'RS.

Come, now, all ye focial pow'rs, Shed your influence

o'er us; Crown with joy the prefent hours, Enliven thofe

before us: Bring the flafk, the mufic bring, Joy fhall

quickly find us; Drink, and dance, and laugh, and fing,

And caft dull care behind us. Bring the flafk, the

mufic bring, Joy fhall quickly find us; Drink, and dance,

and laugh, and fing, And caft dull care behind us.

Love, thy godhead I adore,
  Source of generous paſſion;
But will ne'er bow down before
  Thoſe idols wealth or faſhion,
Bring the flaſk, &c.

Friendſhip, with thy ſmile divine,
  Brighten all our features;
What but friendſhip, love, and wine,
  Can make us happy creatures?
Bring the flaſk, &c.

Why the deuce ſhould we be ſad
  While on earth we moulder?
Grave, or gay, or wiſe, or mad,
  We ev'ry day grow older.
Bring the flaſk, &c.

Then ſince time will ſteal away
  Spite of all our ſorrow;
Heighten ev'ry joy to-day,
  Never mind to-morrow,
Bring the flaſk, &c.

SONG CXLIX.
CATO's ADVICE.

What Cato advises most certainly wise is, Not always to labour, but sometimes to play: To mingle sweet pleasure with search after treasure, Indulging at night for the toils of the day: And while the dull miser esteems himself wiser, his bags to increase, while his health does decay, Our souls we enlighten, our fancies we brighten, And pass the long ev'nings in pleasure

away.

All cheerful and hearty, we set aside party,
    With some tender fair the bright bumper is crown'd;
Thus Bacchus invites us, and Venus delights us,
    While care in an ocean of claret is drown'd:
See, here's our physician, we know no ambition,
    But where there's good wine and good company found;
Thus happy together, in spite of all weather,
    'Tis sunshine and summer with us the year round.

SONG CL.
THE BROWN JUG.

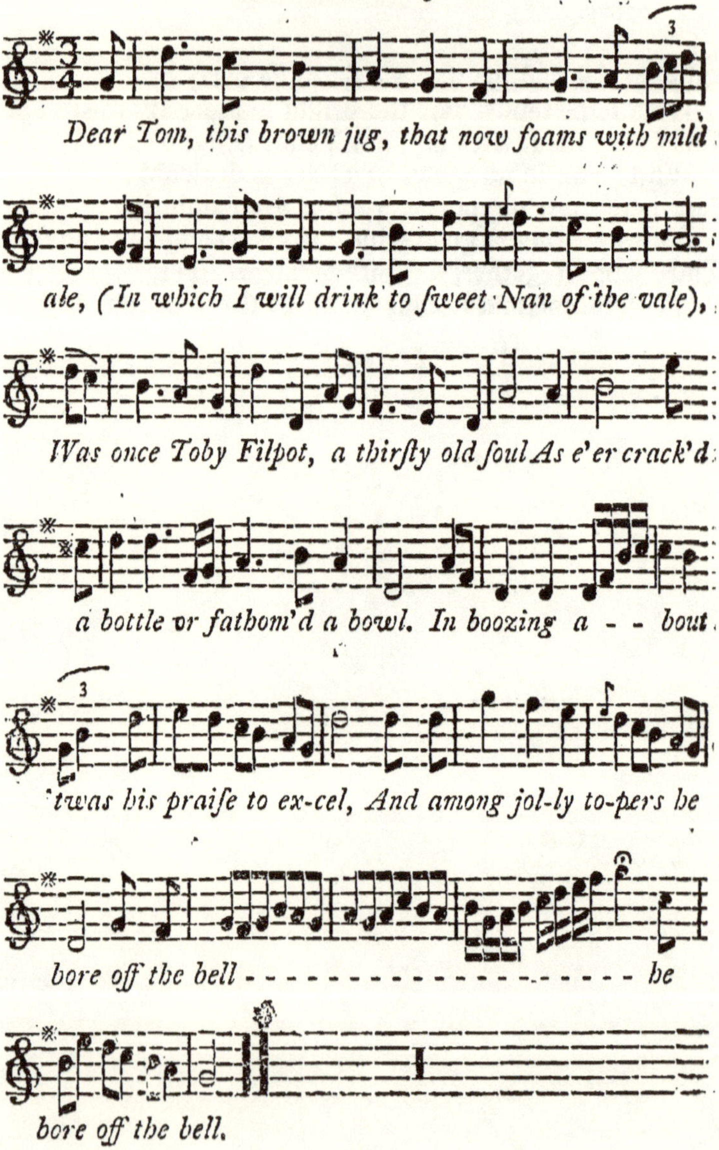

Dear Tom, this brown jug, that now foams with mild ale, (In which I will drink to sweet Nan of the vale), Was once Toby Filpot, a thirsty old soul As e'er crack'd a bottle or fathom'd a bowl. In boozing a - - bout 'twas his praise to ex-cel, And among jol-ly to-pers he bore off the bell - - - - - - - - - - - - - - - he bore off the bell.

It chanc'd as in dog-days he fat at his eafe,
In his flow'r-woven arbour, as gay as you pleafe,
With a friend and a pipe puffing forrow away,
And with honeft old ftingo was foaking his clay,
His breath-doors of life on a fudden were fhut,
And he dy'd full as big as a Dorchefter butt.

His body when long in the ground it had lain,
And time into clay had refolv'd it again,
A potter found out in its covert fo fnug,
And with part of fat Toby he form'd this brown jug.
Now, facred to friendfhip, to mirth, and mild ale;
So here's to my lovely fweet Nan of the vale.

SONG CLI.
THE VICAR OF BRAY.

In good King Charles's golden days, When loyalty no

harm meant, A zealous high-church-man I was, And so

I got preferment. To teach my flock I never miſt,

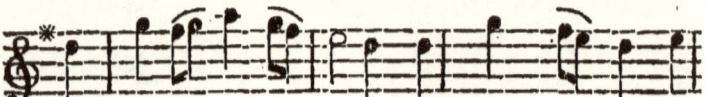

Kings are by God appointed, And damn'd are thoſe that

Chorus.

do reſiſt, or touch the Lord's anointed: And this is

law, I will maintain, Until my dy-ing day, Sir, That

whatfoever king fhall reign, I'll be the Vicar of Bray,

Sir.

When Royal James obtain'd the crown,
   And popery came in fafhion,
The penal laws I hooted down,
   And read the Declaration:
The church of Rome I found would fit
   Full well my conftitution;
And had become a Jefuit,
   But for the Revolution.
     And this is law, &c.

When William was our king declar'd
   To eafe the nation's grievance,
With this new wind about I fteer'd,
   And fwore to him allegiance:
Old principles I did revoke,
   Set confcience at a diftance;
Paffive-obedience was a joke,
   A jeft was non-refiftance.
     And this is law, &c.

When gracious Anne became our queen,
   The church of England's glory,
Another face of things was feen,
   And I became a tory:
Occafional conformifts bafe,
   I damn'd their moderation;
And thought the church in danger was
   By fuch prevarication.
     And this is law, &c.

When George, in pudding-time, came o'er,
  And mod'rate men look'd big, Sir,
I turn'd a cat-in-pan once more,
  And so became a whig, Sir;
And thus preferment I procur'd
  From our new faith's defender;
And almost ev'ry day abjur'd
  The Pope and the Pretender.
    And this is law, &c.

Th' illustrious house of Hanover,
  And Protestant succession;
To these I do allegiance swear—
  While they can keep possession:
For in my faith and loyalty,
  I never more will falter,
And George my lawful king shall be—
  Until the times do alter.
    And this is law, &c.

SONG CLII.

THE WOMEN ALL TELL ME.

The women all tell me I'm falſe to my laſs ; That I

quit my poor Chloe, and ſtick to my glaſs : But to you,

men of reaſon, my reaſons I'll own ; And if you don't

like them, why, let them alone.

Although I have left her, the truth I'll declare ;
I believe ſhe was good, and I'm ſure ſhe was fair :
But goodneſs and charms in a bumper I ſee
That make it as good and as charming as ſhe.

My Chloe had dimples and ſmiles, I muſt own ;
But, though ſhe could ſmile, yet in truth ſhe could frown ;
But tell me, ye lovers of liquor divine,
Did you e'er ſee a frown in a bumper of wine?

Her lilies and roſes were juſt in their prime ;
Yet lilies and roſes are conquer'd by time :
But, in wine, from its age ſuch benefit flows,
That we like it the better the older it grows.

They tell me my love would in time have been cloy'd,
And that beauty's infipid when once 'tis enjoy'd;
But in wine I both time and enjoyment defy,
For, the longer I drink the more thirfty am I.

Let murders, and battles, and hiftory, prove
The mifchiefs that wait upon rivals in love:
But in drinking, thank heav'n, no rival contends;
For, the more we love liquor the more we are friends.

She, too, might have poifon'd the joy of my life
With nurfes, and babies, and fqualling, and ftrife:
But my wine neither nurfes nor babies can bring,
And a big-belly'd bottle's a mighty good thing.

We fhorten our days when with love we engage;
It brings on difeafes, and haftens old age:
But wine from grim death can its votaries fave,
And keep out t'other leg when there's one in the grave.

Perhaps, like her fex, ever falfe to their word,
She has left me—to get an eftate, or a lord;
But my bumpers (regarding nor titles nor pelf)
Will ftand by me when I can't ftand by myfelf.

Then let my dear Chloe no longer complain;
She's rid of her lover, and I of my pain:
For in wine, mighty wine, many comforts I fpy.
Should you doubt what I fay, take a bumper and try.

SONG CLIII.
THE GOSSIPS.

Two gossips they mer-ri-ly met, At nine in the

morning full soon; And they were resolv'd for a whet,

To keep their sweet voices in tune. Away to the tavern

they went; "Here, Joan, I do vow and pro-test, That

I have a crown yet unspent; Come, let's have a cup of

the best.

"And I have another, perhaps
  "A piece of the very same sort;
"Why should we sit thrumming of caps?
  "Come, drawer, and fill us a quart;
"And let it be liquor of life,
  "Canary, or sparkling wine:
"For I am a buxom young wife,
  "And I love to go gallant and fine."

The drawer, as blithe as a bird,
  Came skipping with cap in his hand,
"Dear ladies, I give you my word,
  "The best shall be at your command."
A quart of canary he drew,
  Joan fill'd up a glass and begun,
"Here, gossips, a bumper to you;"
  "I'll pledge you, girl, were it a tun."

"And pray, gossip, did'nt you hear
  "The common report of the town,
"A squire of five hundred a year
  "Is married to Doll of the Crown:
"A draggle-tail'd slut, on my word,
  "Her clothes hanging ragged and foul;
"In troth he would fain have a bird
  "That would give a groat for an owl.

"And she had a sister last year,
  "Whose name they call'd Galloping Peg,
"She'd take up a straw with her ear;
  "I warrant her right as my leg!
"A brewer he got her with child;
  "But e'en let them brew as they bake;
"I knew she was wanton and wild;
  "But I'll neither meddle nor make."

" Nor I, goffip Joan, by my troth,
  " Though neverthelefs I've been told,
" She ftole feven yards of broad cloth,
  " A ring, and a locket of gold ;
" A fmock and a new pair of fhoes ;
  " A flourifhing madam was fhe :—
" But Margery told me the news ;
  " And it ne'er fhall go further for me.

" We were at a goffiping club,
  " Where we had a chirruping cup
" Of good humming liquor, ftrong bub !
  " Your hufband's name there it was up,
" For bearing a powerful fway,
  " All neighbours his valour have feen ;
" For he is a cuckold, they fay—
  " A conftable, goffip, I mean.

" Dear goffip, a flip of the tongue ;
  " No harm was intended in mind :
" Chance words they will mingle among
  " Our others we commonly find.
" I hope you won't take it amifs."
  " No, no, that were folly in us ;
" And if we perhaps get a kifs,
  " Pray, what are our hufbands the worfe ?"

SONG CLIV.
THE POWER OF MUSIC.

When Orpheus went down to the regions below, Which

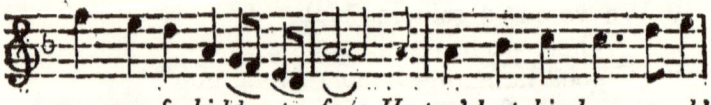

men are forbidden to see; He tun'd up his lyre, as old

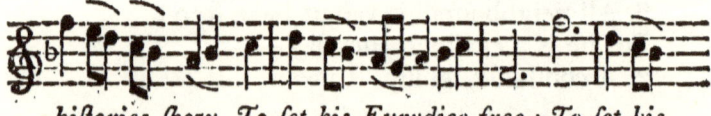

histories show, To set his Eurydice free; To set his

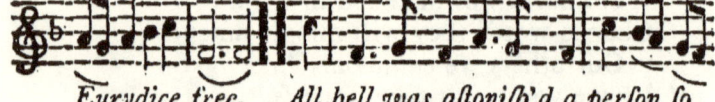

Eurydice free. All hell was astonish'd a person so

wise Should rashly endanger his life, And venture so

far; but how vast their surprise! When they heard that

he came for his wife; How vast their surprise! when

they heard that he came for his wife.

To find out a punishment due to his fault,
  Old Pluto long puzzled his brain;
But hell had not torments sufficient, he thought;
  So he gave him his wife back again.
But pity succeeding found place in his heart;
  And, pleas'd with his playing so well,
He took her again in reward of his art;
  Such merit had music in hell!

SONG CLV.
HOW HAPPY A STATE.

How happy a state does the miller possess, Who would be no greater, nor fears to be less; On his mill and himself he depends for support; Which is better than servilely cringing at court. What tho' he all dusty and whiten'd does go? The more he's bepowder'd, the more like a beau: A clown in this dress may be honester far Than a courtier who struts in his garter and star;

urtier who struts in his garter and star.

ınds are so daub'd they're not fit to be seen,
his betters are not very clean;
polite may as dirtily deal;
ling, will stick to the fingers like meal.
n a pudding for dinner he lacks,
ıout scruple, from other mens sacks;
ıt noble examples he brags,
ıs freely from other mens bags.

:ndeavour to heap an estate,
ıld mimic the tools of the state;
alone their own coffers to fill,
:ern's to bring grist to his mill.
he's hungry, he drinks when he's dry,
hen he's weary, contented does lie;
cheerful to work and to sing:
miller, then who'd be a king?

We harbour no paffions, by luxury taught,
We practife no arts, with hypocrify fraught;
What we think in our hearts you may read in our eyes:
For, knowing no falfehood, we need no difguife.

By mode and caprice are the city dames led;
But we as the children of nature are bred:
By her hand alone we are painted and drefs'd;
For the rofes will bloom when there's peace in the breaft.

That giant Ambition we never can dread;
Our roofs are too low for fo lofty a head;
Content and fweet Cheerfulnefs open our door;
They fmile with the fimple, and feed with the poor.

When love has poffefs'd us, that love we reveal;
Like the flocks that we feed are the paffions we feel:
So, harmlefs and fimple, we fport and we play,
And leave to fine folks to deceive and betray.

SONG CLVII.
AS SURE AS A GUN.

And fo when you're married (poor amorous wight!)
You'll bill it and coo it from morning till night:
But truft me, good Colin, you'll find it bad fun;
Inftead of which you'll fight and fcratch—as fure as a
  gun!

But fhou'd fhe prove fond of her own deareft love,
And you be as fupple and foft as her glove;
Yet, be fhe a faint, and as chafte as a nun,
You're faften'd to her apron-ftrings—as fure as a gun!

Suppofe it was you, then, faid he, with a leer;
You wou'd not ferve me fo, I'm certain, my dear:
In troth, I replied, I will anfwer for none;
But do as other women do—as fure as a gun!

SONG CLVIII.

NO GLORY I COVET.

No glory I covet; no riches I want; Ambition is

nothing to me: The one thing I beg of kind Heaven

to grant Is a mind independent and free.

With paſſions unruffled, untainted with pride,
  By reaſon my life let me ſquare;
The wants of my nature are cheaply ſupplied,
  And the reſt are but folly and care.

The bleſſings which Providence freely has lent,
  I'll juſtly and gratefully prize;
Whilſt ſweet meditation, and cheerful content,
  Shall make me both healthful and wiſe.

In the pleaſures the great man's poſſeſſions diſplay,
  Unenvied I'll challenge my part;
For ev'ry fair object my eyes can ſurvey
  Contributes to gladden my heart.

How vainly, through infinite trouble and ſtrife,
  The many their labours employ!
Since all that is truly delightful in life
  Is what all, if they pleaſe, may enjoy.

SONG CLIX.
THOU SOFT FLOWING AVON.

Larghetto.

Thou ſoft flowing Avon, by thy ſilver ſtream, Of

things more than mortal ſweet Shakeſpear would dream,

would dream, would dream, thy Shakeſpear would dream,

The fairies, by moonlight, dance round his green bed;

For hallow'd the turf is which pillow'd his head: The

fairies, by moonlight, dance round his green bed; For

hallow'd the turf is which pil-low'd his head.

The love-ftricken maiden, the foft-fighing fwain,
Here rove without danger, and figh without pain.
The fweet bud of beauty no blight fhall here dread;
For hallow'd the turf is which pillow'd his head.

Here youth fhall be fam'd for their love and their truth,
And cheerful old age feel the fpirit of youth:
For the raptures of fancy here poets fhall tread;
For hallow'd the turf is which pillow'd his head.

Flow on, filver Avon, in fong ever flow!
Be the fwans on thy borders ftill whiter than fnow!
Ever full be thy ftream; like his fame may it fpread!
And the turf ever hallow'd which pillow'd his head!

SONG CLX.
THE IRISH HUNT.

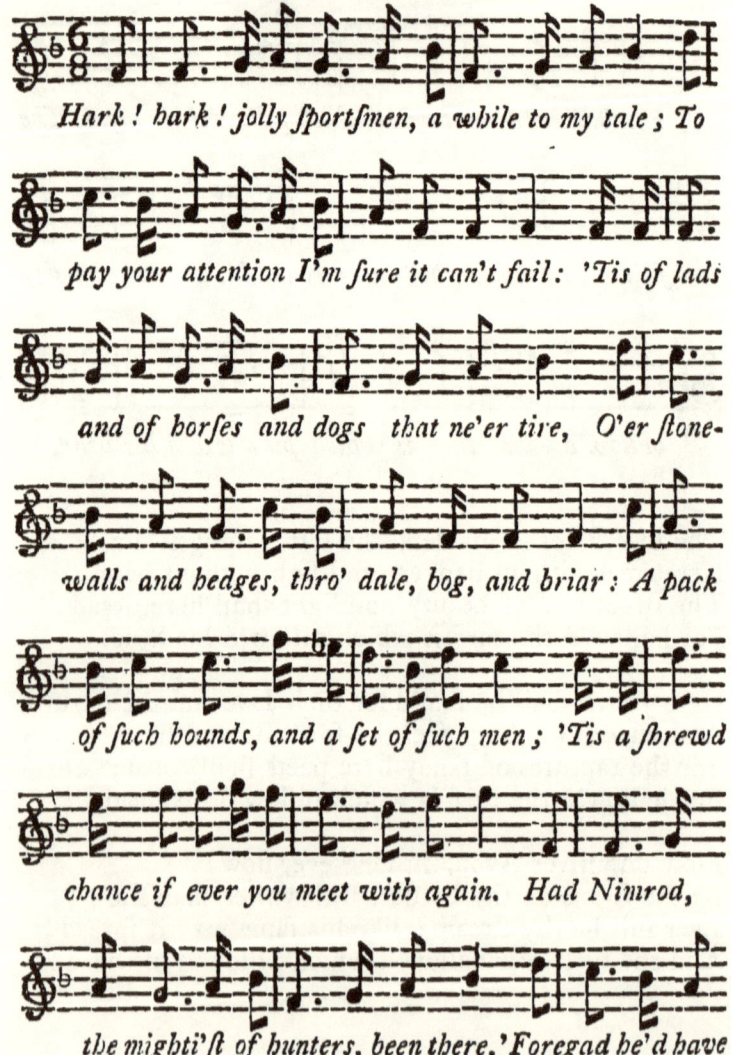

Hark! hark! jolly sportsmen, a while to my tale; To pay your attention I'm sure it can't fail: 'Tis of lads and of horses and dogs that ne'er tire, O'er stone- walls and hedges, thro' dale, bog, and briar: A pack of such hounds, and a set of such men; 'Tis a shrewd chance if ever you meet with again. Had Nimrod, the mighti'st of hunters, been there, 'Foregad he'd have

shook like an aspen for fear.

In seventeen hundred and forty and four,
The fifth of December, I think 'twas no more,
At five in the morning, by most of the clocks,
We rode from Kilruddery in search of a fox.
The Laughlinstown landlord, the old Owen Bray,
And squire Adair, sure, was with us that day;
Joe Debbil, Hal Preston, that huntsman so stout,
Dick Holmes, a few others, and so we set out.

We cast off our hounds for an hour or more,
When Wanton set up a most tunable roar;
Hark to Wanton! cried Joe, and the rest were not slack;
For Wanton's no trifler esteem'd in the pack:
Old Bonny and Collier came readily in,
And ev'ry hound join'd in the musical din;
Had Diana been there she'd been pleas'd to the life,
And one of the lads got a goddess to wife.

Ten minutes past nine was the time of the day
When Reynard broke cover, and this was his play:
As strong from Killegar as though he could fear none,
Away he brush'd round by the house of Kilternan;
To Carrickmines thence, and to Cherrywood then,
Steep Shankhill he climb'd, and to Ballyman-glen;
Bray-common he cross'd, leap'd Lord Anglesey's wall,
And seem'd to say, Little I value you all.

He ran Bushes-grove up to Carberry-burns,
Joe Debbil, Hal Preston, kept leading by turns:
The earth it was open; but he was so stout,
Though he might have got in, yet he chose to keep out:
To Malpas' high hills was the way then he flew;
At Dalkeystone-common we had him in view;

He drove on, by Bullock, through Shrubglanagery,
And ſo on to Mountown, where Laury grew weary.

Through Rocheſtown wood like an arrow he paſs'd,
And came to the ſteep hills of Dalkey at laſt;
There gallantly plung'd himſelf into the ſea,
And ſaid in his heart, Sure none dare follow me:
But ſoon, to his coſt, he perceiv'd that no bounds
Could ſtop the purſuit of ſuch ſtaunch mettl'd hounds;
His policy here did not ſerve him a ruſh,
Five couple of tartars were hard at his bruſh.

To recover the ſhore then again was his drift;
But, ere he could reach to the top of the clift,
He found both of ſpeed and of cunning a lack,
Being waylaid and kill'd by the reſt of the pack.
At his death there were preſent the lads I have ſung,
Save Laury, who, riding a garron, was flung.
Thus ended, at length, a moſt delicate chaſe,
That held us five hours and ten minutes ſpace.

We return'd to Kilruddery's plentiful board,
Where dwells Hoſpitality, Truth, and my Lord;
We talk'd o'er the chaſe, and we toaſted the health
Of the man that ne'er varied for places or wealth.
Owen Bray baulk'd a leap; ſays Hal Preſton, 'twas odd;
'Twas ſhameful, cries Jack, by the great living God!
Says Preſton, I halloo'd, Get on, though you fall;
Or I'll leap over you, your blind gelding and all.

Each glaſs was adapted to freedom and ſport;
For party affairs we conſign'd to the court:
Thus we finiſh'd the reſt of the day and the night
In gay flowing bumpers and ſocial delight:
Then, till the next meeting, bid farewel each brother;
For ſome they went one way and ſome went another.
As Phœbus befriended our earlier roam,
So Luna took care in conducting us home.

SONG CLXI.
WHAT MAN, IN HIS WITS.

What man, in his wits, had not rather be poor, Than

for lucre his freedom to give? Ever busy the means of

his life to se-cure, And so ever neglecting to live.

And so ever neglecting to live.

Inviron'd from morning to night in a croud,
   Not a moment unbent or alone;
Constrain'd to be abject, though never so proud,
   And at ev'ry one's call but his own.

Still repining and longing for quiet each hour,
   Yet studiously flying it still;
With the means of enjoying his wish in his pow'r,
   But accurst with his wanting the will.

For a year must be past, or a day must be come,
   Before he has leisure to rest:
He must add to his store this or that pretty sum,
   And then will have time to be blest.

306   CALLIOPE: OR THE

But his gains, more bewitching the more they increase,
  Only swell the desire of his eye:
Such a wretch let mine enemy live, if he please;
  Let not even mine enemy die.

SONG CLXII.

WOMEN AND WINE.

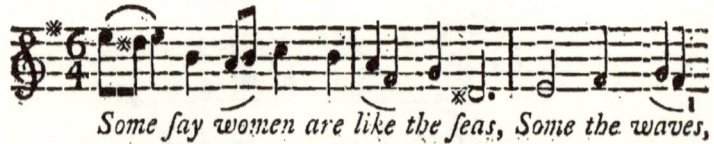
Some say women are like the seas, Some the waves,

and some the rocks; Some the rose that soon decays;

Some the weather, and some the cocks; But if you'll

give me leave to tell, There's nothing can be compar'd

so well As wine, wine, women and wine, They run in

a pa-ral-lel; They run in a pa-ral-lel.

Women are witches when they will,
 So is wine, fo is wine;
They make the ftatefman lofe his fkill,
 The foldier, lawyer, and divine;
They put a gig in the graveft fkull,
 And fend their wits to gather wool:
'Tis wine, wine, women and wine, they run in a parallel.

What is't that makes your vifage fo pale?
 What is't that makes your looks divine?
What is't that makes your courage to fail?
 Is it not women? Is it not wine?
'Tis wine will make you fick when you're well;
 'Tis women that make your forehead to fwell:
'Tis wine, wine, women and wine, they run in a parallel.

SONG CLXIII.
THE UNION.

With women and wine I defy ev'ry care; For life, without these, is a bubble of air; For life, without these, For life, without these, For life without these is a bubble of air; Each helping the other, in pleasure I roll, And a new flow of spirits en-li-vens my soul. Each helping the other, in pleasure I roll, And a new flow of spirits en-livens my soul.

Let grave sober mortals my maxims condemn,
I never shall alter my conduct for them;
I care not how much they my measures decline,
Let them have their own humour—and I will have mine.

Wine, prudently us'd, will our senses improve;
'Tis the spring-tide of life and the fuel of love;
And Venus ne'er look'd with a smile so divine
As when Mars bound his head with a branch of the vine.

Then come, my dear charmer! thou nymph half divine!
First pledge me with kisses—next pledge me with wine:
Then giving and taking, in mutual return,
The torch of our loves shall eternally burn.

But should'st thou my passion for wine disapprove,
My bumper I'll quit to be bless'd with thy love;
For, rather than forfeit the joys of my lass,
My bottle I'll break and demolish my glass.

SONG CLXIV.
PHILLIDA AND CORYDON.

In the merry month of May, In a morn, by break of day, Forth I walk'd by the wood-side, When, as May was in his pride, There I spy'd, all alone, all alone, Philli-da and Co-ry-don.

Much ado there was, God wot!
He would love, and fhe would not:
She faid, never man was true:
He faid, none was falfe to you.
He faid, he had lov'd her long:
She faid, love fhould have no wrong.

Corydon would kifs her then:
She faid, maids muft kifs no men
Till they did for good and all.
Then fhe made the fhepherd call
All the heavens to witnefs truth:
Ne'er lov'd a truer youth.

Thus, with many a pretty oath,
Yea and nay, and faith and troth!
Such as filly fhepherds ufe
When they will not love abufe;
Love, which had been long deluded,
Was, with kiffes fweet, concluded:
   And Phillida, with garlands gay,
   Was made the lady of the May.

SONG CLXV.

THE COUNTRY WEDDING.

Well met, pretty nymph, fays a jolly young fwain, To a beautiful fhepherdefs croffing the plain; Why fo

much in haste? (now the month it was May) Shall I

venture to ask you, fair maiden, which way? Shall I

venture to ask you, fair maiden, which way? Then

straight to this question the nymph did reply, With a

smile on her look, and a leer in her eye, I am come

from the village, and homeward I go; And now, gentle

shepherd, pray why would you know?

I hope, pretty maid, you won't take it amiss,
If I tell you the reason of asking you this;
I would see you safe home, (the swain was in love)
Of such a companion if you would approve.

Your offer, kind shepherd, is civil, I own,
But see no great danger in going alone;
Nor yet can I hinder, the road being free,
For one as another, for you as for me.

No danger in going alone, it is true,
But yet a companion is pleasanter too;
And if you could like (now the swain he took heart)
Such a sweetheart as me, we never would part.
O! that's a long word, said the shepherdess then;
I've often heard say there's no minding you men:
You'll say and unsay, and you'll flatter, 'tis true;
Then leave a young maiden the first thing you do.

O! judge not so harshly, the shepherd replied;
To prove what I say, I will make you my bride;
To-morrow the parson (well said, little swain)
Shall join both our hands, and make one of us twain:
Then what the nymph answered to this is not said;
The very next morn to be sure they were wed.
Sing hey diddle, ho diddle, hey diddle down;
Now, when shall we see such a wedding in town?

SONG CLXVI.

MAY EVE: or, KATE OF ABERDEEN.

The silver moon's en-a-mour'd beam Steals soft-

ly through the night, To wanton with the

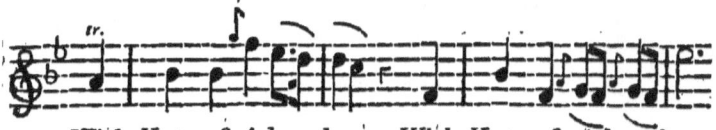

Upon the green the virgins wait,
  In rofy chaplets gay,
Till morn unbar her golden gate,
  And give the promis'd May.
Methinks I hear the maids declare
  The promis'd May, when feen,
Not half fo fragrant, half fo fair,
  As Kate of Aberdeen.

Strike up the tabor's boldeſt notes,
  We'll rouſe the nodding grove;
The neſted birds ſhall raiſe their throats,
  And hail the maid I love:
And ſee—the matin lark miſtakes,
  He quits the tufted green:
Fond bird! 'tis not the morning breaks,
  'Tis Kate of Aberdeen.

Now, lightſome o'er the level mead,
  Where midnight fairies rove,
Like them, the jocund dance we'll lead,
  Or tune the reed to love:
For, ſee, the roſy May draws nigh;
  She claims a virgin queen:
And, hark! the happy ſhepherds cry,
  'Tis Kate of Aberdeen.

SONG CLXVII.

LUCY, THE FAIR QUEEN OF HEARTS.

Farewell to the park and the play, Farewell the

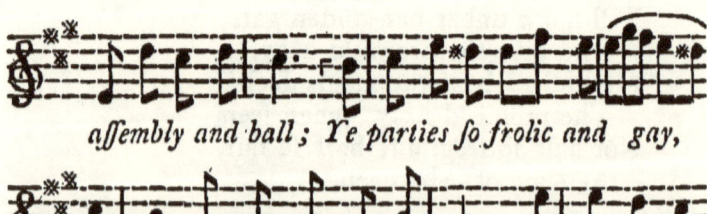

aſſembly and ball; Ye parties ſo frolic and gay,

With pleaſure farewell to you all.   No joys can I

now find in wine, Shot through with sly Cupid's keen

darts ; My freedom, well pleas'd, I resign To Lucy

the fair queen of hearts, To Lucy the fair queen of

hearts. For Lucy I sigh, for Lucy I die, For Lucy

I sigh, for Lucy I die, For Lucy the fair queen of

hearts, For Lucy the fair queen of hearts.

Though beauties are plenty, I own,
    Regardless I view their dull charms,
Nor beauty cou'd conquer alone,
    But beauty and merit disarms.
Insipid to me all their faces,
    In vain they play off all their arts,
Compar'd to the numberless graces
    Of Lucy the fair queen of hearts.
      For Lucy I sigh, &c.

She liftens to all that I fay,
　　She blufhes whenever we meet;
Though with others fhe's lively and gay,
　　With me fhe is grave and difcreet.
To church then I'll lead my fair bride,
　　And, fcorning deceitful bafe arts,
Still happy, whate'er may betide,
　　With Lucy the fair queen of hearts.
　　　For Lucy I figh, &c.

SONG CLXVIII.

THE FRIEND AND THE LOVER.

I'm told by the wife ones a maid I fhall die, They fay I'm too nice, but the charge I deny; I know but too well how time flies along, That we live but few years, and yet fewer are young. But I hate to be

cheated, And ne - ver will buy Whole a - ges of for-

row for moments of joy; I ne - ver will wed till a

youth I can find Where the friend and the lover are

e-qual-ly join'd; Where the friend and the lover, the

friend and the lover, the friend and the lo - ver, are

e-qual-ly join'd.

No pedant, though learned, or foolishly gay,
Or laughing because he has nothing to say,
To ev'ry fair one obliging and free,
But never be fond of any but me:

In whose tender bosom my soul may confide,
Whose kindness can soothe me, whose counsels can guide;
Such a youth I wou'd marry, if such I cou'd find,
Where the friend and the lover are equally join'd.

From such a dear lover as here I describe
No danger shou'd fright me, not millions shou'd bribe;
But, 'till this astonishing creature I know,
I'm single and happy, and still will be so.
You may laugh, and suppose I am nicer than wise;
But I'll shun the vain fop, the dull coxcomb despise;
Nor ever will wed till a youth I can find
Where the friend and the lover are equally join'd.

SONG CLXIX.
COME KISS ME, SAYS HE.

Young Damon was whistling, brisk and gay, With

waistcoat so red, and stockings so grey, Just merrily,

merrily, come from the fair, Just merrily come from

the fair, Just merrily come from the fair. He

He offer'd a ribbon her hair to bind;
Dear Sufan come kifs, and in pity be kind,
Or I'll hang in a fit of defpair;
Defpair, cry'd the maiden, is blind.
  Then kifs me, fays he;
   I won't, fays fhe;
You think that I love you, I don't, I declare.

Shall we go to the parfon, he roguifhly faid?
She curtfy'd, cry'd yes, blufh'd, and held down her head,
With a look that difpell'd all his care;
For fhe found that he wifh'd her to wed:
  Well, kifs me, fays he;
   I will, fays fhe;
I'll kifs when we're wed, not till then I declare.

SONG CLXX.

THO' BACCHUS MAY BOAST.

Tho' Bacchus may boaft of his care-kill-ing bowl,

And fol - ly in thought-drowning re-vels de - light,

Such worfhip, alas! has no charms for the foul,

What soul, that's possess'd of a dream so divine,
With riot wou'd bid the sweet vision begone?
For a tear that bedews Sensibility's shrine
Is a drop of more worth than all Bacchus's tun.

Each change and excefs hath thro' life been my doom,
  And well can I fpeak of its joy and its ftrife ;
The bottle affords us a glimpfe thro' the gloom,
  But love's the true funfhine that gladdens our life.

Come, then, rofy Venus, and fpread o'er my fight
  The magic illufions that ravifh the foul !
Awake in my breaft the foft dream of delight !
  And drop from thy myrtle one leaf in my bowl !
Then deep will I drink of the nectar divine,
  Nor e'er, jolly god, from thy banquet remove ;
But each tube of my heart ever thirft for the wine
  That's mellow'd by friendfhip and fweeten'd by love.

SONG CLXXI.

WHEN THE MEN A-COURTING CAME.

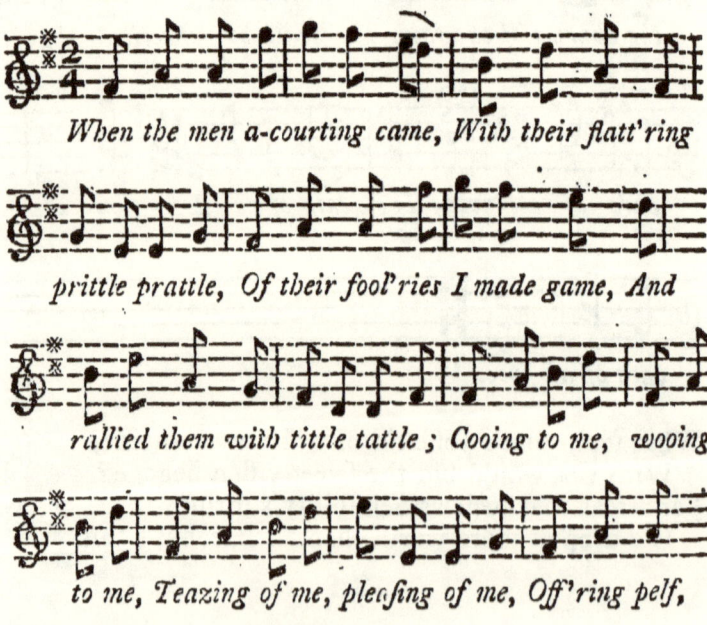

When the men a-courting came, With their flatt'ring

prittle prattle, Of their fool'ries I made game, And

rallied them with tittle tattle ; Cooing to me, wooing

to me, Teazing of me, pleafing of me, Off'ring pelf,

each filly elf Came cooing, wooing, bowing to me.

The divine, with looks demure,
    Talk'd of tithes and eating plenty,
Show'd the profits of his cure,
    And vow'd to treat me with each dainty;
        Cooing, &c.

The learned fergeant of the law
    Show'd his parchments, briefs, and papers;
In his deeds I found a flaw;
    So difmifs'd him in the vapours;
        Cooing, &c.

Phyfic now difplay'd his wealth
    With his noftrums; but the fact is,
I refolv'd to keep my health,
    Nor die a martyr to his practice;
        Cooing, &c.

But, at laft, a fwain bow'd low,
    Candid, handfome, tall, and clever,
Squeez'd my hand, I can't tell how,
    But he won my heart for ever;
        Cooing, &c.
I fent all other wooers from me.

SONG CLXXII.

MY NAME's HONEST HARRY, O.

My name's honeſt Harry, O: Mary I will marry, O;

In ſpite of Nell or I-ſa-bel I'll follow my own va-ga-

ry, O; With my rigdum, jigdum, airy, O, I love lit-tle

Mary, O; In ſpite of Nell or I-ſabel I'll follow my own

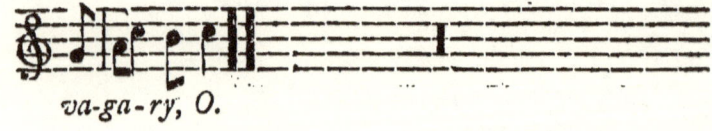

va-ga-ry, O.

Straight ſhe is and bonny, O,
Sweet as ſugar-candy, O,
   Freſh and gay
   As flow'rs in May,
And I'm her Jack-a-dandy, O;
   With my rigdum, jigdum, &c.

Soon to church I'll bring her, O,
Where we'll wed together, O,
And, that done,
Then we'll have fun,
In spite of wind or weather, O;
With my rigdum, jigdum, &c.

SONG CLXXIII.

THE LASSES ARE MAD.

The lasses are mad, the archers are mad, In nimbly footing the ground, Sir; In merry Sherwood no soul shall be sad, While harps with me-lody sound, Sir. In merry Sherwood no soul shall be sad, While harps with me-lo-dy sound, Sir.

We'll tipple till mad, then madly fing
  Madrigals, catches, and glees, Sir;
Chaunt out, like mad, till the welkin ring,
  Under the mifletoe trees, Sir.
    Chaunt out, &c.

We fight like mad when we fall on our foes,
  Shoot arrows wing'd like the wind, Sir;
The fat fallow deer can't 'fcape our bows,
  Nor in fwiftnefs fafety find, Sir.
    The fat, &c.

Then madly we'll fing, and madly we'll dance,
  And madly all roar out, Sir,
And madly make our enemies prance,
  If mad, to try about, Sir.
    And madly, &c.

Brave Scarlet is mad, ftout Allen is mad,
  And John's as mad as the beft, Sir;
Maidens run mad, our hearts are glad,
  Stark mad fhall be ev'ry gueft, Sir.
    Maidens run, &c.

SONG CLXXIV.

LET's SEEK THE BOW'R.

Let's feek the bow'r of Robin Hood, This is his bri-

dal day, And cheerfully, in blithe Sherwood, bride-

maids and bridemen play. Then follow, follow me, my

bonny, bonny lads, And we'll the paſtime ſee; For the

minſtrels ſing, And the ſweet bells ring, And they

feaſt right merrily, merrily; And they feaſt right mer-

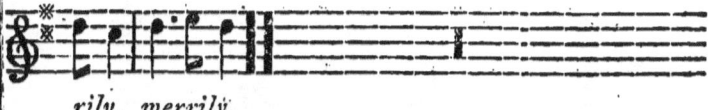
rily, merrily.

The humming beer flows round in pails,
   With mead that's ſtout and old,
And am'rous virgins tell love-tales,
   To thaw the heart that's cold.
Then follow me, my bonny lads,
   And we'll the paſtime ſee;
     For the minſtrels ſing
     And the ſweet bells ring,
And they feaſt right merrily.

There, dancing ſprightly on the green,
   Each light foot lad and laſs,
Sly ſtealing kiſſes when unſeen,
   And gingling glaſs with glaſs.

Then follow me, my bonny lads,
And we'll the paſtime ſee;
For the minſtrels ſing
And the ſweet bells ring,
And they feaſt right merrily.

SONG CLXXV.

MARGARITTA FIRST POSSEST.

Marga-rit-ta firſt poſſeſt, I remember well, my

breaſt, With my row, dow, dow, dow, dow, derro.

With my reſtleſs heart next play'd Martha, wanton

ſloe-ey'd maid, With her tan ta ra ra ra-ro.

She to Katharine gave place,
Kate to Betſey's am'rous face,
  With my row, &c.
Mary, then, and gentle Ann,
Both to reign at once began,
  With their tan ta, &c.

Jenny next, a tyrant fhe,
But Rebecca fet me free,
   With my row, &c.
In a week from her I fled,
And took Judith in her ftead,
   With her tan ta, &c.

She poffefs'd a wond'rous grace,
But fhe wanted Sufan's face,
   With my row, &c.
Ifabella's rolling eye
Eclips'd Sufan's prefently,
   With her tan ta, &c.

Brown fkinn'd Befs I next obey'd,
Then lov'd Nanny, red hair'd maid,
   With my row, &c.
None cou'd bind me, I am free,
Yet love all the fair I fee,
   With my tan ta, &c.

SONG CLXXVI.
WHEN RUDDY AURORA.

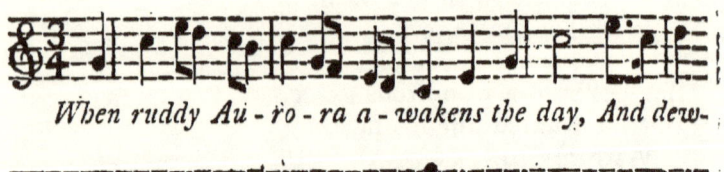
When ruddy Au-ro-ra a-wakens the day, And dew-

drops im-pearl the sweet flow-ers so gay, Sound, sound,

my stout archers, sound horns and a-way; With

arrows, sharp-pointed we go, With arrows, sharp-point-

ed, we go. See Sol now a-ri-ses, in splendor so

bright, I O Pæan, I O Pæan, For Phœbus,

for Phœbus, who leads to de-light, All glorious il-

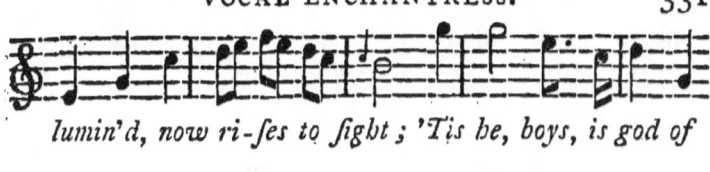

lumin'd, now ri-ses to fight; 'Tis he, boys, is god of

the bow,   is god of the bow,   is god of

the bow, of the bow - - - - - - - - - - - - - -

- - - - - - - - - - - - - - - - - See Sol

now a - ri-ses, In splendor how bright, 'Tis he, boys, is

god of the bow.

Fresh roses we'll offer at Venus's shrine,
Libations we'll pour to great Bacchus divine,
While mirth, love, and pleasure, in junction combine,
    For archers, true sons of the fame.
    For archers, &c.
Bid sorrow adieu; in soft numbers we'll sing;
Love and friendship, love and friendship,
Love, friendship, and beauty, shall make the air ring,

T t ij

Wishing health and succefs to our country and king,
Increafe to their honour and fame.
To their honour and fame,
To their honour and fame,
To their ho - - - nour and fame.
Wishing health and succefs to our country and king,
Increafe to their honour and fame.

SONG CLXXVII.

BOW, WOW, WOW.

I'll *fing you a fong, faith I'm finging it now*

here, I don't mean t'afront either fmall or big bow

wow here: The fubject I've chofen it is the canine

race, To prove, like us, two-legg'd dogs they are a

very fine race. Bow, wow, wow, Fal, lal, lal, ad-

di, addi, Bow, wow, wow.

Like you and I other dogs may be counted fad dogs;
And we won't drink water, fome might think us mad dogs:
A courtier is a fpaniel, a citizen's a dull dog,
A foldier is a maftiff, a failor's a bull dog.
    Bow, wow, &c.

An old maid comes from church, the poor no lady kinder;
A lufty dog her footman, with prayer-book behind her;
A poor boy afks a farthing, and gets plenty of good kicking;
But little Shock, her lap-dog, muft have a roafted chicken.
    Bow, wow, &c.

When filly dogs, for property, uncle, fon, and brother,
Grin and fnarl mighty gruff, and worry one another;
Shou'd they a bit of equity from juftice beg the loan of,
That cunning dog the lawyer, Snap, carries quick the bone off.
    Bow, wow, &c.

A poet's a lank greyhound, for the public he runs game down;
A critic is a cur that ftrives to run his fame down;
And though he cannot follow where the noble fport invites him,
"He flyly fteals behind, and by the heel he bites him."
    Bow, wow, &c.

" You've a choice pack of friends, while to feed 'em
    " you are able;
" Your dog, for his morfel, crouches under your table;

" Your friends turn tail in misfortune or disaster;
" But your poor faithful dog will ne'er forsake his ma-
  " ster."
    Bow, wow, &c.

SONG CLXXVIII.
AS DERMOT TOIL'D.

As Dermot toil'd one summer's day, Young Shelah,

as she sat beside him, Fairly stole his pipe away, Oh,

then, to hear she did deride him, Where, poor Der-

mot, is it gone, Your li-ly li-ly loo - dle? They've left

you nothing but the drone, And that's yourself, you

noo - - dle. Beam, bum, boodle, loodle, loodle, Beam,

bum, boodle, loodle, loo. Poor Dermot's pipe is loſt

and gone, And what will the poor devil do?

Fait now I am undone, and more,
　Cried Dermot—Ah! will you be eaſy?
Did you not ſteal my heart before?
　Is it you have made a man run crazy?
I've nothing left me now to moan;
　My lily lily loodle
That us'd to cheer me ſo, is gone,
　Ah! Dermot, thou'rt a noodle.
　　Beam, bum, boodle, loodle, loodle,
　　Beam, bum, boodle, loodle, loo,
My heart, and pipe, and peace, are gone,
　What next will cruel Shelah do?

Then Shelah, hearing Dermot vex,
　Cried, fait 'twas little Cupid mov'd me,
You fool, to ſteal it out of tricks,
　Only to ſee how much you lov'd me.
Come cheer thee, Dermot, never moan,
　But take your lily loodle;
And, for the heart of you that's gone,
　You ſhall have mine, you noodle.
　　Beam, bum, boodle, loodle, loodle,
　　Beam, bum, boodle, loodle, loo;
Shelah's to church with Dermot gone;
　And, for the reſt—what's that to you?

SONG CLXXIX.
THE SINE QUA NON.

Lord! Lord! without victuals and drink, We po-ets

must give up each strain; It helps us, poor devils, to

think, And thrash with more vigour our brain. With-

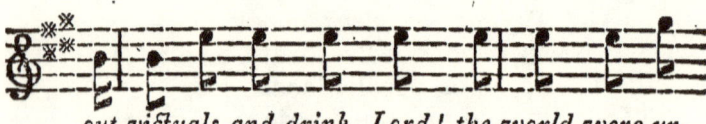

out victuals and drink, Lord! the world were un-

done, 'Tis the soul of the world, 'tis the sine qua non.

'Tis the sine qua non, the sine qua non, The soul of

the world, 'tis the sine qua non.

The foldier, 'midft battle's alarms,
  Without it, could ill face his foe;
So faint would he handle his arms,
  And draw with fuch weaknefs his bow.
Without victuals, &c.

What would ladies and gentlemen do,
  That fay fuch fine things to each other?
They would never be able to coo;
  They could never be father and mother.
Without victuals, &c.

Then hey for good victuals and drink!
  Who is there that would not caroufe?
Wherever he may be, I think
  He's not to be found in this houfe.
Without victuals, &c.

SONG CLXXX.
WHEN FIRST I BEGAN, SIR.

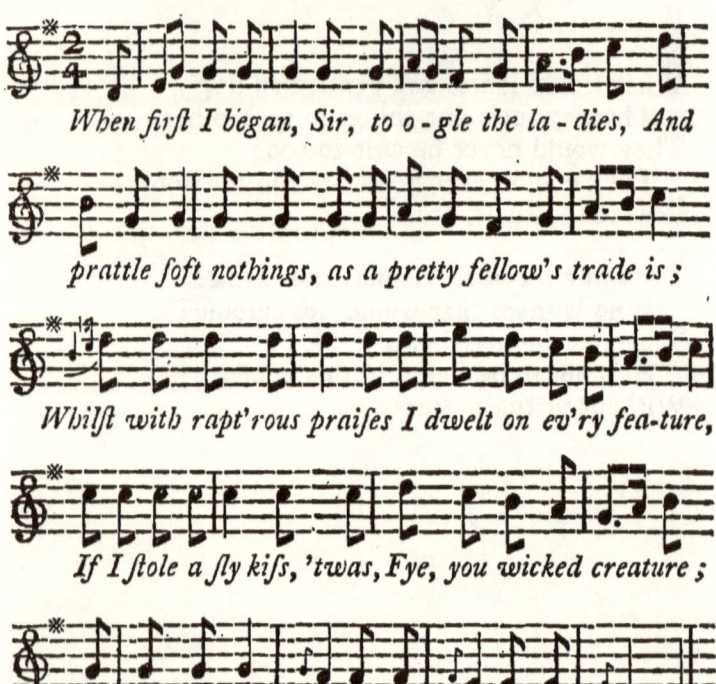

Indeed my attractions no gallantry needed;
Each ev'ning new conquest to conquests succeeded;
Perplex'd how so many fond claims I shou'd parry,
To settle them all, I resolv'd, faith, to marry;
And press'd lovely Laura, in language still sweeter,
Till, blushing, she whisper'd, I'm yours, you wicked creature.

SONG CLXXXI.
TOL DE ROL LOL, SIR.

In vain the ills of life affail; I never yet would

yield me; Nor shall their malice e'er prevail, Whilst

frolic mirth can shield me. Like curs they snarl, but

dare not bite; I heed them not at all, Sir; But laugh

at all their roguish spite, And still sing tol de rol lol,

Sir.

I ever scorn'd, with face of woe,
   Proud dames to dangle after;
With smiles I bent young Cupid's bow,
   And tipt his shafts with laughter:

340   CALLIOPE: OR THE

 Succefs ftill mark'd each merry dart,
  Black, fair, brown, fhort, or tall, Sir;
 I conquer'd ev'ry female heart
  With tol de rol de rol lol, Sir.

 In fpite of Dons fo grave and wife,
  'Till o'er old Styx I ferry,
 I always fhall moft highly prize
  Whatever's blithe and merry.
 May love and laughter ever be
  Attendant on my call, Sir!
 Here's, what I ever lov'd to fee,
  A glafs to tol de rol lol, Sir!

SONG CLXXXII.

YOUNG ROGER THE PLOUGHMAN.

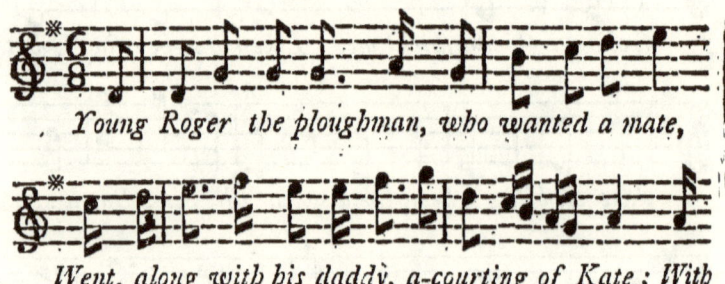
Young Roger the ploughman, who wanted a mate,

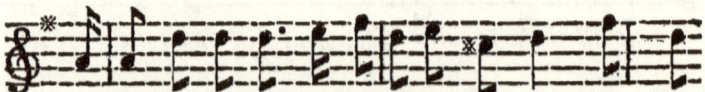
Went, along with his daddy, a-courting of Kate; With

a nofegay fo large, in his ho-li-day clothes, His hands

in his pockets, away Roger goes. Now, he was as

bashful as bashful could be, And Kitty, poor girl, was as bashful as he: So he bow'd, and he star'd, and he let his hat fall, And he grinn'd, scratch'd his head,

and said nothing at all. And he grinn'd, scratch'd his

head, and said nothing at all.

If aukward the swain, no lefs aukward the maid;
She simper'd and blush'd, with her apron-string play'd;
Till the old folks, impatient to have the thing done,
Agreed that young Roger and Kate shou'd be one.
In silence the young ones both nodded assent,
Their hands being join'd, to be married they went:
Where they answer'd the parson with voices so small,
You'd have sworn that they both had said nothing at all.

But, mark what a change! in the course of a week,
Kate quite left off blushing, Rodge boldly cou'd speak,
Cou'd joke with his deary, laugh loud at the jest;
She cou'd coax too, and fondle, as well as the best;

And, asham'd of past folly, they've often declar'd,
To encourage young folks who at courtship are scar'd,
If at first to your aid some assurance you'll call,
When once you are us'd to't, 'tis nothing at all.

SONG CLXXXIII.
WHEN UP TO LONDON.

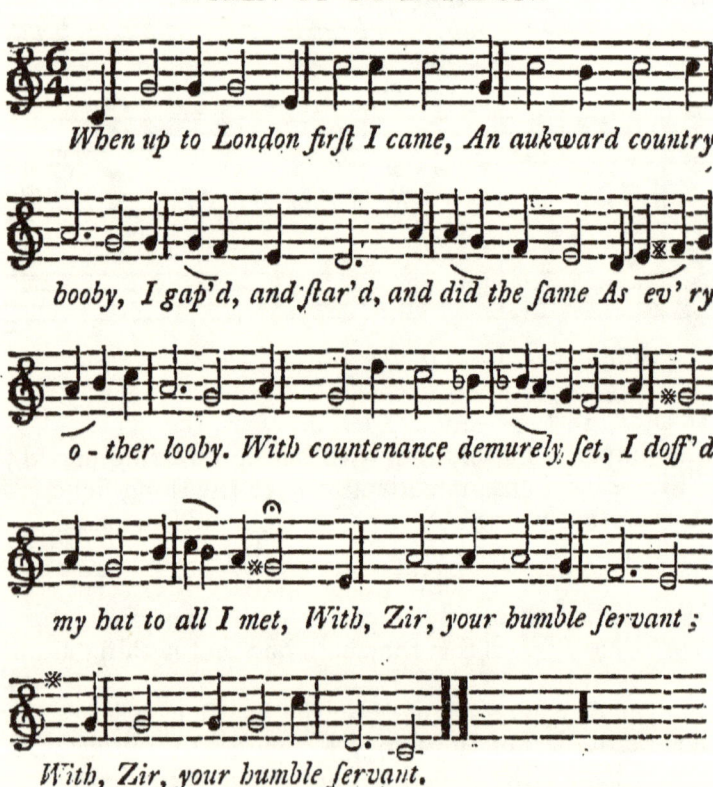

When up to London first I came, An aukward country
booby, I gap'd, and star'd, and did the same As ev'ry
o-ther looby. With countenance demurely set, I doff'd
my hat to all I met, With, Zir, your humble servant;
With, Zir, your humble servant.

Alas! too soon I got a wife;
   And, proud of such a blessing,
The joy and business of my life
   Was kissing and caressing;
'Twas " Charmer! Sweeting! Duck and Dove!"
And I, o'er head and ears in love,
   Was Cupid's humble servant.

She's gone, poor girl; and, in my cot,
   With friend and bottle smiling,
I'd envy not a higher lot,
   The tedious hours beguiling.
If Care peeps in, I'm busy then;
I nod, desire he'll call again,
   And am his humble servant.

Since life's a jest, as wise ones say,
   'Tis best employ'd in laughing;
And, come what frowning cares there may,
   My antidote is quaffing.
I'm ever jovial, gay, and free;
For this is my philosophy;
   And so, your humble servant.

SONG CLXXXIV.

YOU MUST, GOOD SIR, EXCUSE ME.

A fig for all your whining stuff; Fine speeches sweet

as honey; Of love you can't give proof enough Unless

you give your money. Were I your mistress, faith and

troth, Your av'rice soon wou'd lose me; For compliments

are but mere froth, You must, good Sir, excuse me.

Of all the arrows love can boast,
   The golden ones are best, Sir;
And he who boldly bids the most
   Can never be in jest, Sir.
'Tis true that I make rather free;
   But faith you shan't refuse me:
So draw your purse-strings now, d'ye see,
   Or else you must excuse me.

SONG CLXXXV.
LOW DOWN IN THE BROOM.

My daddy is a canker'd carle, He'll nae twin wi'

his gear; My minny she's a scolding wife, Hads a' the

house a-steer; But, let them say, or let them do, It's

a' ane to me; For he's low down, he's in the broom,

That's waiting on me. Waiting on me, my love, He's

waiting on me; For he's low down, he's in the broom,

That's waiting on me.

346   CALLIOPE: OR THE

My aunty Kate fits at her wheel,
    And fair fhe lightlies me;
But weel ken I it's a' envy;
    For ne'er a jo has fhe.
But let them fay, &c.

My coufin Kate was fair beguil'd
    Wi' Johnny i' the glen;
And ay fince-fyne fhe cries, beware
    Of falfe deluding men.
But let her fay, &c.

Glee'd Sandy he came weft ae night,
    And fpeer'd when I faw Pate;
And ay fince-fyne the neighbours round
    They jeer me air and late.
But let them fay, &c.

SONG CLXXXVI.

CONTENTED I AM.

Contented I am, and con-tent-ed I'll be; Refolv'd,

in this life, to live happy and free. With the cares

of this world I'm feldom perplex'd; I'm fometimes

un-ea-fy, but never am vex'd: Some higher, fome

lower, I own there may be; But there's more who

live worfe than live better than me.

My life is a compound of freedom and eafe;
I go where I will, and return when I pleafe;
I live above envy, alfo above ftrife;
And wifh I had judgment to choofe a good wife:
I'm neither fo high nor fo low in degree,
But ambition and want are both ftrangers to me.

Did you know how delightful my gay hours do pafs,
With my bottle before me, embrac'd by my lafs;
I'm happy while with her, contented alone;
My wine is my kingdom; my cafk is my throne;
My glafs is the fceptre by which I fhall reign;
And my whole privy council's a flafk of Champaign.

When money comes in, I live well till it's gone;
While I have it quite happy, contented with none.
If I lofe it at gaming, I think it but lent;
If I fpend it genteelly, I'm always content:
Thus in mirth and good humour my gay hours do pafs
And on Saturday's night I am juft as I was.

SONG CLXXXVII.
BRIGHT PHOEBUS.

Bright Phœbus has mounted the chariot of day, And

the horns and the hounds call each sportsman a-way;

And the horns and the hounds call each sportsman away.

Thro' woods and thro' meadows, with speed, now they

bound, While health, ro-sy health, is in ex-er-cise

found; Thro' woods and thro' meadows, with speed, now

they bound, While health, rosy health, is in ex-er-cise

Each hill and each valley is lovely to view,
While Pufs flies the covert, and dogs quick purfue.
Behold where fhe flies o'er the wide-fpreading plain!
While the loud op'ning pack purfue her amain.
    Hark away, &c.

At length Pufs is caught, and lies panting for breath,
And the fhout of the huntfman's the fignal of death.
No joys can delight like the fports of the field;
To hunting all paftimes and pleafures muft yield.
    Hark away, &c.

SONG CLXXXVIII.

THE TOBACCO-BOX: A Dialogue.

Thomas.

Tho' the fate of battle on to-mor - row wait,

Let's not lose our prattle, now, my charm-ing Kate.

'Till the hour of glory, love shou'd now take place;

Nor damp the joys before you with a fu - - ture case.

Kate. Oh, my Thomas, still be constant, still be true!
Be but to your Kate as Kate is still to you;
Glory will attend you, still will make us blest;
With my firmest love, my dear, you're still possest.

Tho. No new beauties tasted, I'm their arts above;
Three campaigns are wasted, but not so my love;
Anxious still about thee, thou art all I prize;
Never, Kate, without thee, will I bung these eyes.

Kate. Conſtant to my Thomas I will ſtill remain,
  Nor think I will leave thy ſide the whole campaign;
  But I'll cheriſh thee, and ſtrive to make thee bold:
  May'ſt thou ſhare the vict'ry! may'ſt thou ſhare
    the gold!

Tho. If, by ſome bold action, I the halbert bear,
  Think what ſatisfaction, when my rank you ſhare.
  Dreſs'd like any lady-fair from top to toe;
  Fine lac'd caps and ruffles then will be your due.

Kate. If a ſergeant's lady I ſhou'd chance to prove,
  Linen ſhall be ready always for my love;
  Never more will Kate the captain's laundreſs be;
  I'm too pretty, Thomas, love, for all but thee.

Tho. Here, Kate, take my 'bacco-box, a ſoldier's all;
  If by Frenchmens blows your Tom is doom'd to fall,
  When my life is ended, thou may'ſt boaſt and prove,
  Thou'd'ſt my firſt, my laſt, my only, pledge of love.

Kate. Here, take back thy 'bacco-box, thou'rt all to me;
  Nor think but I will be near thee, love, to ſee;
  In the hour of danger let me always ſhare;
  I'll be kept no ſtranger to my ſoldier's fare.

Tho. Check that riſing ſigh, Kate, ſtop that falling tear;
  Come, my pretty comrade, entertain no fear;
  But, may Heav'n befriend us! Hark! the drums
    command:
  Now I will attend you. Love, I kiſs your hand.

Kate.*I can't ſtop theſe tears, tho' crying I diſdain;
  But muſt own 'tis trying hard the point to gain:
  May good Heav'ns defend thee! Conqueſt on thee
    wait!
  One kiſs more, and then I give thee up to fate.

  * Both repeat this verſe, only Thomas ſays, { Conqueſt on me wait!
  { I yield myſelf to fate.

SONG CLXXXIX.

THE MAID THAT TENDS THE GOATS.

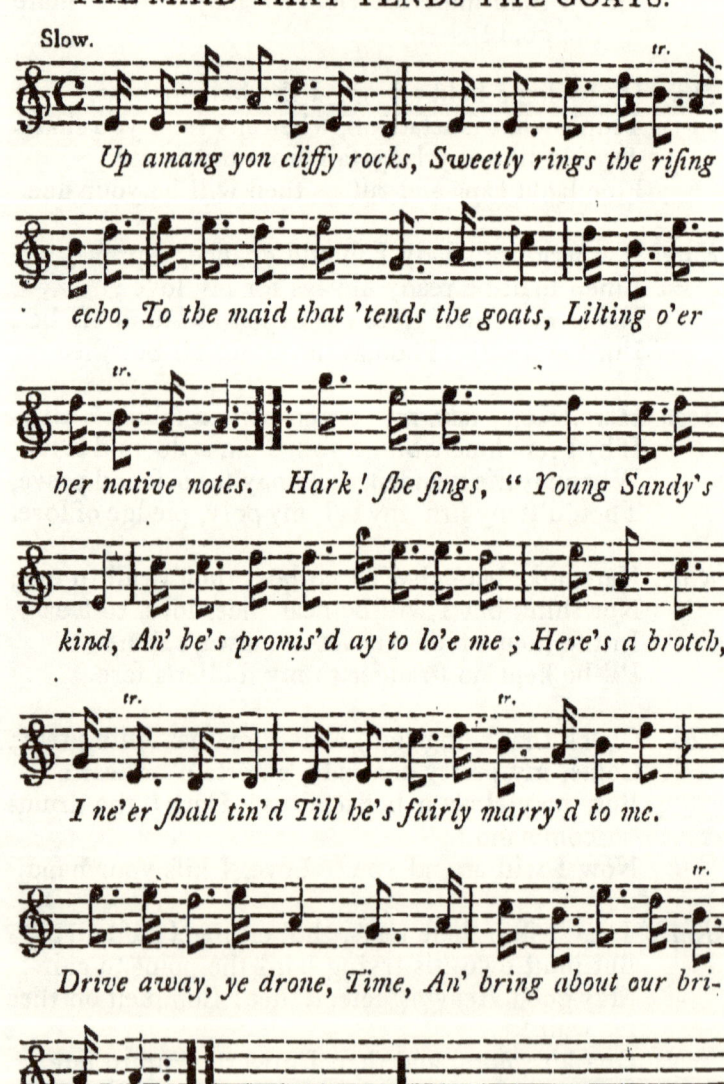

Up amang yon cliffy rocks, Sweetly rings the rising echo, To the maid that 'tends the goats, Lilting o'er her native notes. Hark! she sings, "Young Sandy's kind, An' he's promis'd ay to lo'e me; Here's a brotch, I ne'er shall tin'd Till he's fairly marry'd to me. Drive away, ye drone, Time, An' bring about our bridal day.

" Sandy herds a flock o' sheep ;
" Af'en does he blaw the whistle
" In a strain sae saftly sweet,
" Lammies, list'ning, dare nae bleat.
" He's as fleet's the mountain roe,
" Hardy as the highland heather,
" Wading thro' the winter snow,
" Keeping ay his flock together.
" But a plaid, wi' bare houghs,
" He braves the bleakest norlin blast.

" Brawly he can dance and sing
" Canty glee or highland cronach ;
" Nane can ever match his fling
" At a reel, or round a ring.
" Wightly can he wield a rung ;
" In a brawl he's ay the bangster ;
" A' his praise can ne'er be sung
" By the langest winded sangster.
" Sangs that sing o' Sandy
" Come short, tho' they were e'er sae lang."

SONG CXC.

ALL AMONGST THE LEAVES SO GREEN, O.

In the forest, here, hard by, A bold robber late

was I; With my blunderbuſs in hand, When I bid a

trav'ler ſtand, Zounds! deliver up your caſh, Or your

noddle I ſhall ſlaſh, All amongſt the leaves ſo green,

O. Damme, Sir, If you ſtir, Sluice your veins, Blow

your brains, Hey down, ho down, Derry, derry, down,

All amongſt the leaves ſo green, O.

Soon I'll quit the roving trade
When a gentleman I'm made;
Then, fo fpruce and debonnaire,
Gad! I'll court a lady fair.
How I'll prattle, tattle, chat,
How I'll kifs her, and all that,
All amongft the leaves fo green, O.
    How d'ye do?
    How are you?
    Why fo coy?
    Let us toy;
  Hey down, ho down,
  Derry, derry, down,
All amongft the leaves fo green, O.

But, ere old and grey my pate,
I'll fcrape up a fnug eftate;
With my nimblenefs of thumbs
I'll foon butter all my crumbs;
When I'm juftice of the peace,
Then I'll mafter many a leafe,
All amongft the leaves fo green, O.
    Wig profound,
    Belly round,
    Sit at eafe,
    Snatch the fees,
  Hey down, ho down,
  Derry, derry, down,
All amongft the leaves fo green, O.

SONG CXCI.

WIDDLE WADDLE.

When firſt my perſon bleſs'd her,
    Sir, what d'ye want?
    Sir, what d'ye want?
And, when I'd have careſs'd her,
    Indeed you ſhan't,
    Indeed you ſhan't.
So cunning I addreſs'd her,
    With ſigh and pant,
    With ſigh and pant,
That ſoon I kiſs'd and preſs'd her,
    I'm ſo gallant,
    I'm ſo gallant.

My fair in wit ſo arch is,
    I'm her dawdle,
    I'm her dawdle;
My very ſoul ſhe ſearches,
    Shakes her noddle,
    Shakes her noddle;
My heart with love ſhe parches,
    My blood does coddle,
    My blood does coddle;
And like a duck ſhe marches,
    Widdle, waddle,
    Widdle, waddle.

SONG CXCII.
ROW DE DOW, DOW.

How happy the foldier who lives on his pay, And

ſpends half a crown out of ſixpence a-day; Yet fears

neither juſtices, warrants, or bums, But pays all his

debts with the roll of his drums. With row de dow,

row de dow, row de dow, dow; And he pays all his

debts with the roll of his drums.

He cares not a marvedy how the world goes;
His king finds him quarters, and money, and clothes;
He laughs at all ſorrow whenever it comes,
And rattles away with the roll of his drums.
    With a row de dow, &c.

The drum is his glory, his joy and delight,
It leads him to pleasure as well as to fight;
No girl, when she hears it, tho' ever so glum,
But packs up her tatters, and follows the drum.
  With a row de dow, &c.

SONG CXCIII.

DREARY DUN.

A master I have, and I am his man, Galloping

dreary dun; A master I have, and I am his man,

And he'll get a wife as fast as he can, With his haily,

gaily, gamboraily, giggling, niggling, galloping gallo-

way, draggle tail dreary dun.

I faddled his fteed fo fine and fo gay,
  Galloping dreary dun;
I mounted my mule and we rode away,
  With his haily, &c.

We canter'd along until it grew dark,
  Galloping dreary dun;
The nightingale fung inftead of the lark,
  With his haily, &c.

We met with a friar, and afk'd him our way,
  Galloping dreary dun;
By the Lord! fays the friar, you're both gone aftray,
  With your haily, &c.

Our journey, I fear, will do us no good,
  Galloping dreary dun;
We wander alone, like the babes in the wood,
  With our haily, &c.

My mafter is fighting, and I'll take a peep,
  Galloping dreary dun;
But now I think better, I'd better go fleep,
  With my haily, &c.

SONG CXCIV.

KISS THE COLD WINTER AWAY.

Hey for a lafs and a bottle to cheer, And a thump-

ing bantling every year; Hey for a lafs and a bottle

to cheer, And a thumping bantling every year. With

skin as white as snow, And hair as brown as a

berry; With eyes as black as a sloe, And lips as

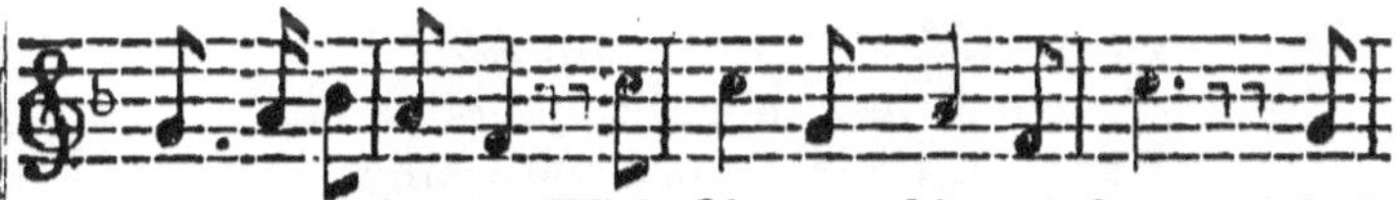

red as a cherry. With skin as white as snow, And

hair as brown as a berry; With eyes as black as a

sloe, And lips as red as a cherry. Sing rousy, tousy,

rantum, scantum, Laugh and lie down is the play:

We'll cuddle together, To keep out the weather, And

kiſs the cold winter away; Kiſs, kiſs the cold winter

away, Kiſs, kiſs the cold winter away.

  Laugh while you live;
   For, as life is a jeſt,
  Who laughs the moſt
  Is ſure to live beſt.
  When I was not ſo old
   I frolick'd among the miſſes;
  And, when they thought me too bold,
   I ſtopp'd their mouths with kiſſes.
   Sing rory, tory, &c.

SONG CXCV.

LIKE MY DEAR SWAIN.

Like my dear ſwain no youth you'd ſee, So blithe,

ſo gay, ſo full of glee; In all our village, who but

he Could foot it up ſo featly? His lute to hear,

from far and near, Each female came, both girl and

dame; And all his boon for ev'ry tune, To kifs 'em

round fo fweetly.

While round him, in the jocund ring,
I've nimbly danc'd, he'd play or fing;
Of May the youth was chofen king,
   He caught our ears fo neatly:
Such mufic rare in his guitar,
But touch his flute the crowd was mute;
His only boon for ev'ry tune,
   To kifs 'em round fo fweetly.

SONG CXCVI.
WHEN BROTHER BOBBY.

When brother Bobby came first to town, By all he

was call'd a country clown; But now, to be sure,

he is alter'd quite, He can do any thing but read

and write: Both hyperbole and common-place, And

that sort of thing he speaks with grace; He bows and

struts with modish swing, And the ladies cry, Lord!

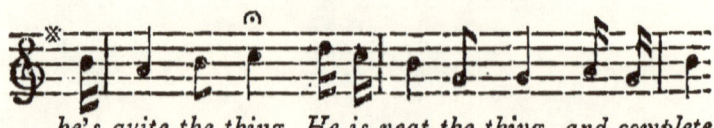

he's quite the thing. He is neat the thing, and complete

the thing, And the ladies cry he is quite the thing;

He bows and struts with modish swing, And the ladies

cry, he is quite the thing.

Then why shou'd Bobby call me a fool,
When I learn'd to write at Launce'ton* school?
Lord Sparkle does my learning praise,
And, when I dance, with rapture gaze.
Both hyperbole and common-place,
I, too, will lisp with modern grace;
And all the town shall henceforth ring
With—Miss Pendragon is quite the thing.
    She's neat the thing, and complete the thing,
And Miss Pendragon is quite the thing;
And all the town shall henceforth ring
With Miss Pendragon is quite the thing.

* Launceston, a town in Cornwall.

SONG CXCVII.

THO' LEIXLIP IS PROUD.

Tho' Leixlip is proud of its close shady bowers,

Its clear fall-ing waters, its murm'ring cascades,

Its groves of fine myrtle, its beds of sweet flowers,

Its lads so well dress'd, and its neat pretty maids:

As each his own village will still make the most of,

In praise of dear Carton, I hope I'm not wrong,

Dear Carton, containing what kingdoms may boaſt of,

'Tis Norah, dear Norah, the theme of my ſong. Dear

Carton, containing what kingdoms may boaſt of, 'Tis

Norah, dear Norah, the theme of my ſong.

Be gentlemen fine, with their ſpurs and nice boots on,
   Their horſes to ſtart on the Curragh of Kildare;
Or dance at a ball, with their Sunday new ſuits on,
   Lac'd waiſtcoat, white gloves, and their nice powder'd hair:
Poor Pat, while ſo bleſt in his mean humble ſtation,
   For gold, or for acres, he never ſhall long;
One ſweet ſmile can give him the wealth of a nation
   From Norah, dear Norah, the theme of my ſong.

SONG CXCVIII.

AULD ROBIN GRAY. Scots Air.

When the ſheep are in the fauld, and the ky at

hame, And a' the warld to ſleep are gane, The

waes o' my heart fa' in ſhow'rs frae my e'e, When

my gudeman lies ſound by me.

New Set of AULD ROBIN GRAY.

Young Jamie lov'd me weel, and aſk'd me for his
bride; But, ſa-ving a crown, he had naething elſe

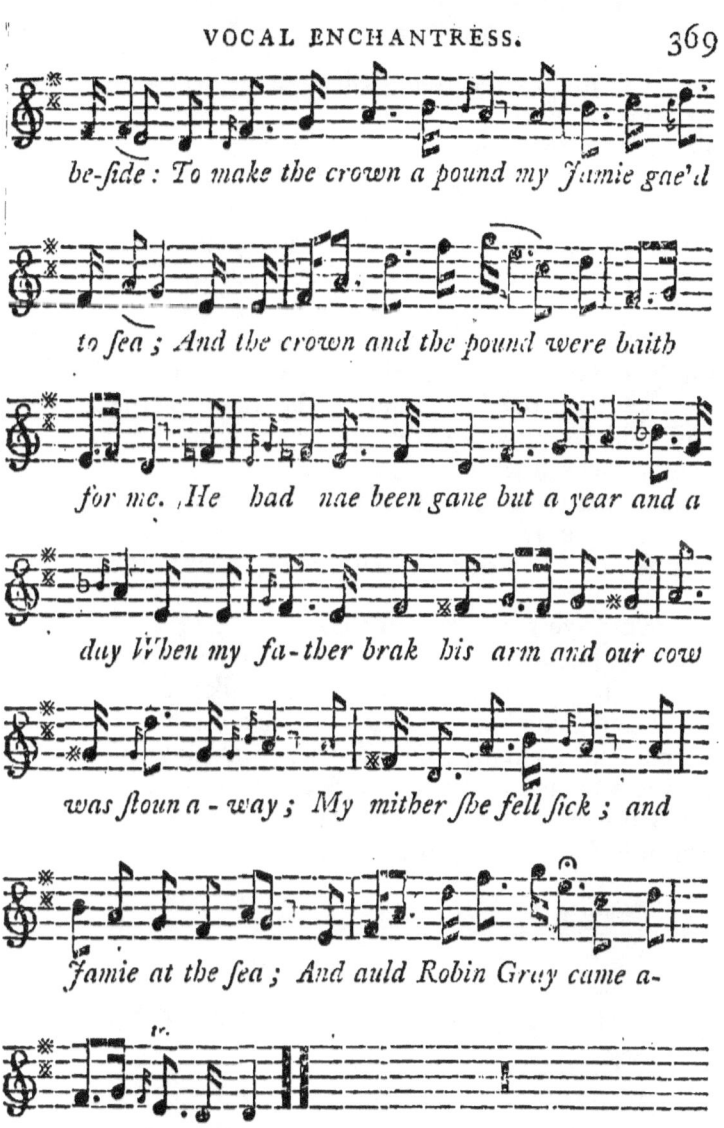

My father cou'dna work ; my mither cou'dna fpin ;
I toil'd day and night ; but their bread I cou'dna win :

Auld Rob maintain'd them baith ; and, wi' tears in his e'e,
Said, Jenny, for their fakes, O marry me !
My heart it faid, Na ; and I look'd for Jamie back :
But the wind it blew hard, and the ſhip it was a wrack ;
The ſhip it was a wrack—why didna Jenny dee :
O why was ſhe ſpar'd to cry, Wae's me ?

My father urg'd me fair ; my mither didna ſpeak ;
But ſhe looked in my face till my heart was like to break :
Sae I gae him my hand, but my heart was i' the ſea ;
And auld Robin Gray was gudeman to me.
I hadna been a wife a week but only four,
When, ſitting ſae mournfully ae night at the door,
I ſaw my Jamie's wraith, for I cou'dna think it he,
Till he ſaid, I'm come hame, love, to marry thee.

O fair did we greet, and little did we ſay ;
We took but ae kiſs, and we tore ourſelves away.
I wiſh that I were dead ; but I'm no like to dee :
How lang ſhall I live to cry, O wae's me ?
I gang like a ghaiſt, and I downa think to ſpin ;
I darena think on Jamie, for that wou'd be a ſin ;
But I'll e'en do my beſt a gude wife to be ;
For auld Robin Gray is ay kind to me.

SONG CXCIX.
THE DEATH OF AULD ROBIN GRAY.

The ſummer was ſmiling, all nature round look'd

gay, When Jenny was attending on auld Robin Gray :

For he was sick at heart, and had nae friend beside,

But only me, poor Jenny, who newly was his bride.

Ah, Jenny, I shall deé, he cry'd, as sure as I had birth!

Then see my poor auld banes, pray, laid in the earth;

And be a widow for my sake a twelvemonth and a

day, And I'll leave you whate'er belongs to auld Ro-

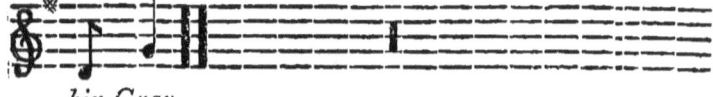

bin Gray.

I laid poor Robin in the earth as decent as I could,
And shed a tear upon his grave ; for he was very good.
I took my rock all in my hand, and in my cot I sigh'd,
O wae's me ! what shall I do since poor auld Robin dy'd ?
Search ev'ry part throughout the land there's nane like me forlorn,
I'm ready e'en to ban the day that ever I was born ;
For Jamie, all I lov'd on earth, ah ! he is gone away,
My father's dead, my mother's dead, and eke auld Robin Gray.

I rose up with the morning sun, and spun till setting day,
And one whole year of widowhood I mourn'd for Robin Gray ;
I did the duty of a wife both kind and constant too ;
Let ev'ry one example take, and Jenny's plan pursue.
I thought that Jamie he was dead, or he to me was lost,
And all my fond and youthful love entirely was cross'd ;
I try'd to sing, I try'd to laugh, and pass the time away ;
For I had ne'er a friend alive since dy'd auld Robin Gray.

* At length the merry bells rung round, I cou'dna guess the cause ;
But Rodney was the man, they said, who gain'd so much applause.
I doubted if the tale was true, till Jamie came to me
And show'd a purse of golden ore, and said it is for thee.
Auld Robin Gray, I find, is dead, and still your heart is true ;
Then take me, Jenny, to your arms, and I will be so too ;
Mess John shall join us at the kirk, and we'll be blithe and gay,
I blush'd, consented, and reply'd, adieu to Robin Gray,

* This verse to be sung quick.

SONG CC.

LOCK'D IN MY CHEST.

Lock'd in my cheſt I've fif-ty pound, With four good

acres of mea-dow ground; For your bonny black

eye, ſweet Lauretta, I ſigh; Marry me, my ſweet laſs,

you'll in plenty abound.

I've two pack-horſes, a jack-aſs, and ſow,
A barrow, a harrow, ſpade, flail, cart, and plough,
Ducks, turkies, geeſe, hens, fourteen ſheep in my pens,
Heifer, calf, cat, and goat, and a fine milch-cow.

A kettle of braſs, and a pot to ſtew,
A waſhing-tub, and a vat to brew,
A warming-pan bright, and a dog barks by night;
Say, will you marry me? and I'll marry you.

SONG CCI.
I PREFER A FLOWING BOWL.

Let the Sultan's wanton care Thousands of the sex

prepare; Gentle, pretty, frisking lasses, Young and

handsome as the Graces; Let him kiss 'em one and all,

What then? what then? this concerns not me at all;

For, like ev'ry thirsty soul, I prefer a flowing bowl.

Chorus.

I prefer a flowing bowl. For, like ev'ry thirsty soul,

I prefer a flowing bowl. I prefer a flowing bowl.

Let the noble duke or peer
Sell his thoufand pounds a-year;
Let him quit his grafs and ftubble,
He'll foon find that life's a bubble;
　Let him rife, or let him fall,
　What then, &c.

Let the valiant foldier go
Seeking dangers to and fro;
Let him, when the trumpets rattle,
Brave the foremoft of the battle.
　Honour fears nor fword nor ball,
　What then, &c.

SONG CCII.

TO THE GREENWOOD GANG WI' ME.

To speer my love, wi' glances fair, The wood-

land lad-die came; He vow'd he wou'd be ay

sincere, And thus he spake his flame: The morn

is blithe, my bon-ny fair, As blithe as blithe can

be; To the green wood gang, my lassy dear, To

the green wood gang wi' me. Gang wi' me,

gang wi' me, To the green wood gang, my laſſy

dear, To the green wood gang wi' me.

The lad wi' love was ſo oppreſs'd
    I wad na ſay him nay;
My lips he kiſs'd, my hand he preſs'd,
    While tripping o'er the brae:
Dear lad, I cry'd, thou'rt trig and fair,
    And blithe as blithe can be;
To the green wood gang, my laddie dear,
    To the green wood gang wi' me.

The bridal day is come to paſs,
    Sic joy was never ſeen;
Now I am call'd the woodland laſs,
    The woodland laddie's queen:
I bleſs the morn ſo freſh and fair
    I told my mind ſo free,
To the green wood gang, my laddie dear,
    To the green wood gang wi' me.

SONG CCIII.
THE BRITISH LION IS MY SIGN.

The British li-on is my sign, A roaring trade I drive on; Right English u-sage, neat French wine, A landla-dy must thrive on. At table d'hôté to eat and drink, Let French and English mingle; And while to me they bring the chink, Faith, let the glasses jingle. Your rhino rattle, Come men and cattle, Come all to Mistress Casey; Of trouble and money, My

jewel, my honey, I warrant I'll make you all eafy.

When drefs'd and feated in my bar,
   Let fquire or beau or belle come;
Let captains kifs me, if they dare,
   'Tis, Sir, you're kindly welcome!
On fhuffle, cog, and flip, I wink,
   Let rooks and pigeons mingle;
And if to me they bring the chink,
   Faith, let the glaffes jingle.
      Rhino rattle, &c.

Let love fly here on filken wings,
   His tricks I ftill connive at;
The lover who would fay foft things
   Shall have a room in private.
On pleafure I am pleas'd to wink,
   So lips in kiffes mingle;
For while to me they bring the chink,
   Faith, let the glaffes jingle.
      Your rhino rattle, &c.

SONG CCIV.
THE FROLICKSOME FELLOW.

In London my life is a ring of delight; In frolics

I keep up the day and the night; I snooze at the

Hummums till twelve, perhaps later; I rattle the bell,

and I roar up the waiter: Your Honour, says he, and

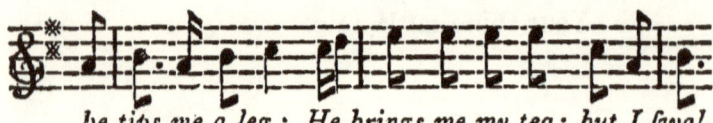

he tips me a leg; He brings me my tea; but I swal-

low an egg: For tea in a morning's a slop I renounce;

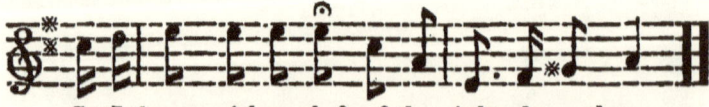

So I down with a glass of the right cherry bounce.

My phaeton I mount, and the plebs they all ſtare;
I handle my reins, and my elbows I ſquare;
My ponies ſo plump and as white as a lilly,
Through Pall-Mall I ſpank it, and up Piccadilly;
Till, loſing a wheel, egad! down come I ſmack,
So at Knightſbridge I throw myſelf into a hack;
At Tatterſal's fling a leg over my nag;
Thus viſit for dinner, then dreſs in a bag.
    With ſwearing, &c.

CALLIOPE: OR THE

I roll round the garden, and call at the Rose;
And then at both playhouses pop in my nose:
I lounge in the lobby, laugh, swear, slide, and swagger,
Talk loud, take my money, and out again stagger:
I meet at the Shakespear a good-natur'd soul;
Then down to our club at St James's I roll:
The joys of the night are a thousand at play;
And thus at the finish begin the next day.
    With swearing, &c.

SONG CCV.

NO HURRY I'M IN TO BE MARRY'D.

No hurry I'm in to be marry'd: But if it's the

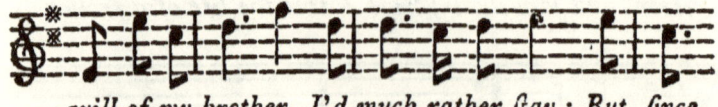
will of my brother, I'd much rather stay; But, since

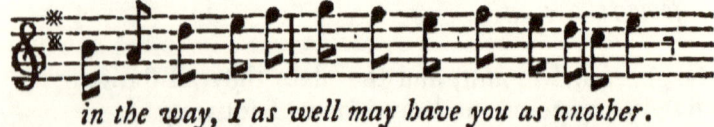
in the way, I as well may have you as another.

I'd much rather stay; Yet, since in the way, I as

well may have you as another.

A strange custom this to be marry'd,
Tho' follow'd by father and mother,
    The grave and the gay;
    But, since in the way,
I as well may have you as another.

A prude, tho' she long to be marry'd,
Endeavours her wishes to smother.
    I'd give you her nay;
    But, since in the way,
I as well may have you as another.

SONG CCVI.

KILKENNY IS A HANDSOME PLACE.

was the lad for me.

But Dublin city bore the bell,
  In ſtreets, and 'ſquares, and houſes fine;
Oh, here young Dick his love cou'd tell,
  And there I told young Dicky mine:
For Dick he was a roving blade,
  And I was hearty, bold, and free;
He lov'd, and I his love repaid;
  Then Dicky was the lad for me.

When Dover ſtrand my happy lot,
  And William there my love did crown,
Young Dick and Jemmy I forgot,
  Kilkenny fair, and Dublin town:
For William was a gentle youth,
  Too baſhful nor too bold was he;
He ſaid he lov'd, and told me truth,
  And William was the lad for me.

SONG CCVII.

TOL, LOL, DE ROL, LOL.

Tol, lol, de rol, lol, My tolly, my tol, With me

when you canter to Wales: For petticoat white, Buff

breeches so tight, Away go needles and flails. Young

Taffy throws by hur wheels; Then Winney kicks up

her heels; With follow, and halloo, and waddle,

and straddle, So merry to see us come. Young Taffy

throws by hur wheels; Then Winney kicks up her heels;

With fiddle, and diddle, and giggle, and niggle, They

give us a welcome home.

   The joy so great,
   So noble we treat,
 An oxen is roasted whole!
   And tho' on the lawn
   The spiggot is drawn
For punch, you may swim in the bowl.
   We give the ladies a ball,
   We foot it away in the hall,
    With follow, &c.

   Miss Howel so nice,
   And Lady ap Rice,
And cousin Sir Evan ap Lloyd ;
   Parson Montgomery,
   Counsellor Flummery,
Ap Morgan, ap Williams, ap Floyd ;
   O, when the stocking is thrown,
   And lovee and I alone,
    Then follow, &c.

SONG CCVIII.
THE HIGH-METTLED RACER.

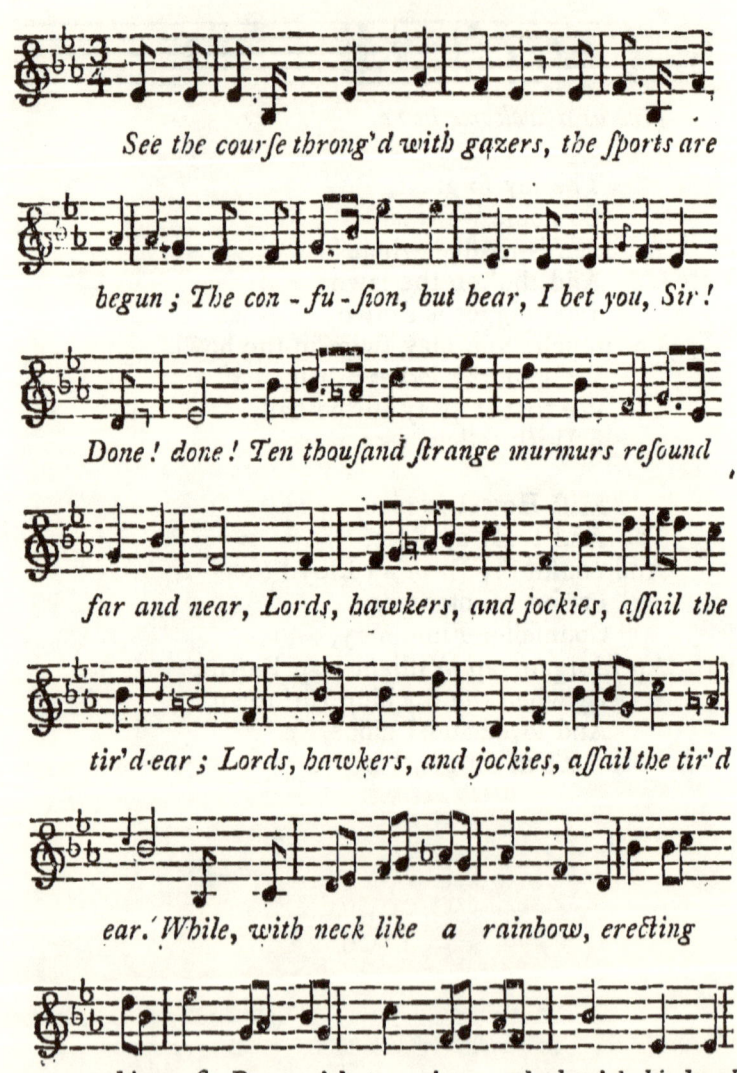

touching his breaſt; Scarcely ſnuff-ing the air, he's

ſo proud and e-late, The high-mettled ra-cer

firſt ſtarts for the plate; The high-mettled ra-cer,

The high-mettled racer, firſt ſtarts for the plate.

Grown aged, us'd up, and turn'd out of the ſtud,
Lame, ſpavin'd, and wind-gall'd; but yet with ſome
    blood:
While knowing poſtilions his pedigree trace,
Tell his dam won this ſweep, his ſire that race;
And what matches he won to the hoſtlers count o'er,
As they loiter their time at ſome hedge alehouſe door;
While the harneſs ſore galls, and the ſpurs his ſides goad,
The high-mettled racer's a hack on the road.

Till at laſt, having labour'd, drudg'd early and late,
Bow'd down by degrees he bends on to his fate;
Blind, old, lean, and feeble, he tugs round a mill,
Or draws ſand till the ſand of his hour-glaſs ſtands ſtill:
And now cold and lifeleſs, expos'd to the view
In the very ſame cart which he yeſterday drew;
While a pitying crowd his ſad relics ſurrounds,
The high-mettled racer is ſold for the hounds.

SONG CCIX.

JACK RATLIN WAS THE ABLEST SEAMAN.

Jack Ratlin was the ablest seaman, None like him could hand, reef, and steer: No dang'rous toil but he'd encounter with skill and in contempt of fear. In fight a li-on; the battle end-ed, Meek as the bleating lamb he'd prove: Thus Jack had manners, courage, me--rit, Yet did he sigh, and all for love.

The song, the jest, the flowing liquor,
   For none of these had Jack's regard:
He, while his messmates were carousing,
   High sitting on the pendant yard,
Wou'd think upon his fair one's beauties,
   Swore never from such charms to rove;
That truly he'd adore them living,
   And dying sigh—to end his love.

The same express the crew commanded
   Once more to view their native land,
Amongst the rest, brought Jack some tidings,
   Wou'd it had been his love's fair hand!
Oh fate! her death defac'd the letter;
   Instant his pulse forgot to move;
With quiv'ring lips, and eyes uplifted,
   He heav'd a sigh—and dy'd for love.

SONG CCX.
TWIGGLE AND A FRIZ.

London town is just like a barber's shop; But, by the Lord Harry, 'tis wond'rous big! There the painted doll, and the powder'd fop, And many a blockhead wears a wig. And I tickled each phiz With a twiggle and a friz; With a twiggle, twiggle, twiggle, and a frizzle, With a twiggle, twiggle, twiggle, And a frizzle, frizzle, frizzle: And I tickled each phiz

With a twiggle and a friz.

A captain of horfe I went for to fhave;
   O, damme! fays he, with a martial frown;
I pois'd my razor like a barber brave;
   I took him by the nofe; but he knock'd me down.
     But I tickled, &c.

I next went to drefs up a fine gallant mifs;
   Down the lady fits and her bofom bares;
Cupid or the devil made me feize a kifs;
   But ere my iron cool'd I was kick'd down ftairs.
     But I tickled, &c.

I went to drefs a lawyer; O rare fport!
   Who had a falfe oath that day for to fwear.
By my fkill fore trouble I fpar'd the court;
   For my iron burnt Six-and-eight-pence's ear.
     So I tickled, &c.

I went for to drefs up an old maid's hair,
   Wrinkl'd and bald as a fcalded pig;
As fhe led the dance down with a fwimming air,
   The poor old lady dropp'd her wig.
     So I tickled, &c.

SONG CCXI.
WHAT CARE I FOR WHOM SHE BE?

Allegretto.

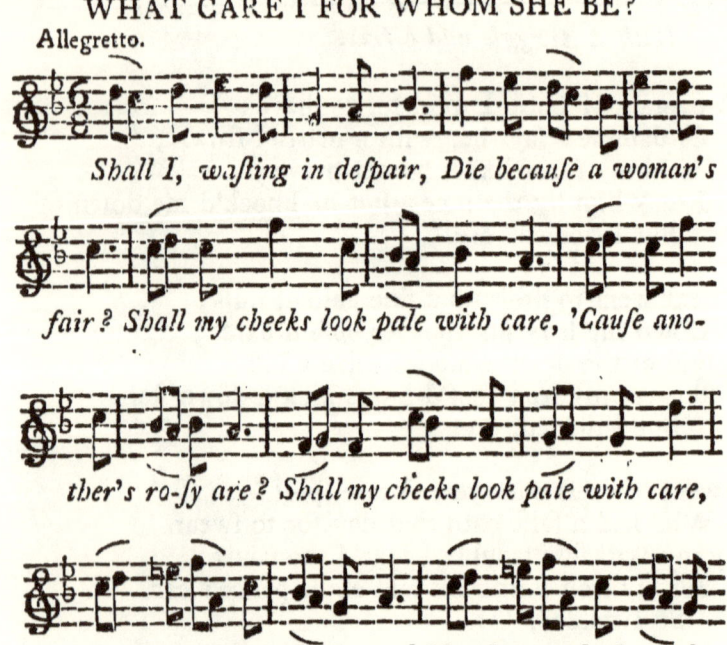

Shall I, wasting in despair, Die because a woman's fair? Shall my cheeks look pale with care, 'Cause ano-

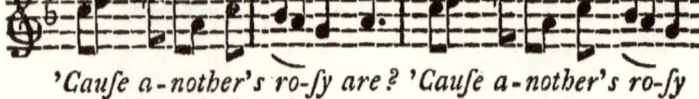

ther's rosy are? Shall my cheeks look pale with care,

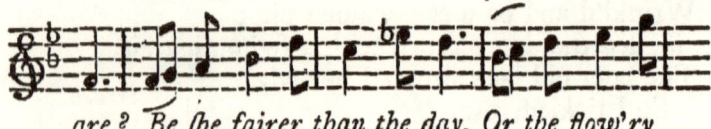

'Cause a-nother's ro-sy are? 'Cause a-nother's ro-sy

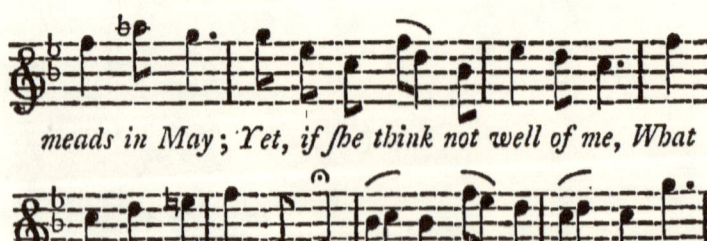

are? Be she fairer than the day, Or the flow'ry meads in May; Yet, if she think not well of me, What care I how fair she be? Be she fairer than the day,

VOCAL ENCHANTRESS.   395

Or the flow'ry meads in May; Yet, if she think not

well of me, What care I how fair she be? What care

I? What care I? What care I how fair she be?

But if she think not well of me, What care I how

fair she be? What care I how fair she be?

Shall a woman's goodnefs move
Me to perifh for her love?
Or. her worthy merits known,
Make me quite forget my own?
Be fhe with that goodnefs bleft
As may merit name the beft;
Yet if fhe be not fuch to me,
What care I how good fhe be?

Be fhe good, or kind, or fair,
I will never more defpair;

3 D ij

If she love me, this believe,
I will die 'ere she shall grieve;
If she slight me when I woo,
I will scorn and let her go.
So if she be not fit for me,
What care I for whom she be?

SONG CCXII.

THE FAITHFUL LOVER.

Alas, my heart! a-las, my heart! On Anna cold my love is placed: For her I sigh, I burn, I die, A flame so strong nought can deface it. For Anna fair is all my care; For her I'd range the world o-ver, If she, inclin'd, wou'd prove more

kind, And pi - - ty me, her faithful lover.

 My friend and pot I've quite forgot,
  My drefs, nay more, my golden treafure;
 With hands o'erlaid I walk the fhade;
  In folitude is all my treafure.
   Chor. For Anna fair, &c.

 Her fhape fo neat, in all complete,
  And lover, fure, fhe ne'er had truer;
 Since love her heart with pangs can't fmart,
  Let gratitude at laft fubdue her.
   Chor. For Anna fair, &c.

 What tho' I've rang'd, and mind oft chang'd,
  And many a dazzling beauty prais'd;
 Now nought my love from her can move,
  'Tis here, and ne'er can be eras'd.
   Chor. For Anna fair, &c.

SONG CCXIII.
BAGATELLE's SO CLEVER.

Ah, ma chere, My pretty dear! Ma charmante

Miss Norah; Oh, I'll sigh and press her, I vill ever

bless her, Cuddle and caress her, Till she cry en-co-ra;

Spite of the fate, She is my mate, Nous danserons

to-ge-dre; Ve can never tire, Frenchman is all

fire! O Bagatelle's so cle-ver! How le beaumonde

vill stare! Pour voir de happy pair! Promenez,

fi ne-gligée, Like de little turtle dove; Always bill-

ing, cooing, Like two puſſeys mewing, Purring out

dere tale of love. O dear me! How ver pretty

Ven ve come to-ge-dre! All de night and day, Sir,

Ve vill kiſs and play, Sir, Oh Bagatelle's ſo cle-ver!

  Vat grand bliſs
  To toy and kiſs
Vid my dear Miſs Norah!
  O ſhe be ſo pretty,
  And ſo very vitty,
It wou'd be much pity
Not to cry encora!
  Oh, mon Dieu!
  Oh, ſacre bleu!
Nous baiſerons for ever;
  Love can never tire,
  Nought can quench his fire,
Oh, Bagatelle's ſo clever!

400   CALLIOPE: OR THE

Ven ve go to de play,
Habillez fo fine and gay,
   Si bien jantée,
   Oh tout a fait,
In our air no embarras;
   Like de grande nobleffe
   Ve fal be careffe,
It vil make grand coup d' eclat;
   How I wifh
   Vid pretty Mifs
To tie de knot for ever!
   I fal live in clover
   Ven it is all over,
Oh, Bagatelle's fo clever!

SONG CCXIV.

MA CHERE AMIE.

Ma chere amie, my charm - - ing fair, Whofe fmiles can banifh ev'- ry care; In kind compaffion fmile on me, Whofe on - - ly care is love of

thee. Ma chere a - mie; Ma chere a - mie;

Ma chere a - mie; Ma chere a - - mie.

 Under sweet friendship's sacred name
My bosom caught the tender flame.
May friendship in thy bosom be
Converted into love for me!
  Ma chere amie, &c.

 Together rear'd, together grown,
O let us now unite in one!
Let pity soften thy decree!
I droop, dear maid; I die for thee!
  Ma chere amie, &c.

3 E

SONG CCXV.
HOW SWEET's THE LOVE.

He lo'ed a lafs wi' fickle mind,
Was fometimes cauld and fometimes kind;
Which made the love-fick laddie rue;
For fhe was cauld when he was true:
He mourn'd and fung, o'er brae and burn,
How fweet's the love that meets return!

One-day a pretty wreath he twin'd,
Where lilacks with fweet cowflips join'd,
To make a garland for her hair;
But fhe refus'd a gift fo fair.
This fcorn, he cry'd, can ne'er be borne;
But fweet's the love that meets return.

Juft then he met my tell-tale een,
And love fo true is fooneft feen:
Dear lafs, faid he, my heart is thine;
For thy foft wifhes are like mine:
Now Jenny, in her turn, may mourn,
How fweet's the love that meets return!

My anfwer was both frank and kind;
I lo'ed the lad, and tell'd my mind:
To kirk we went wi' hearty glee;
And wha fae bleft as he and me!
Now blithe we fing, o'er brae and burn,
How fweet's the love that meets return!

3 E ij

SONG CCXVI.
FY GAR RUB HER O' ER WI' STRAE.

Sweet youth's a blithe and heartfome time;
Then, lads and laffes, while 'tis May,
Gae pu' the gowan in it's prime
Before it wither and decay.

Watch the faft minutes of delyte
  When Jenny fpeaks beneath her breath,
And kiffes, laying a' the wyte
  On you if fhe kepp ony fkaith.

Haith ye're ill-bred, fhe'll fmiling fay,
  Ye'll worry me, ye greedy rook:
Syne frae your arms fhe'll rin away,
  And hide herfelf in fome dark nook.
Her laugh will lead you to the place
  Where lies the happinefs ye want,
And plainly tell you to your face
  Nineteen na-fays are ha'f a grant.

Now to her heaving bofom cling
  And fweetly toolie for a kifs:
Upon her finger whoop a ring
  As taiken of a future blifs.
Thefe bennifons, I'm very fure,
  Are of the gods indulgent grant:
Then, furly carls, whifht, forbear
  To plague us with your whining cant.

SONG CCXVII.

To the foregoing Tune.

DEAR Roger, if your Jenny geck
  And anfwer kindnefs wi' a flight,
Seem unconcern'd at her neglect;
  For women in a man delight:
But them defpife who're foon defeat,
  And wi' a fimple face give way:
To a repulfe then be not blate;
  Pufh bauldly on and win the day.

When maidens, innocently young,
  Say aften what they never mean,
Ne'er mind their pretty lying tongue,
  But tent the language of their een:
If thefe agree, and fhe perfift
  To anfwer a' your love with hate,
Seek elfewhere to be better bleft,
  And let her figh when its too late.

SONG CCXVIII.

WHAT WOMAN CAN DO.

What woman can do I have try'd to be free; Yet, do what I can, I find I love him; And, tho' he flies me, Still, ftill he's the man. They tell me at once he to twenty will fwear: When vows are fo fweet, who the falfehood can fear? So, when you have faid

all you can, Still, ſtill he's the man.

I caught him once making love to a maid,
    When to him I ran;
He turn'd and he kifs'd me, then who could upbraid
    So civil a man?
The next day I found to a third he was kind,
I rated him ſoundly, he ſwore I was blind;
    So, let me do what I can,
    Still, ſtill he's the man.

All the world bids me beware of his art:
    I do what I can;
But he has taken ſuch hold of my heart
    I doubt he's the man.
So ſweet are his kiſſes, his looks are ſo kind,
He may have his faults, but if none I can find,
    Who can do more than they can?
    He ſtill is the man.

SONG CCXIX.

ALL IN THE DOWNS.

All in the Downs the fleet was moor'd, The ſtreamers

waving in the wind, When black-ey'd Suſan came on

board, Oh, where ſhall I my true-love find? Tell me,

ye jo-vial ſailors, tell me true, Does my ſweet Wil-liam,

Does my ſweet William ſail among your crew?

    William, who high upon the yard
      Rock'd with the billows to and fro,
    Soon as her well-known voice he heard,
      He ſigh'd and caſt his eyes below :
The cord glides ſwiftly thro' his glowing hands,
And quick as light'ning on the deck he ſtands.

So the sweet lark, high pois'd in air,
   Shuts close his pinions to his breast,
If chance his mate's shrill call he hear,
   And drops at once into her nest.
The noblest captain in the British fleet
Might envy William's lips those kisses sweet.

O Susan, Susan, lovely dear,
   My vows shall ever true remain!
Let me kiss off that falling tear,
   We only part to meet again.
Change as ye list, ye winds, my heart shall be
The faithful compass that still points to thee.

Believe not what the landmen say
   Who tempt with doubts thy constant mind;
They'll tell thee, sailors, when away,
   In ev'ry port a mistress find.
Yes, yes, believe them when they tell thee so;
For thou art present wheresoe'er I go.

If to far India's coast we sail,
   Thy eyes are seen in diamonds bright;
Thy breath is Afric's spicy gale;
   Thy skin is ivory so white.
Thus ev'ry beauteous object that I view
Wakes in my soul some charm of lovely Sue.

Though battle calls me from thy arms,
   Let not my pretty Susan mourn;
Though cannons roar, yet, safe from harms,
   William shall to his dear return.
Love turns aside the balls that round me fly,
Lest precious tears should drop from Susan's eye.

The boatswain gave the dreadful word,
   The sails their swelling bosom spread;

No longer muſt ſhe ſtay aboard :
They kiſs'd, ſhe ſigh'd, he hung his head.
Her leſs'ning boat unwilling rows to land :
Adieu, ſhe cries, and wav'd her lily hand.

SONG CCXX.

ANDRO WI' HIS CUTTY GUN.

Blyth, blyth, blyth was ſhe, Blyth was ſhe butt and

ben ; And weel ſhe loo'd a Hawick gill, And leugh

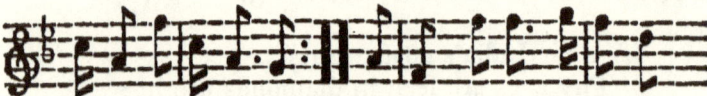

to ſee a tappet hen.   She took me in and ſet me

down, And hecht to keep me lawing free ; But, cunnin'

carlin' that ſhe was, She gar'd me birle my bawbee.

We loo'd the liquor weel enough,
    But, wae's my heart! my cash was done
Before that I had quench'd my drouth,
    And laith I was to pawn my shoon.
When we had three times toom'd our stoup,
    And the neist chappin new begun,
In started, to heeze up our hope,
    Young Andro wi' his cutty gun.
      Blyth, blyth, &c.

The carlin brought her kebbuck ben,
    With girdle-cakes weel toasted brown;
Weel does the canny kimmer ken
    They gar the scuds gae glibber down.
We ca'd the bicker aft about,
    Till dawning we ne'er jee'd our bum;
And ay the clearest drinker out
    Was Andro wi' his cutty gun.
      Blyth, blyth, &c.

He did like ony mavis sing;
    And, as I in his oxter sat,
He ca'd me ay his bonny thing,
    And mony a sappy kifs I gat.
I hae been east, I hae been west,
    I hae been far ayont the sun;
But the blythest lad that e'er I saw
    Was Andro wi' his cutty gun.
      Blyth, blyth, &c.

SONG CCXXI.

TAK' YOUR AULD CLOAK ABOUT YE.

In winter when the rain rain'd cauld, And froſt and ſnaw on il-ka hill; And Boreas, with his blaſts ſae bauld, Was threat'ning a' our ky to kill: Then Bell my wife, wha lo'es nae ſtrife, She ſaid to me right haſti-ly, Get up, gudeman, ſave Crummy's life, And tak' your auld cloak a-bout ye.

My Crummy is a uſeful cow,
   And ſhe is come of a good kyne;
Aft has ſhe wet the bairns' mou',
   And I am laith that ſhe ſhould tyne;

Get up, gudeman, it is fu' time,
　　The fun fhines in the lift fae hie;
Sloth never made a gracious end,
　　Gae tak' your auld cloak about ye.

My cloak was anes a good grey cloak
　　When it was fitting for my wear;
But now its fcantly worth a groat,
　　For I have worn't this thirty year.
Let's fpend the gear that we have won,
　　We little ken the day we'll dee;
Then I'll be proud, fince I have fworn
　　To have a new cloak about me.

In days when our king Robert rang,
　　His trews they coft but half-a-crown;
He faid they were a groat o'er dear,
　　And ca'd the tailor thief and lown.
He was the king that wore a crown,
　　And thou the man of laigh degree,
'Tis pride puts a' the country down,
　　Sae tak' thy auld cloak about ye.

Every land has its ain laugh,
　　Ilk kind of corn it has its hool;
I think the warld is a' run wrang,
　　When ilka wife her man wad rule.
Do ye not fee Rob, Jock, and Hab,
　　As they are girded gallantly?
While I fit hurklen in the afe,
　　I'll have a new cloak about me.

Gudeman, I wat 'tis thirty years
　　Since we did ane anither ken;
And we have had between us twa
　　Of lads and bonny laffes ten:

Now they are women grown and men,
  I wifh and pray well may they be!
And if you prove a good hufband,
  E'en tak' your auld cloak about ye.

Bell my wife fhe lo'es nae ftrife;
  But fhe wad guide me if fhe can:
And, to maintain an eafy life,
  I aft maun yield, tho' I'm gudeman.
Nought's to be won at woman's hand,
  Unlefs ye give her a' the plea:
Then I'll leave aff where I began,
  And tak' my auld cloak about me.

SONG CCXXII.

HOOLY AND FAIRLY.

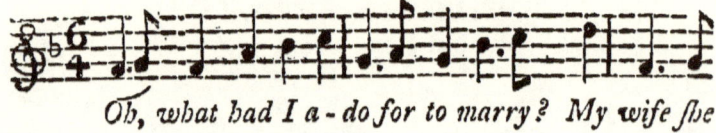
Oh, what had I a-do for to marry? My wife fhe

drinks naething but fack and ca-na-ry; I to her friends

complain'd right airly, O gin my wife wou'd drink

hooly and fairly! Hooly and fairly, hooly and fairly;

O gin my wife wou'd drink hooly and fairly!

First she drank Crummie, and syne she drank Garie,
Now she has drunken my bonny gray marie
That carried me thro' the dub and the larie.
    O gin my wife, &c.

If she'd drink but her ain things I wad na much care;
She drinks my claiths I canna weel spare;
To the kirk and the market I gang fu' barely.
    O gin my wife, &c.

If there's ony siller she maun keep the purse;
If I seek but a bawbee she'll scald and she'll curse;
She gangs like a queen, I scrimpet and sparely.
    O gin my wife, &c.

I never was given to wrangling nor strife,
Nor e'er did refuse her the comforts of life;
E'er it come to a war I am ay for a parley.
    O gin my wife, &c.

A pint wi' her cummers I wad her allow;
But when she sits down she fills hersel fou';
And when she is fou' she's unco camsterie.
    O gin my wife, &c.

She rins out to the cawsey, she roars and she rants;
Has nae dread o' her nibours, nor minds the house wants;
But sings some fool-sang, Cock up your heart, Charlie.
    O gin my wife, &c.

And when she comes hame she lays on the lads,
She ca's the lasses baith limmers and jades,
And I my ainsel an auld cuckold carlie.
    O gin my wife, &c.

SONG CCXXIII.

LEWIS GORDON.

Very Slow.

O send Lewis Gordon hame, And the lad I winna name; Tho' his back be at the wa', Here's to him

that's far awa. Oh, hon, my Highland man! Oh, my

bonny Highland man! Weel wou'd I my true love

ken Amang ten thousand Highland men.

O to see his tartan trews,
Bonnet blue, and laigh-heel'd shoes,
Philibeg aboon his knee!
That's the lad that I'll gang wi'.

The princely youth that I do mean
Is fitted for to be a king:
On his breaſt he wears a ſtar:
You'd take him for the god of war.

Oh, to ſee this princely one
Seated on his father's throne!
Diſaſters a' wou'd diſappear:
Then begins the jub'lee here!

SONG CCXXIV.

Tune Gramachree, page 259.

HAD I a heart for falſehood fram'd, I ne'er could injure you;
For, tho' your tongue no promiſe claim'd, your charms wou'd make me true:
To you no ſoul ſhall bear deceit, no ſtranger offer wrong;
But friends in all the ag'd you'll meet, and lovers in the young.

But when they learn that you have bleſs'd another with your heart,
They'll bid aſpiring paſſion reſt, and act a brother's part:
Then, lady, dread not their deceit, nor fear to ſuffer wrong;
For friends in all the ag'd you'll meet, and brothers in the young.

SONG CCXXV.
HIGHLAND MARCH.

In the garb of old Gaul and the fire of old

Rome, From the heath-cover'd mountains of Scotia

we come: On those mountains the Romans attempted

to reign; But our ancestors fought, and they fought

not in vain. Tho' no ci - ty nor court of our gar-

ment approve, 'Twas presented by Mars, at a fe -

nate, to Jove; And, when Pallas observ'd at a ball

'twou'd look odd, Mars receiv'd from his Ve-nus a

smile and a nod.

No intemperate tables our sinews unbrace;
Nor French faith nor French foppery our country disgrace:
Still the hoarse-sounding pipe breathes the true martial strain,
And our hearts still the true Scottish valour retain.
'Twas with anguish and woe that, of late, we beheld
Rebel forces rush down from the hills to the field;
For our hearts are devoted to George and the laws;
And we'll fight, like true Britons, in liberty's cause.

But still, at a distance from Britain's lov'd shore,
May her foes, in confusion, her mercy implore!
May her coasts ne'er with foreign invasions be spread!
Nor detested rebellion again raise its head!
May the fury of party and faction long cease!
May our councils be wise, and our commerce increase!
And, in Scotia's cold climate, may each of us find
That our friends still prove true, and our beauties prove kind!

SONG CCXXVI.
To the foregoing Tune.

IN the garb of old Gaul, wi' the fire of old Rome,
From the heath-cover'd mountains of Scotia we come;
Where the Romans endeavour'd our country to gain ;
But our anceftors fought, and they fought not in vain.
   Such our love of liberty, our country, and our laws,
   That, like our anceftors of old, we ftand by freedom's caufe ;
   We'll bravely fight, like heroes bold, for honour and applaufe,
   And defy the French, with all their art, to alter our our laws.

No effeminate cuftoms our finews unbrace ;
No luxurious tables enervate our race ;
Our loud-founding pipe bears the true martial ftrain ;
So do we the old Scottifh valour retain.
   Such our love, &c.

We're tall as the oak on the mount of the vale,
Are fwift as the roe which the hind doth affail :
As the full moon in autumn our fhields do appear ;
Minerva would dread to encounter our fpear.
   Such our love, &c.

As a ftorm in the ocean when Boreas blows,
So are we enrag'd when we rufh on our foes ;
We fons of the mountains, tremendous as rocks,
Dafh the force of our foes with our thundering ftrokes.
   Such our love, &c.

Quebec and Cape Breton, the pride of old France,
In their troops fondly boafted till we did advance ;
But when our claymores they faw us produce,
Their courage did fail, and they fu'd for a truce.
   Such our love, &c.

In our realm may the fury of faction long ceafe!
May our councils be wife, and our commerce increafe!
And, in Scotia's cold climate, may each of us find
That our friends ftill prove true, and our beauties prove
    kind!
Then we'll defend our liberty, our country, and our laws,
And teach our late pofterity to fight in freedom's caufe;
That they, like our anceftors bold, for honour and ap-
    plaufe,
May defy the French and Spaniards to alter our laws.

SONG CCXXV.

WHAT IS'T TO US.

What is't to us who guides the ftate? Who's out of favour? or who's great? Who are the mi-ni-fters or fpies? Who votes for places? or who buys? Who are the mini-fters or fpies? Who votes for places? or who buys?

The world will ſtill be rul'd by knaves,
And fools contending to be ſlaves;
Small things, my friend, ſerve to ſupport
Life, troubleſome at beſt and ſhort.

Our youth runs back, occaſion flies,
Grey hairs come on, and pleaſure dies:
Who would the preſent bleſſing loſe
For empire which he cannot uſe?

Kind providence has us ſupply'd
With what to others is deny'd;
Virtue, which teaches to condemn
And ſcorn ill actions and ill men.

Beneath this lime-tree's fragrant ſhade,
On beds of flow'rs ſupinely laid,
Let's then all other cares remove,
And drink and ſing to thoſe we love.

SONG CCXXVI.

BUSH ABOON TRAQUAIR.

Hear me, ye nymphs, and ev' - - ry swain, I'll tell how Peg-gy grieves me; Tho' thus I languish and com-plain, Alas! she ne'er believes me. My vows and sighs, like si-lent air, Un-heed-ed, ne-ver move her, The bon-ny bush a-boon Tra-quair Was where I first did love her.

That day she smil'd and made me glad;
  No maid seem'd ever kinder:
I thought myself the luckiest lad
  So sweetly there to find her.
I try'd to soothe my am'rous flame
  In words that I thought tender;
If more there pass'd I'm not to blame;
  I meant not to offend her.

Yet now she scornful flees the plain,
  The fields we then frequented;
If e'er we meet she shows disdain,
  She looks as ne'er acquainted.
The bonny bush bloom'd fair in May,
  Its sweets I'll ay remember;
But now her frowns make it decay;
  It fades as in December,

Ye rural pow'rs who hear my strains,
  Why thus should Peggy grieve me?
Oh, make her partner in my pains!
  And let her smiles relieve me!
If not, my love will turn despair;
  My passion no more tender;
I'll leave the bush aboon Traquair;
  To lonely wilds I'll wander.

SONG CCXXVII.

ROSLIN CASTLE.

'Twas in that season of the year When all things

gay and sweet appear, That Co-lin, with the morn-

ing ray, A-rose and sung his ru-ral lay. Of

Nanny's charms the shepherd sung, The hills and dales

with Nan-ny rung, While Roslin castle heard the

swain, And e-cho'd back the cheerful strain.

3 H

Awake, sweet muse! the breathing spring
With rapture warms; awake and sing!
Awake and join the vocal throng
Who hail the morning with a song!
To Nanny raise the cheerful lay;
O, bid her haste and come away;
In sweetest smiles herself adorn,
And add new graces to the morn.

O hark, my love! on ev'ry spray
Each feather'd warbler tunes his lay!
'Tis beauty fires the ravish'd throng,
And love inspires the melting song.
Then let my raptur'd notes arise:
For beauty darts from Nanny's eyes;
And love my rising bosom warms,
And fills my soul with sweet alarms.

O come, my love! thy Colin's lay
With rapture calls; O come away!
Come, while the muse this wreath shall twine
Around that modest brow of thine!
O hither haste, and with thee bring
That beauty blooming like the spring!
Those graces that divinely shine!
And charm this ravish'd breast of mine.

SONG CCXXVIII.

To the foregoing Tune.

FROM Roslin castle's echoing walls
Resounds my shepherd's ardent calls;
My Colin bids me come away,
And love demands I should obey.

His melting strain and tuneful lay
So much the charms of love display,
I yield—nor longer can refrain
To own my love, and bless my swain.

No longer can my heart conceal
The painful pleasing flame I feel;
My soul retorts the am'rous strain,
And echoes back in love again.
Where lurks my songster? from what grove
Does Colin pour his notes of love?
O bring me to the happy bow'r
Where mutual love may bliss secure!

Ye vocal hills that catch the song,
Repeating, as it flies along,
To Colin's ear my strain convey,
And say, I haste to come away.
Ye zephyrs soft that fan the gale,
Waft to my love the soothing tale;
In whispers all my soul express,
And tell, I haste his arms to bless.

SONG CCXXIX.

Tune, From the East breaks the Morn, page 230.

LET gay ones and great
    Make the most of their fate;
From pleasure to pleasure they run:
    Well, who cares a jot?
    I envy them not
While I have my dog and my gun.

For exercise air
To the field I repair,
With spirits unclouded and light:
The blisses I find
No stings leave behind,
But health and diversion unite.

SONG CCXXX.

TODLEN HAME.

When I have a saxpence under my thumb, Then I'll

get credit in il-ka town; But ay when I'm poor they

bid me gae by, O po-ver-ty parts good com-pa-ny.

Chorus.

To-dlen hame, To-dlen hame, O cou'dna my love

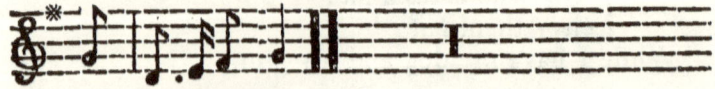

come to-dlen hame,

Fair fa' the goodwife, and fend her good fale!
She gi'es us white bannocks to drink her ale;
Syne if that her tippony chance to be fma'
We'll tak' a good-fcour o't, and ca't awa'.
  Todlen hame, todlen hame,
  As round as a neep come todlen hame.

My kimmer and I lay down to fleep·
And twa pint-ftoups at our bed's feet;
And ay when we waken'd we drank them dry:
What think ye of my wee kimmer and I?
  Todlen butt and todlen ben,
  Sae round as my love comes todlen hame.

Leez me on liquor, my todlen dow,
Ye're ay fae good-humour'd when weeting your mou';
When fober, fae four ye'll fight with a flee,
That 'tis a blithe fight to the bairns and me
  When todlen hame, todlen hame,
  When round as a neep you come todlen hame.

SONG CCXXXI.
OLD SLY HODGE.

Curtis was old Hodge's wife; For virtue none was e-ver such: She led so pure, so chaste a life, She led so pure, so chaste a life, Hodge said it was vir-tue o-ver much: For, says sly old Hodge, says he, For, says old sly Hodge, says he, Great talkers do the least, d'ye see, Great talkers do the least, d'ye see.

Curtis fwore, if men were rude,
  She'd pull their eyes out, tear their hair;
My dear, fays Hodge, you're wond'rous good,
My dear, &c.
  However, let us nothing fwear:
For, fays fly old Hodge, &c.

One night fhe dream'd a drunken fool
  Be rude, in fpite of her, wou'd fain;
She makes no more than with joint ftool,
She makes no more, &c.
  Fell on her hufband might and main.
Still fays fly old Hodge, &c.

By that time fhe had broke his nofe
  Hodge made a fhift to wake his wife;
O Hodge, fays fhe, judge by thefe blows,
Dear Hodge, &c.
  I prize my virtue as my life.
But, fays fly old Hodge, &c.

I dream'd a rude man on me fell;
  However, I his project marr'd.
Dear wife, fays Hodge, 'tis mighty well,
Dear wife, fays Hodge, &c.
  But next time don't hit quite fo hard:
For, fays old fly Hodge, &c.

SONG CCXXXII.

SHE ROSE AND LET ME IN.

The night her silent sable wore, And gloomy were the skies; Of glitt'ring stars appear'd no more than those in Nelly's eyes. When to her father's door I came, Where I had often been, I begg'd my fair, my lovely dame, To rise and let me in.

But she, with accents all divine,
  Did my fond suit reprove;
And while she chid my rash design,
  She but inflam'd my love.
Her beauty oft had pleas'd before,
  While her bright eyes did roll:
But virtue only had the pow'r
  To charm my very soul.

Then who wou'd cruelly deceive,
  Or from such beauty part?
I lov'd her so, I could not leave
  The charmer of my heart.
My eager fondness I obey'd,
  Resolv'd she should be mine,
Till Hymen to my arms convey'd
  My treasure so divine.

Now happy in my Nelly's love,
  Transporting is my joy:
No greater blessing can I prove,
  So bless'd a man am I:
For beauty may a while retain
  The conquer'd flutt'ring heart;
But virtue only is the chain
  Holds never to depart.

SONG CCXXXIII.
LOCHABER NO MORE.

Farewell to Lochaber! and farewell my Jean!

Where heartsome with thee I have mony days been:

For, Lochaber no more, Lochaber no more,

We'll may-be re-turn to Loch-a-ber no more.

These tears that I shed, they are a' for my dear, And

no for the dangers attending on weir; Tho' bore

on rough seas to a far bloo-dy shore, May-be to

return to Lochaber no more.

Tho' hurricanes rife, and rife ev'ry wind,
They'll ne'er make a tempeſt like that in my mind:
Tho' loudeſt of thunders on louder waves roar,
That's naething like leaving my love on the ſhore.
To leave thee behind me my heart is fair pain'd;
By eaſe that's inglorious no fame can be gain'd:
And beauty and love's the reward of the brave;
And I muſt deſerve it before I can crave.

Then glory, my Jeany, maun plead my excuſe;
Since honour commands me, how can I refuſe?
Without it I ne'er can have merit for thee,
And without thy favour I'd better not be.
I gae, then, my laſs, to win honour and fame;
And if I ſhould luck to come glorioufly hame,
I'll bring a heart to thee with love running o'er,
And then I'll leave thee and Lochaber no more.

SONG CCXXXIV.
RULE, BRITANNIA.

The nations not ſo bleſt as thee
  Muſt, in their turns, to tyrants fall;
  Muſt, in their turns, to tyrants fall;
Whilſt thou ſhalt flouriſh—ſhalt flouriſh great and free,
  The dread and envy of them all.
    Rule, Britannia, &c.

Still more majeſtic ſhalt thou riſe,
  More dreadful, from each foreign ſtroke;
  More dreadful, from each foreign ſtroke;
As the loud blaſt that—loud blaſt that tears the ſkies,
  Serve but to root the native oak.
    Rule, Britannia, &c.

Thee haughty tyrants ne'er ſhall tame:
  All their attempts to bend thee down,
  All their attempts to bend thee down,
Will but arouſe thy—arouſe thy gen'rous flame,
  But work their wo and thy renown.
    Rule, Britannia, &c.

To thee belongs the rural reign;
  Thy cities ſhall with commerce ſhine;
  Thy cities ſhall with commerce ſhine;
And thine ſhall be the—ſhall be the ſubject main;
  And ev'ry ſhore it circles, thine.
    Rule, Britannia, &c.

The muſes, ſtill with freedom found,
  Shall to thy happy coaſts repair:
  Shall to thy happy coaſts repair:
Bleſt iſle! with matchleſs—with matchleſs beauty crown'd,
  And manly hearts to guard the fair.
    Rule, Britannia, &c.

Your charms in harmlefs childhood lay
   As metals in a mine;
Age from no face takes more away
   Than youth conceal'd in thine:
But as your charms infenfibly
   To their perfection prefs'd;
So love as unperceiv'd did fly,
   And center'd in my breaft.

My paffion with your beauty grew,
   While Cupid, at my heart,
Still as his mother favour'd you,
   Threw a new flaming dart.
Each gloried in their wanton part;
   To make a lover, he
Employ'd the utmoft of his art;
   To make a beauty, fhe.

SONG CCXXXVI.

Tune, Friend and Pitcher, page 52.

THE filver moon that fhines fo bright,
   I fwear, with reafon, is my teacher;
And if my minute-glafs runs right,
   We've time to drink another pitcher.
      'Tis not yet day, 'tis not yet day;
         Then why fhould we forfake good liquor?
      Until the fun-beams round us play
         Let's jocund pufh about the pitcher.

They fay that I muft work all day,
   And fleep at night, to grow much richer;
But what is all the world can fay,
   Compar'd to mirth, my friend, and pitcher.
      'Tis not yet day, &c.

Tho' one may boaſt a handſome wife,
  Yet ſtrange vagaries may bewitch her;
Unvex'd I live a cheerful life,
  And boldly call for t'other pitcher.
    'Tis not yet day, &c.

I dearly love a hearty man
  (No ſneaking milk-fop Jemmy Twitcher),
Who loves a laſs and loves a glaſs,
  And boldly calls for t'other pitcher.
    'Tis not yet day, &c.

SONG CCXXXVII.

Tune, Corn Rigs are bonny, page 4.

LORD! what care I for mam or dad?
  Why, let them ſcold and bellow;
For while I live I'll love my lad,
  He's ſuch a charming fellow.
The laſt fair day, on yonder green,
  The youth he danc'd ſo well, O;
So ſpruce a lad was never ſeen
  As my ſweet charming fellow.

The fair was over, night was come,
  The lad was ſomewhat mellow;
Says he, my dear, I'll ſee you home;
  I thank'd the charming fellow.
You rogue, ſays I, you've ſtopp'd my breath;
  Ye bells ring out my knell, O;
Again I'd die ſo ſweet a death
  With ſuch a charming fellow.

We trudg'd along, the moon fhone bright;
  Says he, my fweeteft Nell, O;
I'll kifs you here by this good light;
  Lord, what a charming fellow!
You rogue, fays I, you've ftopp'd my breath;
  Ye bells ring out my knell, O;
Again I'd die fo fweet a death
  With fuch a charming fellow.

SONG CCXXXVIII.

Tune, Ceafe, rude Boreas, page 30.

WELCOME, welcome, brother debtor,
  To this poor but merry place;
Where no bailiff, dun, or fetter,
  Dare to fhew a frightful face.
But, kind Sir, as you're a ftranger,
  Down your garnifh you muft lay;
Or your coat will be in danger:
  You muft either ftrip or pay.

Ne'er repine at your confinement
  From your children or your wife:
Wifdom lies in true refignment,
  Through the various fcenes of life.
Scorn to fhow the leaft refentment,
  Though beneath the frowns of fate;
Knaves and beggars find contentment;
  Fears and cares attend the great.

Though our creditors are fpiteful,
  And reftrain our bodies here;
Ufe will make a jail delightful,
  Since there's nothing elfe to fear.

Every island's but a prison,
  Strongly guarded by the sea:
Kings and princes, for that reason,
  Pris'ners are as well as we.

What was't made great Alexander
  Weep at his unfriendly fate?
'Twas because he could not wander
  Beyond the world's strong prison-gate.
The world itself is strongly bounded
  By the heavens and stars above:
Why should we then be confounded,
  Since there's nothing free but love?

SONG CCXXXIX.

BELIEVE MY SIGHS.

Believe my sighs, my tears, my dear, Be-lieve a heart you've won; Believe my vows to you sincere, Or, Jenny, I'm undone. You say I'm fickle, and apt to change At ev'-ry face that's new: Of all the girls

VOCAL ENCHANTRESS.

Chorus.

I e-ver saw, I ne'er lov'd one like you. I ne'er

lov'd one like you, my dear, I ne'er lov'd one like

you; Of all the girls I e-ver saw, I ne'er lov'd

one like you.

My heart was like a lump of ice
   Till warm'd by your bright eye;
And then it kindled in a trice
   A flame that ne'er can die.
Then take and try me, you shall find
   That I've a heart that's true;
Of all the girls I ever saw,
   I ne'er lov'd one like you.
     I ne'er lov'd, &c.

SONG CCXL.
WHAT POSIES AND ROSES.

Such beauties in view I can never praise too high,
Not Pallas's blue eye is brighter than thine; Nor fount
of Sufannah, Nor gold of fair Danæ, Nor moon of
Di-a-na fo clearly can fhine. Not beard of Si-le-nus,
Nor treffes of Venus, I fwear by quæ genus, With
yours can compare; Not hermes caduces, Nor flower
deluces, Nor all the nine mufes, To me are fo fair.

VOCAL ENCHANTRESS.

Chorus.

What posies and roses To noses discloses, Your breath

all so sweet, Your breath all so sweet; To the tip of

your lip, As they trip, The bees lip, Honey sip, Like

choice flip, And their hybla forget.

When girls like you pass us.
I saddle Pegasus,
And ride up Parnassus
  To Helicon's stream.
Even that is a puddle
Where others may muddle;
My nose let me fuddle
  In bowls of your cream!
Old Jove the great Hector
May tipple his nectar;
Of gods the director
  And thunder above:
I'd quaff off a full cann,
As Bacchus or Vulcan,
Or Jove, the old bull, can,
  To her that I love.
    What posies, &c.

SONG CCXLI.

Tune, The Dusky Night, page 250.

WHILE grave divines preach up dull rules,
    And moral wits refine,
The precepts taught in human schools,
The precepts taught in human schools,
    We friars hold divine,
    We friars hold divine.
       Here's a health to Father Paul,
        A health to Father Paul;
       For flowing bowls inspire the souls
        Of jolly friars all.

When in the convent we're all met,
    We laugh, we joke, we sing;
Affairs divine we soon forget,
Affairs divine we soon forget,
    Since Father Paul's our king,
    Since Father Paul's our king.
       Here's a health, &c.

Our beads and cross we hold divine;
    We pray with fervent zeal
To rosy Bacchus god of wine,
To rosy Bacchus god of wine,
    Who does each joy reveal,
    Who does each joy reveal.
       Here's a health, &c.

Here's absolution you'll receive,
    You blue-ey'd nuns so fair;
And benediction we will give,
And benediction we will give;
    So banish all your cares,
    So banish all your cares.
       Here's a health, &c.

So fill your bumpers, fons of mirth,
  Let Friars be the toaft;
Long may they all exift on earth!
Long may they all-exift on earth!
    And nuns their order boaft,
    And nuns their order boaft.
      Here's a health, &c.

SONG CCXLII.

Tune, You the Point may Carry, page 208.

I'M in love with twenty,
  I'm in love with twenty,
And could adore as many more;
  There's nothing like a plenty.
    Variety is charming,
    Variety is charming;
    A conftancy is not for me;
    So ladies take your warning.

For a man in one love,
For a man in one love,
He looks as poor as any boor,
  For a man in one love.
    Variety, &c.

Girls grown old and ugly,
Girls grown old and ugly,
They can't infpire the fame defire
  As when they're young and fmugly.
    Variety, &c.

'Tis not the grand regalia,
'Tis not the grand regalia
Of eaftern kings that poets fings;
  But O the fweet feraglio!
    Variety, &c.

SONG CCXLIII.
THE WAND'RING SAILOR.

The wand'ring sailor ploughs the main, A compe-

tence in life to gain; Undaunted braves the stor-my

seas, To find at last content and ease; To find at

last content and ease: In hopes, when toil and dan-

ger's o'er, To an-chor on his native shore; In hopes,

when toil and danger's o'er, To anchor on his na -

450   CALLIOPE : OR THE

* When round the bowl the jovial crew
The early scenes of youth renew,
Tho' each his fav'rite fair will boast,
This is the universal toast :
This is the universal toast :
   May we, when toil and danger's o'er,
   Cast anchor on our native shore !
   May we, when toil and danger's o'er,
   Cast anchor on our native shore !
   Cast anchor on our native shore !

* These words to be sung to the first part of the tune.

SONG CCXLIV.

ON FRIENDSHIP.

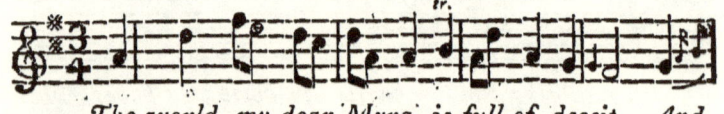
The world, my dear Myra, is full of deceit, And

friendship's a jewel we sel-dom can meet. How strange

does it seem that in searching a-round, That source

of con-tent is so rare to be found ! O friendship !

thou balm and rich fwet'ner of life, Kind parent of

eafe, and compofer of ftrife ; Without thee, alas! what

are rich-es and pow'r, But emp-ty de-lu-fion, the

joys of an hour - - - - - - - - - - But empty

de-lu-fion, the joys of an hour.

How much to be priz'd and efteem'd is a friend
On whom we may always with fafety depend ;
Our joys, when extended, will always increafe,
And griefs, when divided, are hufh'd into peace.
When fortune is fmiling what crowds will appear
Their kindnefs to offer, and friendfhip fincere ;
Yet change but the profpect and point out diftrefs,
No longer to court you they eagerly prefs.

SONG CCXLV.

IN PRAISE OF ALE.

Moderato.

When the chill Si-roc-co blows, And winter tells a

hea-vy tale; When pies and daws and rooks and

crows Sit curſing of the froſts and ſnows, Then give me

ale, Then give me ale, Then give me ale.

Ale in a Saxon rumkin then,
Such as will make Grimalkin prate,
Bids valour burgeon in tall men,
Quickens the poets wit and pen,
      Deſpiſes fate.

Ale, that the abſent battle fights,
And forms the march of Swediſh drum,
Diſputes with princes, laws, and rights,
What's done and paſt tells mortal wights,
      And what's to come.

Ale, that the plowman's heart upkeeps,
And equals it to tyrants thrones,
That wipes the eye that over-weeps,
And lulls in fweet and dainty fleeps,
      The o'er wearied bones.

Grandchild of Ceres, Bacchus' daughter,
Wine's emulous neighbour, if but ftale,
Ennobling all the nymphs of water,
And filling each man's heart with laughter.
      Oh, give me ale!

SONG CCXLVI.
THE CUCKOW SONG.

When daisies pied, and violets blue, And la-dy-

smocks all sil-ver white, And cuckow-buds of yellow

hue, Do paint the meadows with delight; The

cuckow then, on ev'ry tree, Mocks marry'd men, Mocks

marry'd men, Mocks marry'd men; for thus sings he:

Cuckow, cuckow, cuckow, cuckow, cuckow,

cuckow; O word of fear! O word of fear! Un-

pleasing to a marry'd ear; Unpleasing to a marry'd

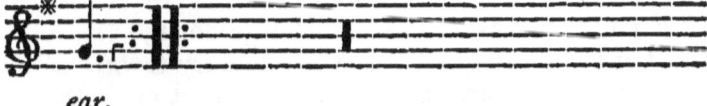
ear.

When shepherds pipe on oaten straws,
    And merry larks are ploughmens clocks,
When turtles tread, and rooks and daws,
    And maidens bleach their summer smocks,
The cuckow then, on every tree,
Mocks married men; for thus sings he:
      Cuckow, cuckow;—O word of fear!
      Unpleasing to a married ear.

SONG CCXLVII.

THE OLD MAN's WISH.

Tune, The Matron's Wiſh, page 58.

IF I live to grow old, as I find I go down,
Let this be my fate: in a fair country town,
Let me have a warm houſe with a ſtone at my gate,
And a cleanly young girl to rub my bald bate.
   May I govern my paſſions with an abſolute ſway;
   And grow wiſer and better as my ſtrength wears away,
   Without gout or ſtone, by a gentle decay.

In a country town, by a murmuring brook,
With the ocean at diſtance on which I may look;
With a green ſpacious plain, without hedge or ſtile,
And an eaſy pad nag to ride out a mile.
   May I govern, &c.

With Horace and Petrarch, and one or two more
Of the beſt wits that liv'd in the ages before;
With a diſh of roaſt mutton, not ven'ſon nor teal,
And clean, though coarſe, linen at every meal.
   May I govern, &c.

With a pudding on Sundays, and ſtout humming liquor,
And remnants of Latin to puzzle the vicar;
With a hidden reſerve of good Burgundy wine,
To drink the king's health as oft as we dine.
   May I govern, &c.

With a courage undaunted may I face my laſt day!
And, when I am dead, may the better ſort ſay,
In the morning when ſober, in the ev'ning when mellow,
He is gone, and has left not behind him his fellow!
   For he govern'd his paſſions with an abſolute ſway;
   And grew wiſer and better as his ſtrength wore away,
   Without gout or ſtone, by a gentle decay.

SONG CCXLVIII.

MY MIND TO ME A KINGDOM IS.

My mind to me a kingdom is; Such perfect joy

therein I find, As far ex-cels all earthly blifs That

God or Nature hath affign'd. Tho' much I want that

moft would have, Yet ftill my mind forbids to crave.

Content I live, this is my ftay;
    I feek no more than may fuffice:
I prefs to bear no haughty fway;
    Look what I lack my mind fupplies.
Lo! thus I triumph like a king,
Content with that my mind doth bring.

I fee how plenty furfeits oft,
    And hafty climbers fooneft fall:
I fee that fuch as fit aloft
    Mifhap doth threaten moft of all.

These get with toil, and keep with fear:
Such cares my mind could never bear.

No princely pomp, nor wealthy store,
   No force to win a victory,
No wily wit to salve a sore,
   No shape to win a lover's eye;
To none of these I yield as thrall;
For why? my mind despiseth all.

Some have too much, yet still they crave;
   I little have, yet seek no more:
They are but poor, though much they have;
   And I am rich with little store:
They poor, I rich; they beg, I give;
They lack, I lend; they pine, I live.

I laugh not at another's loss;
   I grudge not at another's gain:
No worldly wave my mind can toss;
   I brook that is another's bane:
I fear no foe, nor fawn on friend;
I loath not life, nor dread mine end.

My wealth is health, and perfect ease;
   My conscience clear my chief defence:
I never seek by bribes to please,
   Nor by desert to give offence:
Thus do I live, thus will I die:
Would all did so as well as I!

I joy not in no earthly bliss;
   I weigh not Cresus' wealth a straw:
For care, I care not what it is;
   I fear not Fortune's fatal law.
My mind is such as may not move
For beauty bright or force of love.

I wish but what I have at will ;
  I wander not to seek for more ;
I like the plain, I climb no hill ;
  In greatest storms I sit on shore,
And laugh at them that toil in vain
To get what must be lost again.

I kiss not where I wish to kill ;
  I feign not love where most I hate ;
I break no sleep to win my will ;
  I wait not at the mighty's gate ;
I scorn no poor, I fear no rich ;
I feel no want, nor have too much.

The court, ne cart, I like ne loath ;
  Extremes are counted worst of all ;
The golden mean betwixt them both
  Doth surest sit, and fears no fall.
This is my choice : for why ? I find
No wealth is like a quiet mind.

SONG CCXLIX.
DE'IL TAK' THE WAR.

De'il tak' the war, that hurry'd Wil-ly frae me, Who

to love me juſt had ſworn; They made him captain,

ſure to un-do me, Wae is me, he'll ne'er re-turn.

A thou-ſand loons a-broad will fight him, He from

thouſands ne'er will run; Day and night I did

in-vite him To ſtay ſafe from ſword or gun. I

us'd alluring graces, With muckle kind embraces, Now

fighing, Now crying, Then tears dropping fall; And

had he my soft arms Preferr'd to war's alarms, My

love grown mad, Without the man of Gad, I fear in my

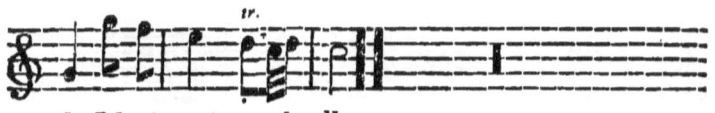
fit I had grant - ed all.

I wash'd and patch'd, to make me look provoking;
   Snares that they told me would catch the men;
And on my head a huge commode sat poking,
   Which made me shew as tall again:
For a new gown, too, I paid muckle money,
   Which with golden flow'rs did shine;
My love well might think me gay and bonny,
   No Scots lass was e'er so fine.
      My petticoat I spotted,
       Fringe, too, with thread I knotted,
Lace shoes, and silk hose garter'd o'er the knee;
      But oh, the fatal thought!
      To Billy these are nought;
Who rode to towns, and rifled with dragoons,
   When he, silly loon, might have plunder'd me.

SONG CCL.
AMYNTA.

My sheep I've forsaken, and left my sheep-hook,

And all the gay haunts of my youth I've forsook;

No more for A-myn-ta fresh garlands I wove:

For ambition, I said, would soon cure me of

love. O what had my youth with ambition to

do? Why left I A-myn-ta? Why broke I my vow?

O give me my sheep, and my sheep-hook re-

store, And I'll wander from love and Amynta no

more.

Through regions remote in vain do I rove,
And bid the wide ocean secure me of love;
O fool! to imagine that ought can subdue
A love so well founded, a passion so true.
 O what had my youth, &c.

Alas, 'tis too late at thy fate to repine!
Poor shepherd! Amynta no more can be thine:
Thy tears are all fruitless, thy wishes are vain;
The moments neglected return not again.
 O what had my youth, &c.

SONG CCLI.
BLOW HIGH, BLOW LOW.

SONG CCLII.
WE'RE GAILY YET.

We're gaily yet, And we're gaily yet, And we're no very fu' but we're gaily yet; Then fit ye a while and tipple a bit; For we're no very fu' but we're gaily yet.

There was a lad and they ca'd him Dick,
He ga'e me a kifs and I bit his lip;
And down in the garden he fhew'd me a trick;
And we're no very fu' but we're gaily yet.
    And we're gaily yet, &c.

There were three lads, and they were clad;
There were three laffes, and them they had;
Three trees in the orchard are newly fprung;
And we's a' get gear enough, we're but young.
    And we're gaily yet, &c.

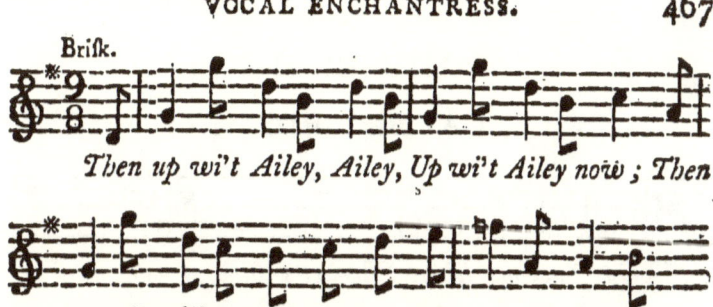

peafe-ftack, Till the mow flew up to her een. Then up wi't Ailey, &c.

Now fye, John Thomfon, rin,
Gin ever ye ran in your life;
De'il get ye, but hie, my dear Jock,
There's a man got to bed with your wife.
  Then up wi't Ailey, &c.

Then away John Thomfon ran,
And I trow he ran with fpeed;
But before he had run his length
The falfe loon had done the deed.
  Then up wi't, Ailey, &c.
(End with the firft verfe, We're gaily yet, &c.)

SONG CCLIII.
GAY BACCHUS.

Gay Bacchus, liking Eſtcourt's wine, A noble meal be-

ſpoke us; And for the gueſts that were to dine Brought

Comus, Love, and Jocus. The god near Cupid drew

his chair; Near Comus Jocus plac'd; Thus wine makes

love forget its care, And mirth exalts a feaſt.

The more to pleaſe the ſpritely god,
    Each ſweet engaging grace
Put on ſome clothes to come abroad,
    And took a waiter's place.

Then Cupid nam'd at ev'ry glaſs
    A lady of the ſky;
While Bacchus ſwore he'd drink the laſs,
    And had it bumper high.

Fat Comus tofs'd his brimmer o'er,
  And always got the moft;
Jocus took care to fill him more
  Whene'er he mifs'd the toaft.

They call'd, and drank at every touch,
  Then fill'd and drank again;
And if the gods can take too much,
  'Tis faid they did fo then.

Free jefts run all the table round,
  And with the wine confpire
(While they by fly reflection wound)
  To fet their heads on fire.

Gay Bacchus little Cupid ftung,
  By reck'ning his deceits;
And Cupid mock'd his ftamm'ring tongue,
  With all his ftagg'ring gaits.

And Jocus droll'd on Comus' ways,
  And tales without a jeft;
While Comus call'd his witty plays
  But waggeries at beft.

Such talk foon fet them all at odds;
  And, had I Homer's pen,
I'd fing ye how they drank like gods,
  And how they fought like men.

To part the fray the Graces fly,
  Who made them foon agree;
And had the Furies felves been nigh,
  They ftill were three to three.

Bacchus appeas'd, rais'd Cupid up,
  And gave him back his bow;
But kept fome dart to ftir the cup
  Where fack and fugar flow.

Jocus took Comus' rosy crown,
  And gaily wore the prize;
And thrice, in mirth, he push'd him down,
  As thrice he strove to rise.

Then Cupid sought the myrtle grove
  Where Venus did recline,
And beauty close embracing love,
  They join'd to rail at wine.

And Comus, loudly cursing wit,
  Roll'd off to some retreat,
Where boon companions gravely sit
  In fat unwieldy state.

Bacchus and Jocus, still behind,
  For one fresh glass prepare;
They kiss, and are exceeding kind,
  And vow to be sincere.

But part in time, whoever hear
  This our instructive song;
For though such friendships may be dear,
  They can't continue long.

SONG CCLIV.

FROM THE COURT TO THE COTTAGE.

From the court to the cottage con-vey me away;

For I'm weary of grandeur, and what they call gay:

From the court to the cottage con-vey me away;

For I'm weary of grandeur, and what they call gay:

Where pride without meafure, and pomp without plea-

fure, Make life in a cir-cle of hurry decay.

Far remote and retir'd from the noise of the town,
I'll exchange my brocade for a plain russet gown;
   My friends shall be few,
     But well chosen and true;
And sweet recreation our evening shall crown.

With a rural repast, a rich banquet for me,
On a mossy green turf, near some shady old tree;
   The river's clear brink
     Shall afford me my drink,
And Temp'rance my friendly physician shall be.

Ever calm and serene, with contentment still bless'd,
Not too giddy with joy, or with sorrow depress'd,
   I'll neither invoke,
     Or repine at Death's stroke,
But retire from the world as I would to my rest.

F I N I S.

www.ingramcontent.com/pod-product-compliance
Lightning Source LLC
Chambersburg PA
CBHW051845300426
44117CB00006B/271